Understanding
OCTAVIO PAZ

Understanding Modern
European and Latin American
Literature

James Hardin, *Series Editor*

volumes on

Ingeborg Bachmann
Samuel Beckett
Thomas Bernhard
Johannes Bobrowski
Heinrich Böll
Italo Calvino
Albert Camus
Elias Canetti
Camilo José Cela
Céline
José Donoso
Friedrich Dürrenmatt
Rainer Werner Fassbinder
Max Frisch
Federico García Lorca
Gabriel García Márquez
Juan Goytisolo
Günter Grass

Gerhart Hauptmann
Christoph Hein
Hermann Hesse
Eugène Ionesco
Milan Kundera
Primo Levi
Boris Pasternak
Octavio Paz
Luigi Pirandello
Graciliano Ramos
Erich Maria Remarque
Jean-Paul Sartre
Claude Simon
Mario Vargas Llosa
Peter Weiss
Franz Werfel
Christa Wolf

UNDERSTANDING

OCTAVIO
PAZ

JOSÉ QUIROGA

UNIVERSITY OF SOUTH CAROLINA PRESS

© 1999 University of South Carolina

Published in Columbia, South Carolina, by the
University of South Carolina Press

Manufactured in the United States of America

03 02 01 00   5 4 3 2

Library of Congress Cataloging-in-Publication Data

Quiroga, Jose, 1959–
    Understanding Octavio Paz / Jose Quiroga.
        p. cm.
    Includes bibliographical references (p.) and index.

    ISBN 1–57003–263–7
    1. Paz, Octavio, 1914—Criticism and interpretation. I. Title.
PQ7297.P28 Z935 1999
861—ddc21   98–25445

Contents

Editor's Preface

Understanding Modern European and Latin American Literature has been planned as a series of guides for undergraduate and graduate students and nonacademic readers. Like the volumes in its companion series Understanding Contemporary American Literature, these books provide introductions to the lives and writings of prominent modern authors and explicate their most important works.

Modern literature makes special demands, and this is particularly true of foreign literature, in which the reader must contend not only with unfamiliar, often arcane artistic conventions and philosophical concepts, but also with the handicap of reading the literature in translation. It is a truism that the nuances of one language can be rendered in another only imperfectly (and this problem is especially acute in fiction), but the fact that the works of European and Latin American writers are situated in a historical and cultural setting quite different from our own can be as great a hindrance to the understanding of these works as the linguistic barrier. For this reason the UMELL series emphasizes the sociological and historical background of the writers treated. The philosophical and cultural traditions peculiar to a given culture may be particularly important for an understanding of certain authors, and these are taken up in the introductory chapter and also in the discussion of those works to which this information is relevant. Beyond this, the books treat the specifically literary aspects of the author under discussion and attempt to explain the complexities of contemporary literature lucidly. The books are conceived as introductions to the authors covered, not as comprehensive analyses. They do not provide detailed summaries of plot because they are meant to be used in conjunction with the books they treat, not as a substitute for study of the original works. The purpose of the books is to provide information and judicious literary assessment of the major works in the most compact, readable form. It is our hope that the UMELL series will help increase knowledge and understanding of European and Latin American cultures and will serve to make the literature of those cultures more accessible.

J. H.

A Note on Translations and Citations

Whenever possible I have followed the standard translations of Paz's works. I have modified these translations in a few specific instances, and I have pointed these out in the text. Translations for works (both primary and secondary sources) that have not been published in English are my own.

At the first mention of each work by Paz, I give the Spanish title, followed by the title in English, in italics if a translation is available, in roman type if it is not. In subsequent references I refer to works that have been translated by their English titles only.

The bibliography at the end of the book provides publication information for first editions of Paz's books and for the critical materials to which I refer.

Chronology

1914	Born in Mixcoac, a suburb of Mexico City, 31 March.
1931	Publishes poems in the literary magazine *Barandal.*
1933	*Luna silvestre* (Wild Moon), Paz's first collection of poems, published.
1934	Paz's father dies.
1937	*Raíz del hombre* (Roots of Man, a long poem, subsequently revised) published. Marries writer Elena Garro, whom he divorces two years later. As a reaction to the Spanish Civil War publishes a plaquette titled *¡No pasarán!* Leaves for Mérida, Yucatán. Writes *Entre la piedra y la flor* (Between the Stone and the Flower). Is invited to participate in the Congreso de Escritores Antifascistas in Spain. Publishes *Bajo tu clara sombra y otros poemas sobre España* (Under Your Clear Shadow and Other Poems on Spain).
1938–1941	In Mexico, collaborates in the journal *El popular* until 1940, from where he resigns after the Russo-German Pact. Publishes poems in the literary magazine *Taller* in 1939 and 1940.
1941	*Laurel,* a literary anthology of poetry in Spanish, is edited by Paz along with Xavier Villaurrutia, Juan Gil-Albert and Emilio Prados. *Entre la piedra y la flor* is published.
1942	*A la orilla del mundo y Primer día* (At the Shore of the World and First Day), *Bajo tu clara sombra* (Under Your Clear Shadow), *Raíz del hombre* (Roots of Man), *Noche de resurrecciones* (Night of Resurrection) are published. "Poesía de soledad y poesía de comunión," a published conference dedicated to San Juan de la Cruz.
1944	Travels to the United States on a Guggenheim fellowship at the end of 1943. Remains for two years, travels to San Francisco and New York, starts writing *The Labyrinth of Solitude.*

1945–1951	Lives in Paris. Meets André Breton and the postwar surrealist group.
1949	*Libertad bajo palabra* (Liberty under Parole, 1st edition) published.
1950	*Labyrinth of Solitude* (1st edition) published.
1951	*¿Aguila o Sol?* (*Eagle or Sun?*, Mexico: Tezontle) published.
1951–1952	Arrives in Bombay in November 1951. Spends the next year in India and in Japan.
1953	Returns to Mexico, becomes an active figure in Mexican literary circles. Collaborates in the *Revista mexicana de literatura,* directed by Carlos Fuentes and Emmanuel Carballo. Receives a scholarship from the Colegio de México in order to finish the manuscript of *The Bow and the Lyre.*
1954	*Semillas para un himno* (Seeds for a Hymn) published.
1956	*The Bow and the Lyre* (1st edition) published.
1957	*Sunstone* published.
1958	*La estación violenta* (The Violent Season) published.
1959	*Labyrinth of Solitude* (2d edition, revised) published.
1960	*Libertad bajo palabra* (2d edition) published. Includes selections from all his previous books of poetry until *Sunstone.*
	Días hábiles, Homenaje y profanaciones (Homage and Profanations) published.
1962	*Salamandra* (Salamander), *Solo a dos voces* (Solo for Two Voices) published.
1962–1968	Becomes chief of the Mexican Embassy in India. Marries Marie José Tramini; visits Sri Lanka, Afghanistan, Nepal, Southeast Asia, Thailand, Singapore, and Cambodia.
1967	The poem *Blanco* published. The collection of essays *The Bow and the Lyre* (2d edition, revised); the collection includes "Los signos en rotación" (Signs in Rotation). *Claude Lévi-Strauss o el nuevo festín de Esopo* is published.
1968	*Libertad bajo palabra* (3d edition) published. Resigns from Mexican diplomatic post in protest over the massacre of Tlatelolco (2 October 1968).
1969	*East Slope, Conjunctions and Disjunctions* published.
1970	*Postdata* (*The Other Mexico: Critique of the Pyramid*) published.

1971 Returns to Mexico. Coedits the literary magazine *Plural* (1971–1976).
Delivers Charles Eliot Norton Lectures at Harvard University during the period 1971–1972. These lectures will be the basis for *Children of the Mire* (1974).

1973 *El signo y el garabato* (The Sign and the Scrawl) published.

1974 *Children of the Mire* published.

1975 *Pasado en claro (A Draft of Shadows)* published.

1976 Resigns, with other collaborators, from *Plural,* protesting governmental editorial interference. In 1977 he organizes and publishes *Vuelta,* a monthly literary magazine published without interruption until 1997.

1979 *Poemas* published. Includes *Libertad bajo palabra* (4th edition, revised), and most of Paz's poetry.

1982 *Sor Juana Inés de la Cruz o las trampas de la fé (Sor Juana Inés de la Cruz or the Traps of Faith)* published.

1988 *Libertad bajo palabra* (5th edition, revised) published.

1990 Is granted the Nobel Prize in Literature.

1993 *Itinerario, La llama doble (The Double Flame)* published.

1995 *Vislumbres de la India* published.

1998 Octavio Paz dies in Mexico City on 19 April.

Abbreviations

AA	*Arbol adentro.* Barcelona: Seix Barral, 1987.
AC	*Alternating Current.* Tr. Helen Lane. New York: Viking, 1973.
AL	*El arco y la lira: El poema. La revelación poética. Poesía e historia.* Mexico City: Fondo de Cultura Económica, 1956. (2d ed., Buenos Aires: Sur, 1965).
Archivo	Ed. Enrico Mario Santí. Mexico City: Ediciones del Equilibrista, 1995.
BL	*The Bow and the Lyre.* Tr. Ruth L. C. Simms. Austin: University of Texas Press, 1973.
CA	*Corriente alterna.* Mexico City: Siglo XXI, 1967 (2d ed. 1968).
CM	*Children of the Mire: Poetry from Romanticism to the Avant-Garde.* Tr. Rachel Phillips. Cambridge: Harvard University Press, 1974.
CP	*Collected Poems of Octavio Paz.* Tr. Eliot Weinberger et al. New York: New Directions, 1987.
EP	*Early Poems, 1935–1955.* Tr. Muriel Rukeyser et al. Bloomington: Indiana University Press, 1973.
ES	*¿Aguila o sol? Eagle or Sun?* Tr. Eliot Weinberger. New York: New Directions, 1976.
LS	*El laberinto de la soledad.* (1950, 1959.) Ed. Enrico Mario Santí. Madrid: Cátedra, 1993.
LSol	*The Labyrinth of Solitude.* Tr. Lysander Kemp, Yara Milos, and Rachel Phillips Belash. New York: Grove, 1985.
MD	*Marcel Duchamp: Appearance Stripped Bare.* Tr. Rachel Phillips and Donald Gardner. New York: Viking, 1978.
OF	*El ogro filantrópico.* Mexico City: Joaquín Mortíz, 1979.
PC	*Pasión crítica.* Barcelona: Seix Barral, 1985.

PL   *Primeras letras (1931–1943).* Ed. Enrico Mario Santí.
            Barcelona: Seix Barral, 1988.

Poemas Poemas   (1935–1975). Barcelona: Seix Barral, 1979.

PRI   Partido Revolucionario Institucional

SG   *El signo y el garabato.* Mexico City: Joaquín Mortíz, 1973.

SO   *Sombras de obras: Arte y literatura.* Barcelona: Seix Barral,
            1983.

SP   *Selected Poetry of Octavio Paz.* Tr. Muriel Rukeyser.
            Bloomington: Indiana University Press, 1963.

Understanding
OCTAVIO PAZ

CHAPTER 1

Overview

> I have been moved by an aesthetic will but also by the idea that the poet who writes is not identical to the man who lives. They are in constant communication and one can say that the man who lives is the inspiration of the poet who writes. But they are not one and the same.
>
> —From Paz's 1990 interview with Anthony Stanton

In awarding Octavio Paz the Nobel Prize for Literature in 1991 for his work's "sensuous intelligence and humanistic integrity," the Swedish Academy recognized the Mexican poet as one of the most influential voices in late-twentieth-century letters. It was a recognition long overdue. For forty years, Paz had been Latin America's most public and prolific essayist, cultural historian, poet, philosopher, and translator. In a sense, Paz shaped and defined the role of the intellectual in contemporary Latin America: he was an active participant in the political and poetical battles of his time—a controversial man of letters who struck a sensitive balance between public discourse and individual, sometimes hermetic, poetic expression. Since the late 1960s, Paz's poetry and essays have been read in the United States in translations by some of the most important American poets and intellectuals. There is no better introduction to Latin America than the polemical and intellectually challenging work of this Mexican man of letters.

Paz's multilayered texts engage the reader in a sophisticated dialogue with history, literature, and philosophy. As an essayist, Paz was heir to a distinguished tradition in Hispanic letters, one that included José Ortega y Gasset and Alfonso Reyes, kindred spirits in the sheer multiplicity of their interests and in the inquisitive tradition of knowledge. Paz's essays on poetry and poetics, in particular *El arco y la lira,* 1956 (*The Bow and the Lyre*) and *Los hijos del limo,* 1974 (*Children of the Mire*), defined modernity as multilayered tradition of rupture in Western poetry, a suggestive paradox that for Paz was emblematic of our present condition. To read Paz on literature is to sense connections well beyond time and place. He joins in one sweeping phrase Rubén Darío and Matsuo Basho, Apollinaire's *calligrammes* and the surviving codices of early Mexican literature. One finds cross-cultural comparisons in the essays of Octavio Paz because he defined tradition (a much maligned word in the modernists' canon) not as a set of rules and strictures but as an open space for the dissemination and articulation of ideas. It is not surprising that the poets and artists of Paz's tradition have all discovered their essence in internationalism.

The same intellectual awareness in Paz's essays can be found in his poetry, in particular in his major collections, *Libertad bajo palabra,* 1949 (revised in 1960, 1968, 1981, and 1988; *Freedom under Parole*) and *Ladera este,* 1969 (*East Slope*). Poetry grounds the multiplicity of Paz's work: it is a form of expression that Paz transformed into the point of encounter between philosophy and aesthetics, thought and sensation, especially in his most ambitious poems, *Piedra de sol,* 1957 (*Sunstone*) and *Blanco,* 1967 (*Blanco*). The connections between the poetry and the rest of the work can be seen in particular in Paz's reading of Mexico, which he re-created as a convergence of different civilizations. In *El laberinto de la soledad,* 1950 (*The Labyrinth of Solitude*), Paz wrote the definitive work on modern Mexico, a country that is for him as enigmatic as a poem can be.

Born on 31 March 1914 in the Mexico City suburb of Mixcoac, Paz was the son of a freethinking lawyer-sympathizer with the popular revolutionary forces of Emiliano Zapata (who was one of the initiators of the Agrarian Reform) and of a Catholic daughter of Spanish immigrants, who sent the young poet to a French school in Mexico at an early age. Paz, by his own admission, grew up surrounded in a world that had been already destroyed by the Mexican Revolution (1910–1920). In this world, *modernismo* was the reigning literary tradition that accounts for some of Paz's initial readings. (It is important to clarify here *modernismo* is not to be confused with Anglo-American *modernism*—which in Spanish America, as in France, is called the *vanguardia* or avant-garde.) *Modernismo* can be seen as Spanish American symbolism, or at least as one of the versions of a fin de siècle ideology—a late-nineteenth- and early-twentieth-century revolution in poetic language and in political thought. *Modernismo* renovated poetic language—exemplified in the exquisite work of the Nicaraguan Rubén Darío—and allowed a pan-Hispanic Spanish Americanism. It was a movement of political and aesthetic rebirth whose profound effects are still felt throughout Spanish American literature.

If *modernismo* informed Paz's early readings, the second part of Paz's literary education took place fully within the *vanguardia* or avant-garde—a second attempt, after *modernismo,* at artistic renewal in Spain and Spanish America starting about 1916. Paz's beginnings as a writer follow at least twenty years of uninterrupted avant-garde experimentation, in a milieu where cultural debates

2

were the norms of the day. The primary nucleus of this cultural debate concerned the relationship between aesthetics and politics, between the solitary task of writers and their responsibility to the community at large. This is a debate that Paz followed in his early years, and it will be present throughout his life. Thus, if one of the branches of the avant-garde took sides with Juan Ramón Jiménez (1881–1958) and his notion of an "arte puro" (an art removed from daily concerns, from the contingent) other sectors of the *vanguardia* opted for open political commitment. Paz's many published critiques of the Mexican avant-garde group Contemporáneos, for example, center on this issue: for Paz, these poets opened Mexican culture to outside influences, but their art remained to a certain extent unconcerned with Mexican reality.

It is important to underscore that Paz sought early on a critical role for art, and early on concerned himself with the issue of social responsibility and its relation to aesthetic freedom. As an attempt to balance these two, Paz founded the magazine *Barandal* in 1931. *Barandal* lasted only seven issues (until March 1932), but the journal can be used as an index of the literary convictions that Paz was trying to negotiate at the time. In his choice of texts he tried to combine a political with an aesthetic avant-garde, including Joyce, Marinetti, Valéry, Alberti, and others. Paz rejected the "pure art" of the Contemporáneos but remained skeptical of political (what would later be called "socialist realist") art. In his "Etica del artista" (Ethics of the Artist) a text he published in *Barandal*, he dealt precisely with the distinction between an art of thesis and a pure art. As Paz succinctly put it: "El artista ¿debe tener una doctrina completa—religiosa, política, etc.—dentro de la cual debe enmarcar su obra? ¿O debe, simplemente, sujetarse a las leyes de la creación estética, desentendiéndose de cualquier otro problema? ¿Arte de tesis o arte puro?" (Should the artist have a complete doctrine—political, religious, etc.—within which he should frame his work? Or must he, simply, confine himself to the laws of aesthetic creation, not involving himself in any other problem? An art of thesis or a pure art?)[1] After considering both options, Paz opts for a critical art, an art of thesis.

This "critical" perspective allows art to be seen as paramount to the modern world, and debates on its role can be seen in Paz's early work, particularly in the dialectical relationship between "pure" and socially committed art. This is the main thrust, for example, of "Poesía de soledad y poesía de comunión," 1943 (Poetry of Solitude and Poetry of Communion)—the kernel out of which *The Bow and the Lyre* was born—and it is directly relevant to *The Labyrinth of Solitude* as well as to Paz's comments on the role of poetry in the contemporary world in the latter *La otra voz,* 1990 (The Other Voice). Paz's work, as well as his standing as an intellectual, are framed by this debate—one that he negotiat-

3

ed throughout his life, opting for a critical middle ground, where aesthetic innovation is complemented by a concern with history, society, and ideological discourse. We cannot understand the complexity of Paz's work as an intellectual without taking into account that the very image of the intellectual that Paz proposed has as its roots a conflict that originates in the 1930s and that reappeared throughout the 1960s, 1970s, and 1980s.

It is important to keep in mind at the outset at least three general lines of development: politics, Mexico, and art. History and politics entered into Paz's life in 1937, when he abandoned Mexico City for Mérida, Yucatán, and felt bound to react to the Spanish Civil War, which had broken out in 1936. His concerns with Mexico and with its problems came to the forefront when he left his country to work on a Guggenheim grant in the United States and then settled in Paris; issues relating to art and technology, East and West were his principal concerns while he lived in India from 1962 until 1968. Politics, Mexico, and art were continually renegotiated in his work since then. By 1941, Paz had already developed the thread that would tie together the most important part of his poetic work: "un vínculo entre historia natural y soledad individual, además del papel saludable, diríase terapéutico, que juega la poesía en relación a estos dos" (a link between natural history and individual solitude, aside from the salutary, even therapeutic role, that poetry plays in relation to these two (49). From then on, his work will continually develop along these lines.

Surrealism, to a certain extent, initially gave these concerns a form. As Jason Wilson explains, for Paz surrealism was a mental attitude, based on the possibility of using poetry in order to transcend the contradictions inherent in life, and in order to make of man a totality, once again, participating and reintegrating himself within experiences that defy temporality. As an aesthetic credo, surrealism gave Paz an aesthetics of the poetic instant.[2] It gave Paz a notion of the world as correspondence, one that links erotics and poetics with politics. Surrealism's emphasis is on the moral dissidence of the poet, the search for a total honesty of voice, the idea that chance puts Humanity in contact with the uncertainty of living and allows us to communicate and commune with others:

> el surrealismo busca un nuevo sagrado extrarreligioso, fundado en el triple eje de la libertad, el amor y la poesía. La tentativa surrealista se ha estrellado contra un muro. Colocar a la poesía en el centro de la sociedad, convertirla en el verdadero alimento de los hombres y en la vía para conocerse tanto como para transformarse, exige también una liberación total de la misma sociedad. Sólo en una sociedad libre la poesía será un bien común, una creación colectiva y una participación universal. El fracaso

del surrealismo nos ilumina sobre otro, acaso de mayor envergadura: el de la tentativa revolucionaria. Allí donde las antiguas religiones y tiranías han muerto, renacen los cultos primitivos y las feroces idolatrías.

Surrealism looks for a new metareligious sacred, founded upon the triple axes of liberty, love, and poetry. The surrealist attempt has hit a wall. To place poetry in the center of society, to turn it into the real food for man and into the way of self-knowledge as well as self-transformation, also demands society's total liberation. Only in a free society will poetry be a common good, a collective creation, and a universal participation. The failure of surrealism also illuminates another, perhaps greater one: that of revolutionary attempts. There where old religions and tyrannies have succumbed, the primitive cults and ferocious idolatries are reborn.[3]

Libertad bajo palabra and *The Labyrinth of Solitude* usher in the mature period of Paz's work. In spite of Paz's voluminous curiosity about all facets of intellectual endeavor, one can see the later Paz (the Paz that writes in the 1950s and, above all, in the 1960s) as engaged in a continuous exploration that reinforces a structure already in place by 1949. This is not to say that Paz "stopped developing" or that his poetry and his prose show no marked change after *Libertad bajo palabra,* but that we shall not find sudden shifts. There is instead a sense of variation and elaboration, as if Paz had understood the key in which he had to write his fugue and proceeded to its variations.

In Paz's work from the 1950s on, the different forms of culture and the different manifestations of history constitute and complement both poetry and prose to the extent that, at times, each becomes a sketch of the other. The comparison with the Chilean Pablo Neruda might be instructive: Neruda, as Emir Rodríguez Monegal saw clearly, is the writer of books of poems, series that give the illusion of a profound multiplicity of voices.[4] Neruda's different registers give the reader the illusion of change, although one could say that this change coexists with a constant sense of self that produces the different modalities of the voice. Paz, on the other hand, is a poet of a more "subterranean" kind of change; his poetry seems to be written all in a single register with no striking variations. What is important in Paz is not the different changes in the poetry but its fundamental sameness. This vision of change as sameness is important in order to track Paz's work after the first edition of *Libertad bajo palabra.* It informs the hidden procedure of Paz's *The Labyrinth of Solitude,* written while he was already living in Paris, and his book on poetry and poetics, *The Bow and the Lyre.*

In Mexico, as well as throughout Latin America, Paz was a commanding intellectual presence. A poet who lived the greater part of the twentieth century torn between the illusions of profound social change and the necessary compromises of democracy, Paz welcomed the end of the cold war as the end to a ruinous dialectical interplay between two systems that had held the world in thrall and whose squabbles and territorial disputes over spheres of influence so afflicted Latin America. At times his positions were polemical, and his relationship with the left, both in Mexico as well as in Latin America, tortuous. He repeatedly criticized the Cuban government for its human rights abuses and its lack of intellectual freedom; he forthrightly denounced the Sandinista government in neighboring Nicaragua for abuses of power, even while they were fighting the Contra rebellion financed by the United States. Because Cuba, Nicaragua, and El Salvador were rallying points for the Latin American intellectual left, Paz's position had been at times condemned and often misunderstood as irresponsible criticism by a prominent intellectual who refused to see the severity of the Central American crisis. When protesters in Mexico condemned what they saw as his one-sided critique of the Latin American left, particularly in *Vuelta,* Paz responded that *Vuelta* also condemned, in its time, the military rightist dictatorships of the Southern Cone. More recently Paz was seen as an apologist for the Mexican Partido Revolucionario Institucional (PRI) that he so criticized during the late 1960s and early 1970s. Paz responded to those attacks by pointing out the relative degree of openness that the PRI has manifested since the 1960s, while Mexico is still in an ongoing process of democratization that can by no means be considered complete. In the midst of the recent turmoil in Mexico, with the Zapatista rebellion in 1994 and the contentious presidential elections of the same year, Paz repeatedly signed and authored editorials warning against further dissolution into chaos, trying to stake out a tenuous middle ground.

Certainly, any book on Octavio Paz could engage in both political and poetical polemics that span not only his political conservatism during the Central American crisis but also his comments on art, aesthetics, love, and other issues. I have chosen to present in this book several possible avenues for criticism of Paz's work. A book that renders Paz in a more polemical mode is outside the strict parameters of this work.

Understanding Octavio Paz examines Paz's poems and essays: the poetry collections that Paz grouped in 1949 under the title *Libertad bajo palabra,* his later *Salamandra,* 1962 (*Salamander*), *Ladera este,* 1969 (*East Slope*), *Vuelta,* 1969–1975 (*Return*), and *Arbol adentro,* 1987 (*A Tree Within*); as well as the essays from *El laberinto de la soledad,* 1950 (*The Labyrinth of Solitude*), *Postdata,* 1970 (*The Other Mexico: Critique of the Pyramid*), and *El ogro filantrópico,* 1974 (*The Philanthropic Ogre*). I include Paz's meditations on the function of the modern state, and on Mexican politics, also collected in the 1993 editions of *The Labyrinth of Solitude* and *Itinerario* (Itinerary), in which Paz has recounted the different stages of his political development. At the same time, and because the different aspects of Paz's work cannot necesarily be seen in isolation, I examine his essays on poetics, including the book-length *El arco y la lira,* 1956; 2d ed., 1967 (*The Bow and the Lyre*), *Los hijos del limo,* 1974 (*Children of the Mire*), and the more recent *La otra voz,* 1990 (*The Other Voice*). I also examine some of his essays on poetry and society, collected in *Corriente alterna,* 1967 (*Alternating Current*); on Eastern and Western culture in *Conjunciones y disyunciones,* 1969 (*Conjunctions and Disjunctions*); on culture, translation, technology, and change in *El signo y el garabato,* 1973 (*The Sign and the Scrawl*); and on poetry in *Las peras del olmo,* 1957 (*The Pears of the Elm Tree*), and *Puertas al campo,* 1966 (*Doors to the Fields*), 1976 (*The Siren and the Seashell*).

Given the enormous quantity and, above all, range, of Paz's work, I have merely mentioned the more important clusters of works. Undoubtedly, I have also been helped in this endeavor by the volume of early Paz writings edited by Enrico Mario Santí (as well as its introduction) titled *Primeras letras,* 1988 (*First Letters*); the interviews collected as *Pasión crítica,* 1985 (*Critical Passion*); the essays on contemporary political issues collected in *Tiempo nublado,* 1983 (*Stormy Weather*), *Pequeña crónica de grandes días,* 1990 (*Minor Chronicle of Great Days*), and by the innovatively designed work titled *Solo a dos voces,* 1973 (*Solo for Two Voices*) where Octavio Paz and Julián Ríos square off in a project that seems almost utopian: book, interview, collection of photographs—truly a chronicle of the late 1960s and early 1970s.

Of necessity, some works have been eliminated from discussion: Paz's *Renga,* 1972; a collective poetry project, *Sor Juana Inés de la Cruz o las trampas de la fé,* 1982 (*Sor Juana Inés de la Cruz or the Traps of Faith*); Paz's lucid reading of structural anthropology titled *Claude Lévi-Strauss o el nuevo festín de Esopo,* 1967 (*Claude Lévi-Strauss: An Introduction*); *El mono gramático,* 1974 (*The Monkey Grammarian*); and *La llama doble,* 1993 (*The Double Flame*). Perhaps closer attention to these books would yield a different *version* of Paz, but I doubt it would lead to a *different* Paz. All in all, I think readers will find in this book a comprehensive vision of one of the major poets in this century, whose work needed to be reexamined as a whole, not only in light of new publications but also in terms of Paz's own revision of himself. Among the books of criticism that have been most useful, I mention those of Enrico Mario Santí, Pere Gimferrer, Rachel Phillips, Jason Wilson, John Fein, Julia Kushigian; the collections edited by Alfredo Roggiano, Mario Valdés; and, last but not least, the trenchant critique by Jorge Aguilar Mora.

As a poet who was fundamentally concerned with change, Paz nevertheless surprises us by the smoothness with which he passes from one "version" of himself to another. From aesthetics to politics, from art to society, from art criticism to anthropology, Paz continually re-read himself; he went back to explore previously unexplored areas, or revisited earlier work to synthesize and join what seemed to be dialectically opposed elements into a new image. I have tried to give detailed readings of Paz's poetry collections in terms of aesthetics, while at the same time allowing the biographical context to explain areas or problems that may not be readily apparent while reading the poetry itself. At times, given Paz's penchant for revisiting previous work, I have also used a thematic organization—particularly regarding the multiple offshoots of his major books *Libertad bajo palabra, The Labyrinth of Solitude, The Bow and the Lyre.*

It is not tendentious to say how much easier, perhaps, this critical work would have been, if Paz were a novelist or prose writer. Poetry entails collection and assembly, dispersal and communion; a single poem lives within a book, and the book's organization of sometimes disparate poems speaks of a centripetal but also a centrifugal force. Indeed, as we study the body of Paz's work, we see that he fundamentally altered some of the poems in his earliest collections, included or excluded them in various reprints, and so on. By the same token, some of his essays appear under different titles and in different versions at different times. This is why any reader that approaches the work of Paz is confronted with the problematic notion of text as a tissue of metamorphoses, of change. In this sense, some of the sections of *Libertad bajo palabra,* are directly relevant to *The Labyrinth of Solitude,* as well as to *The Bow and the Lyre* and to *Alternating Current.* Similarly *El signo y el garabato* contains work that is important for the understanding of poems that were written before the collection (such as *Blanco*) and so on. To follow a chronological imperative blindly does not make sense; to discard it completely, however, would have also been uncalled for in a book that proposes a comprehensive view of Paz.

I interrogate Paz in terms of his literary and historical positions by noting how his texts coalesce to form a kind of narrative, while at the same time leaving sufficient space to prevent the narrative from closing itself on its own circle. This overview has given biographical and general information on Paz. Chapter 2, on *Libertad bajo palabra,* examines themes in the collection as a whole, moving then to a book-by-book analysis of the collection. Chapter 3 reads Paz's work on Mexican society and politics, starting with *The Labyrinth of Solitude* and taking into account Paz's more recent opinions on Mexico and the Mexican state. In chapter 4 I have included Paz's work on poetics, particularly *The Bow and the Lyre, Los signos en rotación,* and *Children of the Mire.* I have included the poetry written immediately before and during Paz's long stay in India in a separate chapter, chapter 5, as critics generally agree that this is the most important period of Paz's life. Because *Blanco* is Paz's most ambitious text, I have devoted a full chapter to it, chapter 6. Finally, chapter 7 takes into account Paz's work after his return to Mexico from the East. As I explain in the conclusion to this work, if I have given more emphasis to Paz's earlier work, it is because in it we follow a progression of thought that is then submitted to multiple variations. We can see the author fashioning himself as he wants to be.

Sadly, as this book was off to press, President Ernesto Zedillo, returning to Mexico from the 1998 Summit of the Americas in Santiago, Chile, formally announced that Octavio Paz had died in Mexico City on 19 April, after a long illness. It is clear that Paz's death closes off a chapter in Mexican and Latin American literary history—a chapter whose outlines and contours we can merely glimpse at this time, without the benefit of distance and time. For a book of criticism on Paz, there is the temptation to go over, once again, to render all present tense verbs into a closed off past, to formally render a certain kind of closure to life. I have resisted this temptation at this time, and although I have eliminated what are now the sad inaccuracies of a life that is no longer with us, I have chosen to render Paz in the present tense of writing—a present tense which is also that of his poems, and of his work as a whole.

All critics who attempt to examine Paz's work comprehensively end up apologizing for the gaps in their texts. But then again, Paz beckons his readers toward a synthesis that eludes the poet himself—while also warning us against the fallacy of subsuming multiplicities into one coherent whole. This book is but the prelude to other readings, attempts to fill in the gaps of a work that is always, essentially, addressed to the future reader.

CHAPTER 2

Libertad bajo palabra

Libertad bajo palabra (Freedom under Parole), Paz's own collection of his first books, has never been published in English under that title. Most of the poems appear in different collections, such as *Selected Poems of Octavio Paz* (1963) and *Early Poems, 1935–1955* (1973). The English-speaking reader, then, has no access to the multiple versions of this book that Paz has created throughout the years. In 1949 Paz collected seventy-four poems—most of which had been published in his youth—and gave the collection the title of a prose poem, "Libertad bajo palabra," that from then on would appear as the collection's first text. *Libertad bajo palabra* has gone through five editions (the last one in 1988): in the process Paz has not simply reorganized the book into different sections; he has also included or excluded various texts from various revisions. As Enrico Mario Santí remarked in his introduction to the most recent edition, *Libertad bajo palabra* is the title of not one but of many texts: a book of seventy-four poems published in 1949; a collection that appeared in 1960; a third edition of 1968 in which many poems of the second edition are rearranged or excluded; and a fourth version that appeared as the first part of Paz's 1979 collection published under the title. Even though *Libertad bajo palabra,* constantly assembled and reassembled, collects poems written before—and after—1949, neither the sections nor the poems are presented according to dates of publication. Instead, chronology and aesthetics are combined according to a principle Paz names in one of his "advertencias" to the collection of 1960 as "afinidades de tema, color, ritmo, entonación o atmósfera" (affinities of theme, color, rhythm, beat or atmosphere).[1]

Libertad bajo palabra's organization and reorganization over time speaks of a desire to collect and circumscribe a particular period of Paz's life (1935–1957) in a manner not unlike that of Charles Baudelaire in *Les Fleurs du mal,* Walt Whitman in *Leaves of Grass,* Ezra Pound in *Cantos,* and the Spanish poet Luis Cernuda in *La realidad y el deseo* (Reality and Desire). Paz's model might be closest to Cernuda's, for Cernuda's book, like Paz's, attempts to establish a tenuous symmetry between two elements: reality and desire for Cernuda, words and freedom for Paz. The idea of order in Cernuda, however, is temporal and chronological; Paz, on the other hand, attempts to create some kind of "ideal history" that does not exactly correspond to the lived experience "outside" of the book. For example, *Entre la piedra y la flor* (*Between the Stone and the Flower*), the fifth book that Paz published in 1941 (but wrote during the late 1930s) appears, in the 1979 edition of *Poemas,* subsumed within *Libertad bajo palabra* under the section *Calamidades y milagros* (Calamities and Miracles); when readers reach this section, they have already read many of the poems written by Paz *after* his departure for the United States in 1943. Such rearrangements occur throughout the book; what I underscore is that *Libertad bajo palabra* is not meant to be a linear account of Paz's poetic life.

The ideal history of *Libertad bajo palabra* changes through time. This history may be seen not only as the poet's biography, but as different versions of it, as these are told and retold over time. By virtue of the corrections and emendations to which the texts have been submitted, we can follow the different versions of the narration that Paz makes out of his own life. *Libertad bajo palabra* also reveals texts that can be plotted over time; the same text written in different forms at different periods. For example, it is important to distinguish the 1941 version of the poem *Between the Stone and the Flower* from the version that is found in *Libertad bajo palabra.* The first version of *Between the Stone and the Flower* consists of 242 lines; the second is much reduced. Because the poem is about the social condition of Yucatecan peasants, Paz later justified the change as one in which the "ideologue" disappeared only to allow the essence of reality to appear: "En la primera, yo veía al explotado; en la segunda, veo también a la cultura india humillada." (In the first, I saw the exploited; in the second, I also see the humiliated Indian culture.)[2] The trappings of rhetoric removed, the poem aims towards the timelessness of the aesthetic object. Paz uses his rewritings to turn, in a sense, poems into essays. The poems explain themselves as the poet tries to bring out the original motivation for the poem itself.

Paz's desire to collect his early poetry in one book was a process that predates the first edition of *Libertad bajo palabra.* In 1942, Paz first joined his previous books (*Bajo tu clara sombra, Raíz del hombre, Primer día, Noche de resurrecciones*) in *A la orilla del mundo* (On the Shore of the World) a collection that does not include the book written on his experiences in Yucatán, *Between the Stone and the Flower.* After *A la orilla del mundo,* his first collection, in the proper sense of the term, there was a marked change in Paz's work. He left for the United States in 1943, discovered the more colloquial voice of American poets (including William Carlos Williams), and wrote most of the poems of *Calamities and Miracles* and *Condición de nube* (Condition of Clouds); both books were later included in *Libertad bajo palabra.* It was only in 1947 and in

Paris, and via the urging of the Mexican critic Alfonso Reyes, that the first edition of *Libertad bajo palabra* appeared, in 1949.

The first edition of *Libertad bajo palabra,* as Enrico Mario Santí has explained, has the form and the shape of a sonata in three movements: a central allegro section flanked by two, more somber moods.[3] The structural "trunk" of the book is composed of *A la orilla del mundo* plus two other sections, *Asueto* (Rest) and *El girasol* (Sunflower)—most of them written in the United States and in Paris—and two more sections: *Puerta condenada* (Condemned Door) and the long poem "Himno entre ruinas" (Hymn among the Ruins). This initial compilation has suffered many mutations over time. In the 1988 edition, for example, Paz incorporates "Hymn among the Ruins" as the beginning of the section titled *La estación violenta* (The Violent Season), which was originally compiled in 1958 after *¿Aguila o sol?* 1951 *(Eagle or Sun?)* and *Semillas para un himno,* 1954 (Seeds for a Hymn). What was used to symbolize the end of an epoch, signaled by the inclusion of "Hymn among the Ruins" at the end of the first edition of *Libertad bajo palabra,* is now joined to other sections that were written outside of Mexico, along with other books that were published separately in the intervening years (between the first and the second edition of *Libertad bajo palabra*). *Libertad bajo palabra,* then, does not only grow, but is actually amplified, and its expansive growth affects all of its branches—in a given period of time, other books are incorporated, older poems rearranged and revised. Time itself, according to a tenet that Paz will insist on since the 1960s, is linked to space, and the poem's space is as elastic as time. The image that underlies *Libertad bajo palabra* is that of the tree, an image that recurs in the latter period of Paz's work (see, for example, his 1987 collection *Arbol adentro* (*A Tree Within*).

The prose poem that gives *Libertad bajo palabra* its title was written in Paris, and joins all of the previous work written before that time; the title recalls *Parole en libertà,* by the Italian Futurist Filippo Tomasso Marinetti. Paz plays on the title in order to talk about two elements—freedom and words—that circumscribe each other as he shuffles a number of tightly woven concepts: liberty, language, form, along with *vigilia* (vigil), a state that is not quite that of the surrealist dream nor that of total consciousness. For Paz, *Libertad bajo palabra* means that art conditions liberty; art is that to which liberty submits. Another way of reading the title is that language or words are concrete and material signifiers of freedom; the freedom of language is the guarantee for all other kinds of freedom. The relationship between the two terms is particularly complex for Paz; art has its own laws and its own rules, and poets must abandon their sense of law and consciousness in order to seek whatever it is that gives art its sense of structure.

Because freedom is not the central item of this equation (*palabra,* "word," is), Paz warns that the rejection of form, the abandoning of words in (or to) liberty, does not necessarily entail a gain in freedom. Hence his criticism of certain versions of the avant-garde, particularly that of Futurists, who desired freedom from grammar and syntax only to be enslaved to the very principle of a liberty (from grammar and syntax) that *they* subjectively defined. Paz's critique of surrealism's automatic writing follows the same rationale, for automatic writing confuses freedom with automatism, which is merely one of the principles, or possibilities, of language. By placing words over freedom, the poet is always in an attitude of expectant discovery. Paz's position is closer, in this sense, to Heideggerian phenomenology than to existentialism; as he will explain in *The Bow and the Lyre,* words and liberty are joined together as being is to nonbeing.

"Libertad bajo palabra" underscores from the onset Paz's statements with regard to form and its relationship to liberty. First, the poem is markedly different from most of the others of the collection (with the exception of those included in *Eagle or Sun?*). It is a prose poem in six paragraphs, and it articulates a particular relationship between form and content by using a "hybrid" form. (Note how Paz situates a "hybrid" structure such as the prose poem, at the outset of a book that gives an account of his beginnings as a poet.) "Libertad bajo palabra" talks about borders, but it is also, as a poem, a border in itself:

Allá, donde terminan las fronteras, los caminos se borran. Donde empieza el silencio. Avanzo lentamente y pueblo la noche de estrellas, de palabras, de la respiración de un agua remota que me espera donde comienza el alba.

Out there, where the frontiers end, roads are erased. Where silence begins. I go forward slowly and I people the night with stars, with speech, with the breathing of distant water waiting for me where the dawn appears. (*EP* 3)

"Out there" ("Allá") is always a space that goes beyond the poem but that returns to the poem itself. Unlike other texts by Paz, "Libertad bajo palabra" is less about the aesthetic instant of time, but about the very unfolding of a truth. As such, its position at the beginning of the book corresponds to the idea Paz has of the book as a whole. "Libertad bajo palabra" is a kind of travelogue that begins and ends and consumes itself on the page; it is a poem about the creation of poetry always as a search for the margins where silence and words are joined. "Libertad bajo palabra" thus ends by positing a state of reciprocity: the word *is* freedom by being situated *under* freedom, and freedom itself keeps the world in a state of perpetual invention. Most of the poem is a meditation on the realities that the poet and the word invent as they go along. The poem's beat and rhythm, its continuous shifts, its stops and starts—all give the impression of the inner voice of a panting wanderer, situated at the limit of a known world. The poem's form allows Paz to pursue a seemingly deranged sense of poetic imagery. Paz's poetry questions an "other" whose identity is never clear, but who seems to bear a relationship with the poet as divided self. Part of the poet's destiny, as Paz reminds us, is to have a conversation with a self that is precisely an other—in a relationship similar to, but also profoundly dissimilar to, the one that words have with themselves. The poet borrows not only words, but also the very silence that these words inhabit. Silence is defined as a border-state in *Libertad bajo palabra,* but this silence is also the otherness of language, something in which language itself gets lost.

For Paz, writing entails a particular awareness of the opacity of words, joined to an understanding of the poet's otherness to himself. The poet invents but is also invented by reality; nature is composed of binary dualities that need to be apprehended as a whole. This awareness of totality, at the same time, entails understanding loss: the poet is always a trembling presence amid the beautiful and the debased, both seen as translations, or versions, of the sublime. Paz is not afraid of to reveal himself as both the passive bearer of desire and the sadistic torturer of words; he knows that in this system the one who punishes is also the one who desires. In other words, the complex interaction that Paz reveals in terms of otherness, and in terms of his own relationship to poetry, entails an awareness of the poet as judge, victim, and witness. As he explains in "Libertad bajo palabra": "el juez, la víctima, el testigo. Tú eres esos tres. ¿A quién apelar ahora y con qué argucias destruir al que te acusa? Inútiles los memoriales, los ayes, los alegatos. Inútil tocar a puertas condenadas. No hay puertas, hay espejos." ("the judge, the victim, the witness. You are all three of them. To whom will you appeal now and with what sophistries will you annihilate the accuser? Petitions, appeals, allegations, all useless. Useless to knock on condemned doors. These are not doors, but mirrors" [*EP* 3].)

Paz's poetic voice can be seen as a center that moves, that achieves some kind of inner balance precisely from its combinations. Paz swerves out of the dramatic oppositions of Romantic poetry by inventing himself as a fluid, instead of an antinomial, poet. For Paz, the poet is the one that loses himself to the extent that he can contemplate the "other" and know that this other is himself. One of the most used adjectival forms in Paz entails precisely a blending of contraries, as the title of his first collection, "Bajo tu clara sombra" (Under Your Clear Shadow) implies. This is why Paz's poetry gives an account of a constantly shifting presence. This presence resembles that of poets, who proclaim their own mutability. Paz projects himself upon a surface where the exchange between self and other becomes an eternal dialectical interplay. He does not oppose words to silence but shows, on the contrary, how poets give meaning to silence by continually inventing language.

The idea that Paz develops in his early poetry—its achievement, in a sense—is the creation of a poetics of movement, of metamorphosis, where authenticity does not entail immutability, or even an essence impervious to time. This is why the poet needs to allow words to become the center of his poetics: words in freedom change and thus serve as an analogy for the poet's self. Paz will recall this idea in every one of the books included in *Libertad bajo palabra,* but the collection should be seen as, in a sense, the embodiment of this idea of progress. Neither the poems, nor the poet, nor the book, are ever fixed. In the introduction to his collection of *Poemas* in 1979, Paz explains: "Los poemas son objetos verbales inacabados e inacabables. No existe lo que se llama 'versión definitiva': cada poema es el borrador de otro, que nunca escribiremos" (*Poemas* 11). (Poems are verbal objects both unfinished as well as "unfinishable." There is no "definitive version" of a poem: each poem is the draft of another, that perhaps we will never write.)

Nonetheless, the poetics of change has a slow evolution in Paz. For Paz, a book is but a tissue of relationships given in the form of fragments. The reader always begins with ruins, with bodies that have become nature, with a space that is completely colonized by the idea of form (or even, for the critic, by Paz's own essayistic writing on his own poetry). There are avenues, there are things that are not said in Paz's work, but one has to arrive at them after completely reading the space as a whole. This is why we shall examine *Libertad bajo palabra* first, thus reading the poetry according to the nonchronological order in which the poet, as one of the primary readers of his own work, has chosen to collect it. As he says, in *Corriente alterna:* "Las verdaderas ideas de un poema no son las que se le ocurren al poeta *antes* de escribir el poema sino las que *después,* con o sin su voluntad, se desprenden naturalmente de la obra"(7). ("The real ideas of a poem are not those that occur to the poet before he writes his poem, but rather those that appear in his work afterward, whether by design or by accident" [*AC* 6].)

Libertad bajo palabra is divided into five major sections: *Bajo tu clara sombra* (Under Your Clear Shadow), *Calamidades y milagros* (*Calamities and Miracles*), *Semillas para un himno* (Seeds for a Hymn), *¿Aguila o sol? (Eagle or Sun?),* and *La estación violenta* (The Violent Season). Each of these books is subdivided into different sections; in most cases one of the sections names the book itself. For example, *Bajo tu clara sombra* is divided into six: "Primer día"

(First Day), "Bajo tu clara sombra" (Under Your Clear Shadow), "Raíz del hombre" (Root of Man), "Noche de resurrecciones" (Night of Resurrection), "Asueto" (Rest), and "Condición de nube" (Condition of Cloud). *Calamidades y milagros* is divided into two sections: "Puerta condenada" (Condemned Door) and "Calamidades y milagros"; *Semillas para un himno* is divided into three: "El girasol" (Sunflower), "Semillas para un himno," and "Piedras sueltas" (Loose Stones); *Eagle or Sun?* is introduced by the poem that, as in *Libertad bajo palabra,* names the collection as a whole, and is then subdivided into three books; "Trabajos del poeta" (The Poet's Works), "Arenas movedizas" (Shifting Sands), and "Eagle or Sun?" Only *La estación violenta* is not divided into sections; rather, it is composed of nine long poems, concluding with *Piedra de sol* (*Sunstone*). As we can see, the books that form *Libertad bajo palabra* name themselves out of a particular nucleus that is found within each of the sections, as if the original kernel would produce the later offshoots. This is the book's aesthetic mode of operation; it is important to keep it in mind as we read the different sections of the work. That Paz has rearranged his earlier books not in chronological order, but by means of an aesthetic contruct, proves that one cannot read Paz solely in terms of his biography. That he names and revisits his biography in longer poems such as *Sunstone* as well as in *Pasado en claro,* 1974 (*A Draft of Shadows*) reveals that Paz is constantly linking an aesthetic to a historical reading of his life. It is important, therefore, to examine his life as he has poetically rearranged it, and to rescue the other, apparently more linear, construct that structures that life.

Poetic Beginnings: *Bajo tu clara sombra*

Primer día (1935)

The 1979 edition of Paz's *Poemas* begins in 1935, although Paz had previously published, in 1933, a small edition of poems titled *Luna silvestre,* that he has never since republished. Granted, the initial date placed at the onset of *Libertad bajo palabra* (1935–1957) is somewhat misleading: the book actually contains, although rearranged in later sections (most notably, in *Calamities and Miracles*), poems like "Nocturno" (Nocturne), "Insomnio" (Insomnia), and "Espejo" (Hope) written in 1932, 1933, and 1934, respectively. That Paz rearranges these poems within a later book, one that contains texts written precisely after the first major change in Paz's life (his departure for Yucatán in 1937) without changing even the dates of the collection as a whole, is significant in terms of the organization that Paz imposes on the revised editions of *Libertad bajo palabra.* If the young Paz reacted against the "pure poetry," or the

16

overaestheticized stance of his immediate precursors in the period around 1937, the later Paz has revisited earlier aesthetic positions in order to strike a balance between aesthetics and history, between art and contingency. It is this balance that is most evident in his decision to arrange the initial sections of *Libertad bajo palabra* without necessarily following a chronological arrangement, eventually positioning some of the initial poems later in the book.

Primer día is a slim collection, its central section a series of five sonnets, flanked by three short poems that introduce them ("Tu nombre" [Your Name], "Monólogo" [Monologue], and "Alameda" [Poplar Grove]) and one longer poem ("Mar de día" [Sea at Daytime]) written completely in heptasyllables (seven-syllable verse) that concludes the series. What is valued in "Primer día" is precisely the poem as object. As befits a book that has been revised at a later time, what stands out in "Primer día" is the series of images anticipating those that Paz will use throughout his work: hair is compared to summer lightning (for Paz summer is "la estación ardiente" [the ardent season]) in a relationship of mobility / immobility: "immovil en la luz, pero danzante" (immobile in the light, but dancing). This dialectics between movement and stasis, between names and time, appears in "Primer día" as a paradoxical immobility that allows the poem to be a formal construction, rotating and fixed, "preso en su movimiento ensimismado" (imprisoned in its pensive movement) at the moment when the body dislodges itself from itself: "tu cuerpo de sí mismo se desata" (your body undone from itself).

In "Primer día" the body contains nature within a system of correspondences that Paz will explore later in his work. To go inside the body is to go inside nature; oblivion does not entail dissolution into space but actually getting lost in its absolute surface. It is matter itself that gives the poet the raison d'être for dissolution: one does not dissolve in air, but into surface, into body. One of Paz's central concepts in this book is that a fragment is capable of defining the world around it; the book itself is a fragment that promises the reader access to the totality of his work.

Bajo tu clara sombra (1935–1938)

Bajo tu clara sombra y otros poemas sobre España first appeared in Valencia in 1937, in the midst of the Spanish civil war, with a note written by the Spanish poet Manuel Altolaguirre. The book included a poem titled *¡No pasarán!* that Paz had actually published before he left for Spain in 1937, as a chapbook where he established his solidarity with the republican faction in Spain. In its original form, *Bajo tu clara sombra* was an extensive meditation written in ten cantos, celebrating the purity of love and the unity of man and woman with the earth.

Another edition is published in the collection *Tierra nueva* in 1941, and a third edition from 1942 collects these poems with those of earlier and later collections, like *Primer día, Raíz del hombre,* and *Noche de resurrecciones.*

Like those of *Primer día,* the poems in *Bajo tu clara sombra* have been heavily corrected, and again the corrections are done in terms of form, in order to release an "essential" idea buried within rhetoric. These revisions underscore the poems' status as epiphanies—in other words, as poems that appear to be written on the spur of the moment. Paz's poetics of ecstasy does not allow for a rhetorical torrent of emotions; because the moment is so defining in itself, his poems are cut up, divided into sections, as in "Entre la piedra y la flor," "Elegia" (Elegy), and "El Ausente" (The Absent One), from *Calamities and Miracles.* This way of arranging and fragmenting poetic expression will change in the later, longer poems, like *Sunstone.*

In Paz's *Poemas* (1979), *Bajo tu clara sombra* is divided into five sections, each based on a particular speaking situation: the poet talks about the loved one indirectly; the poems are addressed to an Other that is, at different times, either the loved one, the reader, or the poet himself. In the first section Paz names one adressee, "Bajo tu clara sombra / vivo como la llama al aire, / en tenso aprendizaje de lucero" (27) (Under your clear shadow / I live like the flame in air / in a tense apprenticeship of star) that changes in the second section ("Tengo que hablaros de ella" [I must tell you about her]), which then dissolves itself into a generalized "tú" in the third section ("Mira el poder del mundo, / mira el poder del polvo, mira el agua." [Look at the world's power / look at the power of dust, look at the water]) in order to transform itself into the Earth: "Deja que una vez más te nombre, tierra" (84) (Let me name you once again, earth). There are fundamentally three persons (or three voices) in these poems, and they come into being precisely out of the articulation of a triangular structure: lover–loved one–reader ("amante–amado–lector"). There is a direct link between Paz's expressive obliqueness or indirection, and the self-evidence of the object (Woman); the woman to whom the poet is speaking about is fundamentally *spoken about* to someone else. The first poem defines the speaker, and the second poem is about words and speech ("Tengo que hablaros de ella") as if the poet were driven by necessity to talk about her. It is in this poem that the speaker and the addressee (the "I" that speaks to a "you" to whom the poem is addressed) are in indirect relationship to the one who is being discussed. The third poem is addressed directly to the reader, it seems—a reader that has been transmuted, to a certain extent, into some kind of lover. It is a poem about the gaze, or looking: "Mira el poder del mundo" a looking that is manifested precisely in the subject. *Bajo tu clara sombra* renders visible the triangulation within Paz's erotic poetry.

Raíz del hombre (1937)

Raíz del hombre, in three sections, is one of the most revised of Paz's poems. Goetzinger states that from its first publication on, *Raiz del hombre* changes from a poem of 541 verses, to one of 232, and then to one of 55 verses.[4] Given such enormous change in the poem itself, it is impossible to read it without taking into account Paz's later poetics unless one has the first edition at hand. But if we follow Paz's ideas on correction, then the later version should be able to tell us more concisely what the earlier one was attempting, as for Paz correction brings out the original intentions of the poem.

In the 1988 edition of *Libertad bajo palabra,* the three fragments or meditations in "Raíz del hombre" concern the same subject, linked by the emblem of the tree and by the invisible circulation of a blood that flows throughout the text. The first section places the poet as a naked ephebe under a tree. The landscape is one that is in either future or anterior time, even though the poet insists on the immediacy of this landscape by means of deictics, shifters that point to a concrete object ("Este es el cielo más inmóvil, / y ésta la más pura desnudez" [This is the most immobile sky, this is the purest nakedness]) repeated throughout the poem. The second poem begins with a poetic imperative to burn voices and lips, and thus detain time. If in the first section nakedness was an attribute of the poet, at the end of the second section it is night itself that is naked of words ("la noche desnuda de palabras"). Paz does not make clear, at the end of this section, if he is speaking of himself as a lover (as opposed to the loved woman) or to another that is *himself* as a lover. The poem works by means of absolute negations ("Nadie sabe tu nombre ya" [Nobody knows your name any more]) and by providing details of a minimal landscape, composed of a flower and the tree itself ("the great tree of my blood" as he says in the first poem). Man and Woman are joined by the same tree and the same blood, and this exchange of fluids is the theme of the third section, where the blood comes out into the open in order to join both beings as part of the same circulatory system. The bodies disappear in this third poem to allow the blood to come forth and link them both to each other, as well as to the same system that is joined by the tree as well as by the three branches that compose the work.

In Paz's poetic diary "Vigilias: Diario de un soñador," we can trace the poet's original intentions: he quotes there the first section of the poem while talking about love as a force that is capable of revealing, by means of woman, the visible forms of the world. This is the argument of the poem: love is the "root of man"; it is precisely love that allows man and woman to abandon their individual beings in order to commune with a nature that is both within and without. There are nonetheless two further points to be made about this text. First, the idea of necessity that appears in the previous *Bajo tu clara sombra* ("tengo que hablaros de ella") is transformed here into strength and force. Second, these two are communicated by means of insistent shifters, and what the shifters name is as important as what they try to name and visualize. When Paz says, "Este es el cielo más inmóvil" (This is the most immobile sky) or "Esta es tu sangre" (This is your blood) he is not only trying to isolate the present; he is, by means of the immediacy given in the shifter, trying to render the object itself invisible. In other words, the deictic functions in a double mode: it insists on the immediacy of the object in order to give the reader the illusion that the object itself disappears or should disappear.

Written entirely in the present tense, *Raíz del hombre* is an important poem that anticipates Paz's later aesthetic concerns. This present is always in tension with its own attempt at immediacy, an immediacy in itself predicated on the illusion of disappearing subjectivities. But the poem can only name the "roots of man" by presenting us with ruins that the reader will reconstruct. Its fragments are doubly significant, for they isolate three instances of time that cannot be named as a whole.

Noche de resurrecciones (1942)

The fourth section of *Bajo tu clara sombra* is a poem similar to *Raíz del hombre,* at least in terms of its outward organization: a fragmented work in three sections. It was first published in fragmentary form in *Taller* in 1940, and it appears for the first time as a complete poem in Paz's first collection of books, *A la orilla del mundo* (1942), assembled after he returns from Spain to Mexico. However, *Noche de resurrecciones* is also a poem about form. The first section is written in free verse, the second in chained, assonanced tercets that echo Dante's (except for the last stanza), while the third poem is composed of an hendecasyllabic quartet. It would seem that what is resurrected within this night is an idea of form that Paz is working on at this time—one that, at least in its outward expression, is also to be found in the later chained tercets of "Mediodía" (Noon) from "Asueto."

Addressed to a lover, the first poem of *Noche de resurrecciones* talks about the movement of the body in a river. The manner in which Paz names this fluid mobility is by constructing it first as an immobile word, as if it were a bolt of lightning: "Lates entre la sombra, / blanca y desnuda: río" (*Poemas* 34). (You beat within the shade / river: white and naked). If the river appears as an image (followed by the abrupt beat signaled by the colon), the poem's first word, "Lates" (You beat) holds the key to the movement of the poem as a whole: the heartbeat can be seen as marking the appearance and disappearance of the loved body within the river. While the body floats in a river (or within a river), the poem signifies this movement toward silence. The woman is of the same substance of the water that moves toward the silence of rock: "Entre riberas impalpables quedas, / blanca y desnuda, piedra" (*Poemas* 34). (Amidst impalpable margins you remain / white and naked, stone). The verse moves from that sense of the "impalpable" to the solidity of "rocks." After the poet has immobilized this figure, after he has framed it, so to speak, within its own immobility as an object, the poem can "resurrect" the body in tercets, a form that dates back to antiquity. These tercets of the second poem are given in the first person plural, and they take the form of an address to the night. Enveloped by a night that is also a realm of primordial water, the poet lives on earth and brings forth a painful reed (*espiga*) as a creation that will help the poet dream toward a rebirth.

Noche de resurrecciones puts the reader in the midst of an Orphic scene repeated throughout Paz's work. The poet will be like the earth itself, creating out of himself a poetry that will take its place as nature: a refractory *being* that will resurrect the soul of the poet. A minor deity in this respect, as Paz mentions in the brief quatrain that is the third section of the poem, man himself is able to bring forth daylight.

Asueto

Paz's poetry collections aim toward a particular scene that is always imminent, yet always beyond reach. The images repeat themselves from book to book, and out of the recurrence of images a primordial landscape is produced. This landscape is almost minimalist; it is composed out of similar objects or elements: thunderbolt, river, strands of hair, sunlight. And out of these objects, Paz not only creates a scene but an idea of form—one that is constantly recombining its elements.

The title *Asueto* signals a moment of productive and creative rest, in which the pure materiality of things is apprehended. *Asueto,* the fifth subsection of the first major part of *Libertad bajo palabra,* is composed of twelve poems that differ in length and form: from the tercets of "Mediodía" (tercets also appear, as we saw, in *Noche de resurrecciones*) to sonnets like "Junio" (June) (similar, once again, to the sonnets of "Primer día"). Most of the poems are about particular sites ("Lago," "Jardín," "Arcos") or about a notion of a time becoming space, as in "Mediodía," "Medianoche" (Midnight), "Noche de verano" (Summer Night), "Junio," or "Primavera a la vista" (Spring Ahead). Paz can describe a particular scene and place the reader within it in few words; words turn into bolts of lightning that illuminate with precision.

In "Mediodía," one of Paz's most important early poems, the poet is blind-ed by a particular "resplandor" (splendor) that produces an empty circle of self-consuming light. "Mediodía" is also one of Paz's more difficult poems, because its sense of classic grandeur ("Sombras del mundo, cálidas ruinas" [Shadows of the word, warm ruins]) is based on a vision of static time where nothing hap-pens except for the poem's act of utterance. The poem, like many of Paz's, needs to be read in relation to the set of signifiers that it mobilizes in the tercets them-selves, with their chains of words and concepts. The text leads to a question that then resolves itself in a statement introduced by a dash, which in Spanish is gen-erally (although not exclusively) a marker for dialogue. Thus, precisely at the moment of falling, the subject understands himself as a voice:

> ¿éste caer en una entraña obscura
> es de la misma luz del mediodía
> que erige lo que toca en escultura?

> —El cuerpo es infinito y melodía.

> this falling on an obscure inside
> is of the same light as that of noon
> that erects what it touched into sculpture?

> —The body is infinite and noon.

One way of understanding this tercet is by noticing how its question is addressed to a notion of identity, to a vision of similarities among contraries that have played themselves out in the text. In this sense, a bottomless sense of falling is equated to ascending to the highest domains of light; falling is equated to its opposite. And the poem concludes with another perfect equation: that of the silent and absent sense of light at noon, with the hidden melody that the poet rescues from its depths. Paz responds to blindness with insight, in the latter's more literal meaning—an "inner sight" that rescues the hidden concordance, or melody, of nature. The infinite body without borders is thus apprehended with the vision of order given by melody.

"Medianoche," the companion poem to "Mediodía" that Paz places at a later point in the book, can only be defined by opposition. Here, the soul ascends toward heaven as fire, music, pure silence, or river. Song (not melody) is the cen-ter of this poem, where free verse allows for a tranquil song—in opposition to the ecstatic agonies of "Mediodía." In "Medianoche" there is precisely the expansive feeling of that which needs only the slightest circumscription, which Paz accomplishes by repeating the first line of the poem at the beginning of the last stanza. But this repetition is a welcome echo that the poem sees itself as pure song, wanting to achieve the vague contours of form. As in the best Romantic tradition, night is the realm of emanation, and here the reader can be certain that none of the jagged edges of light will interrupt the poem's flow.

"Mediodía" and "Medianoche" allow us to see two different but complementary sides of Paz. In one, the poet creates an object that communicates its own anguish by means of perfectly constructed tercets; in the other, tranquillity leads to self-reflection, but also to a song enamored of itself. That Paz is aware of the deceptive nature of these Romantic chiaroscuros, where the enchanted soul can sing of itself, is what leads him to face the terrifying clarity of "Mediodía." Hence, Paz's best compositions from *Libertad bajo palabra* (including its masterpiece, *Sunstone*) are also immensely problematic; the achievement of the perfect form seems at times a mode of self-punishment, of controlling precisely the boundlessness of the sublime, by turning the text into an object. In many ways, "Mediodía" is a terrifying poem, where eyes blindly rotate in their orbits, where the certainties of insight are blinded by an inner search.

Paz's notion of the poetic word is that it writes itself *over* itself, that it repeats other words proferred at another time. This repetition is key to what is exact and what is equivocal about the word itself. Like words, time is also the carbon copy of another time, one that copies itself ad infinitum. The eternal return is apprehended in an instant of pure transparency. Time and words are made of the same fabric. *Asueto,* as a moment of rest, is merely one that allows the poet to apprehend the transparency of all.

Condición de nube

Condición de nube (1944) is the last major section of the first part of *Libertad bajo palabra.* It is composed of twenty poems assembled as a collection after Paz leaves Mexico for the United States, including "Los novios" (Engaged) , "Dos cuerpos" (Two Bodies), and "La rama" (The Branch).

Condición de nube speaks of change arrested into form. Remember that Paz has collected here poems already written after his departure for the United States in 1943, even if he includes very few poems that deal with his life during these years. The central image of clouds reveals, in an aesthetic mode, Paz's vision of his life during the years, before his departure, whereas most of the poems of "Calamities and miracles" (the section of *Libertad bajo palabra* immediately following) are concerned with concrete images of life in the United

States. Amid the larger layout of Paz's book of books, *Condición de nube* presents the reader with a moment of stasis in the poet's vacillating between life and aesthetics. His condition is like that of clouds (as he implies in one poem) tenuously balancing water and air at any given moment. Clouds imply an awareness of dissolution, and this dissolution appears in tragic form in two poems of the collection that deal specifically with the bodies of man and woman: "Los novios" and "Dos cuerpos." In "Los Novios," a boy and a girl lie on the grass and exchange objects that are then turned into metaphors: "Comen naranjas, cambian besos / como las olas cambian sus espumas." ("Sucking their oranges, giving their kisses / like waves exchanging foam" [*EP* 9].) In the second stanza the boy and the girl on the beach exchange lemons and kisses "como las nubes cambian sus espumas" (like clouds exchanging foam). Finally, in the third stanza, the dead boy and the girl prolong the condition of life into death by undertaking a metaphoric exchange that takes place even as a negation; Paz literally repeats the verb of the first stanza in the third: "No dicen nada, no se besan, / cambian silencio por silencio" (Saying nothing, never kissing / giving silence for silence). Death in "Los Novios" is like the shadow of the blinding light of "Mediodía"—an alternate state, a state of otherness, metaphor itself.

In "Dos cuerpos" (Two Bodies) Paz writes five tercets that repeat the same initial verse as a motif: "Dos cuerpos frente a frente" (Two bodies face to face). But these tercets are then structured within the poem as a whole by means of chained links that add one point of comparison, and then a third term (night) that then rewrites the second point of comparison as a synecdoche of the third:

> Dos cuerpos frente a frente
> son a veces dos olas
> y la noche es océano.

(Poemas 52)

> Two bodies face to face
> are at times two waves
> and night is an ocean.

(EP 11)

The effect highlights the initial term (which is composed of the duality of two bodies face-to-face) and submits them to another metaphor—which then turns the whole composition into a triangular structure underlying the amorous situation. This triad repeats, in a different key, the tripartite structure of the poems included in "Bajo tu clara sombra," where the reader overhears the poet's speech to an Other that at times could be confused with language itself. With a slight variation precisely on the third stanza, which anticipates the conclusion of the fifth, bodies are, then, waves, stones, roots, knives, and stars, while the night is ocean, desert, and sparks. The third stanza varies the composition in the concluding verse of the tercet, and the last stanza takes up this variation once again. The bodies here become stars that fall on an empty sky—the emptiness of the sky itself an element that is not metaphorized. In "Los Novios," as in other poems included in *Condición de nube,* Paz creates a form that argues for its own volition, for its collapse in an amorous moment of dissolution. Dissolution itself is part of an eternal cycle of creation-destruction and re-creation.

Worlds of Conflict: *Calamities and Miracles* (1937–1947)

Calamities and Miracles is the second of the five major divisions of *Libertad bajo palabra,* but it spans roughly the same dates as *Entre tu clara sombra.* These first two divisions correspond to the period in Paz's life that immediately precedes his leaving Mexico City for the first time in 1936 in order to live in Mérida, and then his Spanish sojourn in 1937–1938 in the midst of the Spanish civil war, as well as his stay in the United States in 1943. *Calamities and Miracles* goes one step further and includes the period when Paz works as a cultural attaché in Paris in 1946 and encounters surrealism in Paris. In the developing structure of *Libertad bajo palabra,* these years are pivotal for Paz; he makes the transition from the politically committed poetry that he wrote prior to his experiences in the Spanish civil war, to his encounter with André Breton and the surrealists in Paris in the late 1940s.

The period that begins with Paz's return to Mexico from Spain and Paris in 1938 is the period of *Taller,* at the time the most ambitious and important literary magazine for which Paz wrote, and of his feud with Pablo Neruda over Neruda's refusal to allow his texts to be included in *Laurel.* To these markers (at times buried under Paz's corrective pen) that can be seen in the poetry, it is important to add the sequence of historical events and texts that surround the poems of *Calamities and Miracles.* The late 1930s and early 1940s, when Paz is in México, are the years of the Hitler-Stalin pact (1940), Trotsky's assassination in Mexico (1940), and the Second World War. Paz's stay in the United States in 1945 coincides with the founding of the United Nations; and the heady postwar artistic climate of France (where Paz hears of Stalin's gulag in the Soviet Union).

Paz's sojourn in the United States will be examined in more detail in *The Labyrinth of Solitude,* the book that includes perhaps the best account of Paz's preoccupations during those years. At this point Paz is working on his ideas of the poet's solitary craft and of poetry's place within the wider communities of a world ravaged by war and by demands for political action. That he will find a tentative solution to these dialectics in surrealism in a sense closes off the period marked by the first edition of *Libertad bajo palabra* in 1949, as well as the first edition of *The Labyrinth of Solitude* in 1950. The image of the poet's place in the modern world is bracketed, first of all, by Paz's early reading of T. S. Eliot's "The Hollow Men" and *The Waste-land* in Mexico in 1930 and 1931, and then editing in *Taller* a supplement titled *Poemas de T. S. Eliot* in 1940, to his encounter with Breton and Peret's surrealism in Paris.[5] Thus the poems of *Calamities and Miracles,* more than others in the collection, define a shift in Paz's mode of writing.

Even if the chronological arrangement does not always give an idea for Paz's rationale when it comes to ordering his work in *Libertad bajo palabra* (let us notice that "Asueto" and "Condición de nube" also carry similar dates) it is clear that Paz has chosen in this book to give an account of his changes in perception and style. The wider construction that can be perceived in *Libertad bajo palabra* allows Paz to become a discursive poet who speaks of both history and aesthetics.

Puerta condenada (1938–1946)

Although this section includes some of his earliest poems, written at the time of the first *Bajo tu clara sombra,* Paz wants us to understand "Puerta condenada" as the account of a self that is imprisoned in an ego (or "I") that needs communion and liberation. Here Paz combines shorter poems like "Otoño" and "La calle" with longer pieces like "La sombra," along with other compositions fragmented into sections like "La caída" (two sonnets), "Crepúsculos de la ciudad" (five sonnets), "Conscriptos U.S.A." (a longer poem in two parts, the second part subdivided within itself into three poems), "Cuarto de hotel," (three sections) and, closing the book, "La vida sencilla," a longer poem with a final coda.

Critics have pointed out how important the discourse of liberty is in Paz, but his idea of liberty is born out of the sense of imprisonment that seems to surround modern man. In an entry written in September 1935, in "Vigilias: Diario de un soñador," Paz clarifies the pivotal ideas for his work:

> La libertad se define, siempre, concretamente, en función de un contrario. En sí misma, como abstracción, la libertad es una idea vacía. . . . La libertad no es una idea "autónoma," independiente; depende siempre de sus contrarios y para pensarla es necesario pensar en aquello de que depende y huye. Se es libre con referencia a algo . . . hasta me atrevería a decir, violentando un poco los términos, que la libertad es el verdadero con-

tenido de la esclavitud, ya como simple rebeldía, ya como sumisión aceptada. (*PL* 71–72)

Liberty is defined, concretely, in relation to a contrary. In itself, as abstraction, liberty is an empty idea. . . . Liberty is not an "autonomous," independent idea; it always depends on its contraries and in order to think about it one needs to think about that upon which it depends on and flees from. One is free in reference to something . . . I would even say, forcing the terms a bit, that the real content of liberty is slavery, either as simple rebellion, or as accepted submission.

I have quoted Paz at length at this point because the ideas on liberty written in the mid-1930s, in the midst of his inner political and aesthetic debates, are central to Paz's concept of freedom, which gives meaning to *Libertad bajo palabra* by illuminating the poetry in formal terms. Paz's poetry is not "free" in the formal sense; Paz will grow increasingly disenchanted with the outporing of emotion associated with the ego; he will also distance himself from the surrealists' automatic writing. In "Vigilias," Paz's notion of liberty is already conditioned by language, and it yields to a counterpoint where the constraints of form lead to a sense of authentic liberation.

Freedom underlies the "Condemned door" of the first part of this book, where the idea of man as prisoner that leads to the concluding poem of the second part—dedicated to the marquis de Sade—is central to Paz's reading of the conscripts that he notices in the United States. For Paz, what gives man his liberty is his awareness that certain doors allow access only to spaces that have already been condemned. If we follow Paz's statements at this point, liberty does not exist in a vacuum but in a context of lucidity and rationality, where at all moments human beings must be aware of which precincts cannot be literally revisited. Endless time entertains human beings with fictions and fictive choices. Man's liberty allows him freedom from the anonymous emptiness of being and liberates him from time as this is measured by modern society. The poet's journey consists in circumscribing those fictive spaces, and understanding where true freedom lies. This understanding of freedom as something other than the ability to choose any convenient route, or enter any door, is what gives Paz's notion of freedom its profoundly moral stance. True freedom entails an awareness of its constraints, of its demands; if Man is to define himself by virtue of freedom, then he has to understand himself precisely from the point of view of subservience, of freedom's negation. But the negative dialectics that Paz pursues in this collection are not merely confined to images of condemned doors or to the attempt to grasp the self by means of dialectical plunging into the nonself. The Poem, as Paz will explain later in *The Bow and the Lyre,* is related to philosophy not merely as the illustration of an idea, but rather as a negation of the very concept of philosophical thought; the instant of time which it enacts in writing is essentially irreducible to all other modes of expression.

The sequence of sonnets titled "Crepúsculos de la ciudad" are vignettes of urban life, introducing in Paz's work the theme of the city—a theme that will reappear in some of his best longer poems, particularly from the later *Return.* Paz has reorganized the sequence at different times. The sonnets were initially a sequence of eight, and then six, until the fourth edition of *Libertad bajo palabra* in the *Poemas* edition of 1979. Starting with Santí's edition, "Crepúsculos de la ciudad" now consists of five sonnets, with the original fifth sonnet now separated as a different poem, titled "Monumentos" (Monuments). As they stand, the sequence speaks, first of all, of a particular circuit of desire that awakens at dusk. This desire is first sought in terms of death and sex, and culminates in the poet's search for himself in the last sonnet: it is with this vision of a solitary poet in a process of self-discovery that the sequence concludes. All of these sonnets take place precisely at the twilight hour, where the oposition between light and dark allows the true being of the city to come to the surface. This twilight hour for Paz is a chiaroscuro that devours one sense of clarity in order to bring forth the kind of song of the self that was already seen in "Medianoche," from the almost contemporaneous sequence of "Asueto." In the first sonnet, the sun devours the dregs of the day, allowing nature to wake up from the blinding clarity of a sun. Nature wakes up in an act of love but also of celebration, and offers itself to the sun's death. Not unlike nature, the poet also offers himself to the dying sun, and partakes of the nocturnal landscapes of a reawakened nature in the empty signs of the city's streets and buildings. Nevertheless, like a nocturnal sun, the poet will decipher and penetrate with a different kind of clarity that which has been buried in the city's walls.

A devouring sun, as well as a nature that offers itself to its death, reappear in the second sonnet of "Crepúsculos de la ciudad" (to which Paz has appended a long note in the *Poemas* edition of 1979). The origins of this sonnet are in Paz's noticing that the city's red-light district was also the street where many funeral parlors were located. The solitary wanderer lives in a crepuscular, rapacious zone of life and death that is analogous to nature. If in the first sonnet the trees had offered themselves to the last rays of the sun, at night the whores come out on city streets in order to channel the hidden desires awakened by the sun's absence. In the third sonnet, the onset of night allows the poet to rediscover his true being, as well as his real body. Once again, the inner light brought forth by the onset of darkness repeats the process of "Mediodía" and "Medianoche," although in the fourth sonnet of "Crepúsculos" the sky at dusk is seen as indifferent, as impenetrable as the light in "Mediodía." The parenthetical space opened by the dissappearance of the sun and before the moon and the stars appear says nothing: it is sheer boundlessness, lack of perspective and frame. As in "Mediodía," faced with such an image of unlimited expanse, the soul has no option but that of delving within itself to find its own sense of materiality within its precipitous fall. This search for materiality will also be the theme of the fifth sonnet of the collection, where the poet reveals himself as impatient for the onset of day.

The sense of discursive narrative that can be uncovered in "Crepúsculos de la ciudad" is more evident in "Conscriptos U.S.A.," a poem in two sections that deals with the reality Paz encountered on the border between Mexico and the United States. The first, "Conversación en un bar" (Conversation in a Bar), introduces the reader to a series of voices; the second section, subdivided in three parts, is titled "Razones para morir" (Reasons for Dying). In the first section, Paz presents five voices—although it is not clear whether these five voices are actually one—that narrate what seems to be an escape from army duty. This poem is one of the first where Paz essays a procedure that will reappear in "Hymn among the Ruins": the juxtaposition, within the same discourse, of different times, places, or voices. But in "Conscriptos U.S.A." the voices speak with a sense of aesthetics that defines a kind of peasant poetic language that would only be explored later in the work of the Mexican short story writer Juan Rulfo. As in Paz's earlier "Between the Stone and the Flower," the voices that speak in this poem are consumed by the overwhelming presence and power of nature. The narrative thread concerns the conscripts' desire for women—a desire that lands these voices into jail. By means of the metaphorical tissue of his commentary, the poet implies that the men's desire is analogous to that of nature. As in much of Paz's poetry, nature here is seen as a body. But in "Conscriptos" the primary dialectics between nature and man opposes a corporealized nature to the disembodied voices of the conscripts. This natural "flow" given in the parenthetical, poetical statements, also breaks down already fragmented voices. On the one hand, the poet's voice tries to give the poem its sense of flow but finds itself interrupted by the conscripts' utterance. Like the disembodied Yucatecan peasants in "Between the Stone and the Flower" the conscripts have been rendered prisoners of nature. Only in the last section of the poem, as Jason Wilson points out, does the notion of freedom appear as transformation.[6]

Freedom implies an awareness, as well as an acceptance, of change; "Puerta condenada" collects poems written in the midst of Paz's personal struggle with change that would be resolved in Paris in the late 1940s. Along with *Eagle or Sun?* this collection includes some of Paz's darker poems, like "Las palabras." But the sense of imprisonment that Paz feels at the time—torn between the aesthetics of solitude and commitment that will lead to *The Laberynth of Solitude* in 1950—allows for the particular sense of freedom underlying this book, one that includes an extraordinary variety of styles and modes of writing. Perhaps "Words," with its bestialized and brutalized words, suggests that the poet is fighting against the very fabric of his craft. But it is important to underscore that this brutality aimed at words also reverts to the self-punishing poet that will reappear in the late 1940s and early 1950s in *Eagle or Sun?* This central moment of crisis plays itself out over several of the books included in *Libertad bajo palabra*. But the axis of change is found particularly in "Puerta condenada" and in the following section, "Calamities and Miracles."

"Calamities and Miracles" (1937–1947)

Paz indirectly explained the title for this book in his many accounts of contemporary life. For Paz, what is calamitous is the imprisonment in which modern civilization holds the individual; even if we have been given the possibility of freedom, it is only through an awareness of both—imprisonment and freedom—that we can understand the measure of our conditions and possibilities.

"Calamities and Miracles" opens with "Between the Stone and the Flower," one of Paz's earliest and most revised poems, and it concludes with "El prisionero (Homenaje a D.A.F. de Sade)" (The Prisoner), one of the most important poems in the collection. "The Prisoner" unites many of the themes that Paz will explore in future books, and it is also the most Bretonian of his works (one of its lines, "el semen, la sangre y la lava" is directly quoted from Breton's reading of an episode from Sade's *La nouvelle Justine,* as Paz mentions in his essay "André Bréton o la búsqueda del comienzo").[7]

It is clear that Paz considered "El prisionero" an important poem: it survived every purge in *Libertad bajo palabra* and it was chosen by Paz for translated collections of his work. Paz also dedicated a full-length essay on the importance of the marquis de Sade for modernity, for the surrealists, and for Paz's own poetry. "The Prisoner" is one of the first poems in this collection that is accompanied by an attempt to understand the modern tradition philosophically. That this understanding is done via the figure of the marquis de Sade should not surprise readers acquainted with Breton's surrealism: Sade was a central figure in the surrealist pantheon, not so much for his style of writing but for his uncompromisingly rebellious social attitude. However, as Jason Wilson explained, Paz differed from Breton in his assessments on Sade. For Paz, Breton was much closer to Rousseau and to his tradition of liberty, love, and desire, than to the cold and mechanistic rationality that one associates with Sade. This is why the poem is also a critique on the surrealists' penchant for Sade, which cannot be but paradoxical for Paz. The Sadean love is egotistic; it is predicated on the submission of the other, who becomes an instrument for self-knowledge and not, as in Paz's poetry, a means of communicating with nature. The libertine marquis de Sade becomes the prisoner of his own desires; by elevating himself as the parameter for his own sense of freedom he can only condemn himself to solitude. As Wilson states, Paz agrees with Breton that Sade separates morality from passion, and thus liberates our natural instincts from the repressive forces of taboos.[8] Nevertheless, Paz disagrees with Breton's ultimate assessment on Sade; the philosopher's system condemns him to the solitary prison (and here Paz recalls that Sade spent more than twenty years in prison) in which he is placed in the poem: "Prisionero en tu castillo de cristal de roca" (121). ("Prisoner in your castle of crystal of rock" [*EP* 91].)

Paz's "El prisionero" is a discursive text. Quoting from Sade's testament, it focuses on the fact that Sade's last wishes have been denied since his death. If Sade wanted to leave no trace of his physical presence on earth, history has played him an ironic twist: "No te has desvanecido. / Las letras de tu nombre son todavía una cicatriz que no se cierra" (*Poemas* 120). ("You have not disappeared / The letters of your name are still a scar that will not heal" [*EP* 89].) History has played a sadistic game with Sade: his constant presence throughout the twentieth century has turned him into an object, in much the same way as he turned lovers into instruments of his will. From the beginning, the poem as a whole is a sadistic homage—a trope—on Sade; thus we should not expect here a paean to the philosopher but rather an excoriating assessment of his importance. Paz focuses immediately on his subject: he dissects it without pity, and with the same calculating bent that he finds in Sade's work, he enters directly into the situation of utterance. History has fused the philosopher's name with a practice; in doing so, however, it has also turned the philosopher's name into an enigma, for acts cannot, in essence, speak of that which they name. This is why Sade's cold and calculating rationality creaks like a machinery that has no sense of its function, while the philosopher as figure remains intact, hidden and laughing in the second stanza, behind a pink mask. Paz sees the historical game played on Sade as part of an ironic construction, where the one who insisted on his own isolation and sense of rebellion has become the leader of countless and nameless acts of vengeance upon society. The libertine becomes the paradigm for the revolutionary, but also for the torturer, who sees the world in his own image. Paz sees Sade, finally, as a tragic figure; his imprisonment does not allow him to change; it keeps him forever confined to the name that he gave to himself. Paz thus seeks to reanimate Sade; he ushers a command that is an invitation to partake of the boundlessness of existence. But the conclusion to this poem can only be in the mode of paradox, a paradox that the hyper-rational Sade, with his tortured apparatus, could not understand. Reanimating Sade as a historical figure is as fruitless as reanimating the real Sade. At the poem's conclusion the apostrophe has confused subject and object, and Paz fuses with Sade and addresses the command to another who can only be an image of himself:

> Atrévete:
> la libertad es la elección de la necesidad.
> Sé el arco y la flecha, la cuerda y el ay.
> El sueño es explosivo. Estalla. Vuelve a ser sol.
>
> En tu castillo de diamante tu imagen se destroza y se
> rehace, infatigable.
>
> (Poemas 122)

> Now dare:
> freedom is willingness toward necessity.
> Be the arrow, the bow, the chord and the cry.
> Dream is explosive. It bursts. Become again sun.
>
> In your diamond castle, your image destroys itself,
> remakes itself, tireless.
>
> (EP 93)

The figure of Sade was more than a negative example for Paz. A poet who designs "Calamities and Miracles" to conclude with "El prisionero" cannot be a poet who can sustain an image of the marquis de Sade at a hygienic distance from the self. The poet that opens his book with a rewritten statement of political solidarity with exploited Yucatecan peasants, and who is then disenchanted when he understands how solidarity itself is twisted and misused by others—to the extent that he recoils toward himself in anguish, solitude and exile—cannot see Sade as merely an object for the self. Paz's poetics insists that we understand Sade as an other for the poet, as the very real possibility of a poetic imprisonment caused by fear of the necessary laws of the world. Paz's surrealism, based as it is on the transcendent powers of love, demands that he understand the sadist in himself, and that he expose himself as overcoming the temptations entailed by Sade. This process will continue throughout Paz's contact in Paris with surrealism, as will be seen in his struggles with poetry in *¿Aguila o sol?*

Intimations and Epiphanies: *Semillas para un himno* (1943–1955)

Libertad bajo palabra is a discourse that readers must order by themselves. The idea of ordered progression can be seen in the space that takes the reader from "Semillas para un himno" to *¿Aguila o sol?*, finally concluding, in *La estación violenta,* with "Himno entre ruinas" and *Sunstone.* Even if the ultimate idea of order may be subjective (but no less illusory), from "Semillas," to "Piedras sueltas," to *Sunstone,* readers can see that Paz has laid open the construction of his mature phase by spreading it out over a series of books. The period from 1943 to 1948, represented by poems from "Asueto," "Condición de nube," "Puerta condenada," "Calamities and Miracles," and "El girasol" represents the preparatory phase for a new period that will begin in 1948, with *La estación violenta* in particular, and with *Sunstone.* That this is only one of the many fictions entertained by the organization of *Libertad bajo palabra,* is evident for a reader that follows closely Paz's biography. Seen from the point of view of aesthetics, the reader has to wait until *La estación violenta* to appreciate the insights given in "El prisionero." But the period that is accounted for in *Semillas para un himno* (1943–1955) is more than the preparatory phase that the fictional construction of *Libertad bajo palabra* wants us to imagine. Once again, the particular order of the book speaks of a different narrative, but both in real life as well as in its literary account in the collection, the years 1948–1950, are at the center of this discourse. These are the years when Paz lives in Paris and when he publishes the first edition of *Libertad bajo palabra,* as well as *The Labyrinth of Solitude.* Although they are rearranged in this collection, they are nevertheless represented with particular clarity in the poet's decision to introduce this period with *Semillas para un himno,* and following these poems with *¿Aguila o sol?*

Semillas para un himno is the third major section of *Libertad bajo palabra.* It contains three further subdivisions: *El girasol,* composed of ten poems; *Semillas para un himno,* composed of eleven poems, including the one that gives the title to the section and the volume; and *Piedras sueltas.* The idea of seeds is related to the notion of fragmentation and both are important for Paz. In *Alternating Current,* he explains, "La semilla es la metáfora original: cae en el suelo, en una hendidura del terreno, y se nutre de la sustancia de la tierra. La idea de caída y la de espacio desgarrado son inseparables de nuestra imagen de la semilla" (26). ("The seed is the original metaphor: it falls on the ground, into a crack in the earth, and is nourished by the earth's substance. The idea of a Fall and that of spatial separation are implicit in our image of the seed" [*AC* 23].) There is a kind of perpetual recomposition here: words, fruits, stars, wings—the universe is composed of these fragments of things that in turn recompose themselves. It is clear that they are not really fragments but objects that are always analogous to words.

El girasol (1943–1948)

There are ten poems in the section *El girasol* and in these Paz shows the marked preference for a longer poetic line that was already seen in the latter poems of *Calamities and Miracles. El girasol* seems a more tightly organized collection than others, perhaps because the book is apparently built on fragments that are in the process of solidifying into wholes. But this may also be an impression given by the fact that, like the sunflower, the poems in this book allow for the continuous rotation of a number of already constant symbols in Paz: rivers that flow as life, bodies that flow like a river, eyes that create or recreate the world in their image. Throughout, Paz shows himself to be the poet of desire that he anticipated by placing "El prisionero" at the end of the previous collection. The poems included in "El girasol" insist on the poet's desire for words to bring about change. A good example of this is "Escrito en tinta verde." The poem begins in the first stanza by equating the poet's ink with the nature that he draws on the page:

> La tinta verde crea jardines, selvas, prados,
> follajes donde cantan las letras,
> palabras que son árboles,
> frases que son verdes constelaciones.
>
> (*Poemas* 128)
>
> Green ink makes garden, forest, fields,
> trees full of leaves where letters sing,
> words that are trees,
> phrases appearing as green constellations.
>
> (*SP* 33)

It is the ink, the surface of writing, as opposed to the signified itself, that creates the illusion of nature. Metaphor is rendered as a surface: words are not responsible for the creation of alternate realities, but the ink as a surface is capable of creating leaves inhabited by letters, and words that are trees and constellations. Two progressions are clear in the first stanzas of the text, as if they were two

34

equivalent spirals: from ink, to letters, to words, to phrases, and then from gardens to leaves, to trees, and then to constellations. Both the linguistic progression, as well as what we may term the "natural" process, end in the "green constellations" that are the point of contact between both processes. But this statement of utopian trust in language is shown as desire:

> Deja que mis palabras desciendan y te cubran
> como una lluvia de hojas a un campo de nieve,
> como la yedra a la estatua,
> como la tinta a esta página.
>
> (*Poemas* 128)

> Permit my words' descent cover your whiteness
> like a rain of leaves on a field of snow,
> like ivy on the statue,
> ink on this page.
>
> (*SP* 33)

The creative certainty of the first stanza is changed in the second. Here, desire opens a wedge between the realities that the poet had constructed with his green ink. The verb "deja" (let) with its implicit desire for consent, reveals that the loved one's body is beyond the nature created by the poet, and is never so passive as that "other" nature is. At the same time, the poet is creating another reality, by formulating his desire on a double set of analogies that are once again predicated as green on white. Thus, the snowed field leads, further on in the text, to a statue, which in turn leads to the page where the poet is writing. The third stanza joins the disparate fragments of the body, "Brazos, cintura, cuello, senos" (Arms, waist, throat, breasts) in order to conclude, in the fourth, with the final articulation of both series:

> Tu cuerpo se constela de signos verdes
> como el cuerpo del árbol de renuevos.
> No te importe tanta pequeña cicatriz luminosa:
> mira al cielo y su verde tatuaje de estrellas.
>
> (*Poemas* 129)

> Your body is constellated in green images
> like a tree's body, covered with green shoots.
> Never mind the scar, little and luminous:
> look up at the sky and its green tattoo of stars.
>
> (*SP* 35)

The body is totally consumed by the green signs that the poet has created on its surface, although this new surface is not able to cover the body completely—nor does it want to, for the object of writing is not to colonize another surface, but to permit a kind of double vision that the poet sees on the surface of night. The combination of the series of white and green is here completed by the articulation of green stars, which are like the tattoos of the sky. In this way, "Written in Green Ink" can be read as a poem on the act of writing. Like many other texts in Paz's work, it is difficult to distinguish at what point the poem ceases to be a love poem and turns into a meditation on poetics. But what is ultimately important is that for Paz, writing and love are never completely distinguished from each other: poetics always seems like part of an *ars amatoria* contained in the poems themselves.

Semillas para un himno (1950–1954)

In 1953, Paz returned to Mexico. In 1954 he gave a lecture on surrealism that provoked angry commentary; surrealism was not only seen as dead and passé, but completely alien to the "Mexican" character, according to many of Paz's contemporaries. Paz's return to Mexico followed the publication of *The Labyrinth of Solitude* and of the poems included in *¿Aguila o sol? Semillas para un himno* was the first book of poems that he published upon his return, and within an aggressively nationalistic Mexican context, these poems could not but provoke the indignation and bafflement of many of Paz's contemporaries. Paz as surrealist was offering another vision of the engaged artist. But this engagement had little to do with the concrete economical and political context of the time; it was concerned more with a revolutionary practice within the space of the page than outside of it. This is not to say that Paz did not participate in the political and social polemics of his time—*The Labyrinth of Solitude* is a powerful indictment of the Mexican intellectual class—only that the poetry seemed to have liberated itself from the "tyranny" of context in order to explore other realms of thought.

The lack of puncuaction in all of these "Semillas para un himno" creates the illusion of visions that coexist within moments of ecstasy. Whereas Paz had previously framed those moments of ecstasy in shorter poems almost engulfed by the white space of the page, in these texts emptiness itself is populated or filled with words. We can see here the beginning of Paz's conceptual aesthetics of the page as a reality that is part of the poem. In "Semillas para un himno," this spatial poetics repeats the words "Infrecuentes" and "Instantáneas" formatted at different sides of the page. The poetic measure here interplays form along with scansion and rhythm. In great measure, "Semillas para un himno" is placed at this point in the ordered progression of *Libertad bajo palabra* to show how Paz plays with a different notion of rhythm in verse.

Paz shows that the rhythm and beat that he now uses in his poetry is in great measure an internal, or inner beat—found within the line and then echoed from one line to the other. "Semillas para un himno" is also full of images of interiority, alerting the reader to the fact that something is happening inside the verse. This inner rhythm Paz relates to memory; it is as if involuntary memory had found the beat that announces its appearance. "Estrella interior," for example, starts with an image of night opening itself up as if it were a flower, inviting the poet for a rebirth, and much of *Semillas para un himno* is about a process of emanation or rebirth that allows a hidden, inner truth, to reappear. In "Semillas para un himno" Paz opens an instant of time as if he were short-circuiting the space between one phrase and the other, in order to bring about poetic revelation. This procedure allows for a sense of delay, as in the first lines, where the poetic discourse meanders in order to come back to the same phrase:

> Infrecuentes (pero también inmerecidas)
> Instantáneas (pero es verdad que el tiempo no se mide
> Hay instantes que estallan y son astros
> Otros son un río detenido y unos árboles fijos
> Otros son ese mismo río arrastrando los mismos árboles)
> Infrecuentes
> ———Instantáneas noticias favorables.
>
> (*Poemas* 150)

> Seldom (but nevertheless undeserved)
> Sudden (but certainly time is not moderate
> There are moments that explode and become stars,
> Some are a river in check and a few unmoving trees
> Some are that same river uprooting those same trees)
> Seldom
> ———Sudden good news.
>
> (*EP* 39)

In coming back to the same phrase, however the phrase develops and changes within time itself. The words describe an elusive event (in the seventh line this is seen as "noticias favorables" [good news]). If the emphasis on "seeds" preordains the reader to expect a poem that is full of images of earth, the predominant image of this poem is that of a ship. It is an image that undergoes various mutations during the course of the poem; first, it takes the form of a girl that opens time in two; then it is a game that is remembered from childhood; finally, it is a ship that the poet puts in motion in order to transport the formidable news of letters that turn into words and then into images. If in terms of rhythm the poem is moved by the beat given in its two recurrent words, the ship serves as an image that opens up spaces and times within the very fabric of discourse constructed by Paz.

The "news" that Paz is talking about is instants or wedges in the fabric of time. But they come into being precisely within time itself, as they do in "Estrella interior." His descriptions of these instants are contained throughout "Semillas para un himno": the lightning bolts that are indirectly named as explosive instances, the sudden immobility of rivers and trees, as well as the sublime vision of matter itself as surface. These elements might be said to contain Paz's three versions of the poetic sublime, appearing infrequently but instantaneously. These are the two axes on which the text gyrates, the poem itself divided into two movements. The first, following the section quoted above, is crowned by the vision of a young girl as a boat that divides time in two; the second follows a series of parenthetical statements that repeat the first statement (on "infrecuentes" [infrecuent] and "instantaneos" [instantaneous]), quoted above, in order to express that those instantaneous and infrequent moments are events that do not always appear in the guise of words. The poem concludes with the image of the poet putting a ship in motion, a ship full of words (literally, "iniciales" as if these were the Morse codes of poetry) that will turn into images.

"Semillas para un himno" marks an important change in Paz's poetry. The period of his return to Mexico was one fraught with agony and impatience; the reencounter with his native land a difficult one, where the poet's idea of the revolution in terms of poetic language did not appeal to most of his contemporaries. But if one reads *Libertad bajo palabra* as we have done here, following Paz's notion of organization, it is obvious that Paz considers this one of the first poems where the idea of play is exposed. Play appears not only in the concrete scene of the poet's remembering games in his childhood in order to motivate the central image of the ship in the poem, but also in the general ludic tone of the piece, whose sense of ecstasy is given by means of an erotic play with the reader. It is a play of ecstasy addressed to time, in its infinite variations as well as in the general infrequency of the images that the poet complains about. But it is also addressed to space: this poem, along with "Himno entre ruinas" is one of the first where Paz introduces a poetics of words in space that will culminate in *Blanco*.

Piedras sueltas (1955)

Paz positions *Piedras sueltas* before the more sustained experimentation of *¿Aguila o sol?* The section is important for the sense of architectonics that permeates *Libertad bajo palabra;* these are meant to be the seeds of the much larger "hymn" that Paz will offer in the following sections. But these poems actually seem more like the archaeological remains of a much vaster project. The adjective "sueltas" leads the reader in different directions: not only to the poems as the remains of some previous structure, but as incarnations of these "seeds" that will bear fruit in Paz's later poetry. I note again the chronological displacement of *Libertad bajo palabra,* as many of the books placed after *Piedras sueltas* chronologically precede these poems, which are roughly contemporaneous to Paz's *The Bow and the Lyre* (1956). The book is divided into three sections, "Lección de cosas" (Lesson on Things), "En Uxmal" (In Uxmal), and "Piedras sueltas." As a whole, *Piedras sueltas* presages the vision of Mexico and of the East that Paz will explore during the 1960s; these are not necesarily short, epiphanic moments like those of his earlier poetry, but point more toward the creation of a poetry of the object, a cross between Latin American *modernismo* and the Japanese tradition of the haiku. The first section, "Lección de cosas" examines various objects, principally figurines: a mask of the Aztec god Tlaloc, a sugar skeleton used in Mexico during the Day of the Dead, an Aztec goddess. The last poem of the series of ten is precisely titled "Objetos"; it is a short, three line piece:

> Viven a nuestro lado,
> los ignoramos, nos ignoran.
> Alguna vez conversan con nosotros.
>
> (*Poemas* 155)

> They live alongside us
> we do not know them, they do not know us
> But sometimes they speak with us.
>
> (*EP* 45)

To the general disregard that we have toward objects, Paz already imposes a mutual disregard, one that equates subjects and objects. It is not only that the objects are ignored by us, but that within the life that they secretly lead, they are oblivious to our gaze. The language of objects is elusive, and the mode of conversation is silence. If nature is seen in most of Paz's poems as a "communicative" nature, these objects are immersed in silence. But at the same time, readers are meant to think that these poems are short precisely because the language of objects is much vaster than the language of men—vaster in the sense of its being written in a different language. This parenthetical silence here precedes a book such as *¿Aguila o sol?* where all of nature seems to speak to the poet in a terrifying language.

Poetic Crisis: *¿Aguila o sol?*

One of the longest sections of *Libertad bajo palabra*, *¿Aguila o sol?* is one of Paz's most unusual books, accounting for a period of experimentation that took place, according to Paz's own dates, between 1949 and 1950, thus coinciding not only with the initial collecting of the early poetry into *Libertad bajo palabra* but also with *The Labyrinth of Solitude*. *¿Aguila o sol?* is therefore the record of an experience, of a period in time, while the poet in Paris worked at the Mexican diplomatic corps. The context for this exploration—which will be seen in more detail in the section on *La estación violenta*—was Paz's growing sense of isolation and despair as a result of the confusing political and ideological alliances produced by the first postwar period. As he says in *Itinerario:* "La escritura me abrió espacios inexplorados. En breves poemas en prosa—¿poemas o explosiones?—traté de penetrar en mí mismo. Me embarcaba en cada palabra como en una cáscara de nuez" (98). (Writing opened up unexplored spaces. In brief poems in prose—poems or explosions?—I tried to penetrate myself. I embarked myself in each word as if in a nutshell.) The context for this exploration is Paris, and the heightened sense of national affiliation that Paz gained as a foreigner in the most cosmopolitan center of Europe, receptive not only to foreign ideas but also to alternate visions of a reality that seemed more "authentic" or less contaminated by European rationalism. Not only is Breton's surrealism an important precedent for these poems—Breton's *L'amour fou* (1937) and *Arcane 17* (1945) could also be considered poems in prose, and the surrealists saw Lautréamont's prose poetry in *Les Chants de Maldoror* as a direct precursor—but also the works of Paz's friend Henri Michaux, inveterate prose poet and explorer of the inner realms of surrealism.

With the exception of *The Monkey Grammarian* (an account of Paz's experiences in the Orient written for the French collection *Les Sentiers de la Création* in 1970), the prose poem is not one of Paz's habitual modes, unless we include certain epiphanic moments where parts of his essays lead to an ecstatic communication in prose. In *The Bow and the Lyre* Paz clarifies that his vision of poetry is beyond the sociohistorical classifying of verse and prose; indeed, he explains that novelistic discourse in the twentieth century is at times closer to what is generally considered "poetry," principally at those times when the discourse seems to turn in upon itself. In any case, he sees the traditional genre distinctions as fallacious, particularly after the example of Lautréamont's *Les Chants de Maldoror.* Paz's experimentation with the prose poem, both in this book as well as in *The Monkey Grammarian* implies an exploration of himself, as well as of his writing. Both in *The Monkey Grammarian* as well as in *¿Aguila o sol?* the prose poem becomes an open genre, one that is able to capture all sorts of disparate things and place them within the apparently formless totality of the page. In both books—significantly included, along with his play *La hija de Rapaccini,* 1956 (Rapaccini's Daughter) in his 1979 edition of *Poemas*—Paz is able to blend both internal and external reality with a divided and alienated poetic self. In *The Monkey Grammarian,* the account of a pilgrimage is both internal and external; in *¿Aguila o sol?* the poet explores his two sides as a Mexican in Paris and tosses them like the game alluded to in the book's title— a tossing of the Mexican coin whose two sides represent an eagle or a sun. As in William Carlos Williams's *Kora in Hell* (see *PC* 90), or Baudelaire's prose poems, the poet recounts a journey of self-discovery as a solitary being in the midst of civilization, wandering the city streets. But Paz's own vision is also predicated on models closer to the Latin American tradition. The second section, "Arenas movedizas," at times seems closer to Rubén Darío's *modernista* exper- imentations in prose, particularly where the prose poem has a clear-cut storyline as in "Mi vida con la ola" (My Life with the Wave). Spanish American *mod- ernistas* were also, in a sense, inner exiles, and Paz rescues in *¿Aguila o sol?* a sense of a double exile and an attempt at a double reconciliation: of the poet with his surrealist and more specifically Parisian aesthetics, and of these aes- thetics with Aztec (non-Western) and indigenous roots. The book's first edition was illustrated by Rufino Tamayo, who also attempted to combine his Mexican roots with the figurative traditions of the West, and who steered clear of the more political art of Mexican muralists such as Diego Rivera. Paz dedicated one of his prose poems ("Ser natural") to Tamayo—who was also admired by Breton— and he has also written extensively on his art.

    ¿Aguila o sol? breaks with Paz's lyrical poetry: the writing leads in multiple directions, not only toward poetry but also toward the short story or the vignette, the allegory, parable, or manifesto. This is also important for *¿Aguila o sol?,* where the coin is a synecdoche for a wider set of choices that are constantly being made in this book, one that is a continuous game of chance. As Paz says in the opening text, "Comienzo y recomienzo. Y no avanzo. Cuando llego a las letras fatales, la pluma retrocede: una prohibición implacable me cierra el paso" (*Poemas* 163). ("I begin and begin again. And do not move forward. When I reach the fatal letters, my pen falls back: an implacable prohibition blocks the way" [*ES* 3].) These words allude to one of the central motifs, present in all of

Paz's experimentations with prose poetry: the idea of a route or of a road. The opening poem of *Libertad bajo palabra,* is also concerned with the idea of journey and route: "Allá, donde terminan las fronteras, los caminos se borran. . . . Avanzo lentamente y pueblo la noche de estrellas, de palabras." ("Out there, where the frontiers end, roads are erased. . . . I go forward slowly and I people the night with stars, with speech" [*EP* 3].) But it is a route that, in *¿Aguila o sol?,* carries within itself the sense of an impasse, of a wall that the poet cannot cross. Paz's later awareness of writing as possessing its own sense of route—a road that leads to self-discovery—has to be seen in relation to the aims of a book such as *¿Aguila o sol?* since the stories in this book are either extended meditations upon a single theme or a single metaphor, and even, at times, fantastic incarnations of a particular image. The sense of an impasse is linked to insomnia, a recurrent theme in *¿Aguila o sol?* Neither sleep nor lucidity, insomnia, like Paz's *vigilias,* is a kind of middle state, where the poet is prey to conflictive demons and extraordinary situations that keep turning him away from himself in order to fling him back to himself once again, in a spiraling frenzy. What the poet searches for here is a route that will lead toward a new beginning; the book as a whole closes with the promise of a rebirth in "Hacia el poema (Puntos de partida)" (Toward the Poem [Starting points]). In *¿Aguila o sol?* the sense of an impasse appears in poem 14 of "Los trabajos del poeta" (The Poet's Works), but this sense of violent travail is present throughout the book, as the poet seeks to uncover and recover at the same time his original expression.

¿Aguila o sol? is divided into three sections: the first, "Trabajos del poeta," is a series of sixteen prose poems; the second, "Arenas movedizas," (Shifting Sands) is a series of ten short poetic short stories, or vignettes. The third and longest, "*¿Aguila o sol?*" once again is a series of twenty-two prose poems. "Trabajos del poeta" reveals the poet's delusions: he is prey to demonic visitors at night, against whom he fights. The poet is a warrior who needs to think of his military strategy. He has to be careful to hold these beings at bay yet allow them to reappear. The poet cannot pretend to be either too strong or too secure of himself; the visitors are ungodly presences and their appearance is profoundly ambivalent. This ambivalence produces the poet's violence; the apparition of these beings of night is also related to the desired apparition of the Word.

Violence is the most important and disturbing element in "The Poet's Works." The kind of creative narration that Paz insists upon in this book entails an erotic and violent encounter with the word. The creative process is a struggle, and the poet is always in an erotic state of expectation; either he encounters the word at a particular moment or the word fails to materialize. What is important here is that the word is absolutely centralized within the process of creation, that it is not a reality itself that the poet wants to capture in words, as poetry is generally understood, but that words precede the particular reality that is named. Because words are material things, they also possess life. The poet experiments with those words as if he were a scientist in a laboratory. In order to effect this operation, a certain arbitrariness between the signifier and the signified has to be eliminated. The words are transformed into grotesque bodies: foreheads with a hole, bodies fed to such an extent that they explode, hunchbacked beauties, talons that trample upon heads with mechanical frenzy. The poet is here a kind of prisoner like the marquis de Sade in "El prisionero," and both he and his words are engaged in sadistic and masochistic acts whose ultimate purpose is a derangement of the senses, the end result of a process of embodiment in language.

"¿Aguila o sol?," the longest of the three sections of the book, opens with "Jardin con niño" (Garden and Child), a picture of a garden, already for Paz a utopian space. The text begins with the account of an older poet, apparently lost in the midst of his quotidian life. He finds the enclosed, protected space of the garden of his childhood. The tone is nostalgic and elegiac. The poet finally reaches the very center of his memory, from which he is again violently returned to the present. But his present is already that of fallen man, an Other who is himself and who writes, who looks at himself while writing. "Jardin con niño" starts with a vision of a journey—"A tientas, me adentro" (Uncertainly, I enter)—in order to conclude with a vision of otherness. The older poet has looked at himself while writing, and his Other is a child. This is also the sense in "Viejo poema" (Old Poem) where the poet enters into the precinct of childhood, this time not a garden but a house. As in "Garden and Child," the particular melancholia is produced because the man is abandoning, once and for all, the realm of childhood. In these two texts, poetry closes the door of childhood, allowing the poet to enter into those precincts to exorcise them, to abandon them forever. As Paz says in "Hacia el poema" (Toward the Poem), the last poem of the collection and one of the many *ars poeticae* in *Libertad bajo palabra*: "Damos vueltas y vueltas en el vientre animal, en el vientre mineral, en el vientre temporal. Encontrar la salida: el poema" (*Poemas* 228). ("We turn and turn in the animal belly, in the mineral belly, in the belly of time. To find the way out: the poem" [*ES* 119].)

¿Aguila o Sol? ends with this state of reconciliation. Gone are the particular travails, the sense of condemnation, the sadism of "Trabajos del poeta." The texts are liberatory fantasies that have accomplished their therapeutic work.

Epiphanies: *La estación violenta* (1948–1957)

La estación violenta is the most important collection in *Libertad bajo palabra:* it contains the longest and most important poems in the book and it signals Paz's definitive move to another "phase." As it appears in the edition of *Poemas* (1979) it is structured in chronological fashion, from the earliest poem, "Himno entre ruinas" written in 1948, to the major achievement of Paz's early poetry, *Sunstone,* dated 1957. These are texts written mostly in postwar Europe, especially France, the foremost meeting ground for political and intellectual debate, with Sartre the most polemical and important figure. Paz has declared, however, that because he had been a reader of Ortega y Gasset, he was not over-whelmed by Sartrean existentialism (*Itinerario* 81)—aside from the fact that Sartre was not, unlike Heidegger, an admirable reader of poetry. For his politi-cal and ideological thought, Paz gravitated toward Camus (whom he meets in an act of homage, in a memorial act to the poet Antonio Machado [*Itinerario* 86]) and André Breton and Benjamin Peret—although he claims not to have been influenced by their concrete thoughts on politics on history, but by their friend-ship and example.

Paz declared, with a mixture of irony and regret, that he accepted his diplo-matic post in 1945 to Paris with the hope that he would be present, in Europe, to a major proletarian uprising after the war (*PC* 71–72). *La estación violenta* can be seen as the chronology of that difficult period in European thought—the confusing and, to a certain extent, aimless years of the postwar period—that would finally lead to the cold war, when already all talk of revolution had been quenched for the sake of separating the world into the different and opposing camps signaled by the United States and the USSR. At this point, which Paz dates around 1947 and 1948, Paz read two books by Raymond Rousset, *L'universe concentrationnaire* and *Le Jours de notre mort,* which explore Nazi concentration camps as a distorted reflection of society. It was also, by the efforts of Rousset, that news began to filter out about the existence of concen-tration camps in the USSR. At this point, the Western intelligentsia condemned Rousset as an agent of Western imperialism, for the sake of solidarity with the Soviet Union, even though Rousset had proved without doubt the existence of these camps as well as of a Code of Corrective Work. Paz decided to publish the important documents of the code, as well as an introduction, in the Argentine journal *Sur*, with the help of José Bianco and Victoria Ocampo. It was to Bianco that Paz dedicated the poem "Máscaras del alba," one of the more important and least studied in *La estación violenta.*

The title of the collection, then, gives an account of these difficult years in terms of politics; what the end of the war produces, according to Paz, is pre-cisely the violent confusion of the postwar years. Paz feels isolated at this time; because of the publication of anti-Soviet documents in *Sur,* he was separated from the more dogmatic left. It is within this context that Paz spent the year, between 1951 and 1952, in India and in Japan. In Delhi he wrote "Mutra," 1952 and in Tokyo "¿No hay salida?" 1952 (The Endless Instant). These are, then, the first texts that Paz writes in the Orient, to which he will return in 1962 (to India) for six years. These are also the years when Paz begins to write what will later become *The Bow and the Lyre.*

In *La estación violenta* Paz confronts the ruins of Western civilization by traveling around Europe and the East. From "Himno entre ruinas," the poem that opens the collection, to "Máscaras del alba," "Fuente," and "Mutra," Paz focuses on what is left of a civilization, he insists on a kind of architecture of a past that haunts the present—not only in Avignon, in Sicily, and in India (the locales where these poems take place) but also in "El prisionero" his poem-homage to Sade written also in 1948. These are poems that communicate the relationship between past and present in terms of mutual and destructive dissolution. With the exception of the first two poems ("Himno entre ruinas" and "Máscaras del alba") most of the others are written in long stanzaic forms. Paz's later work, with the possible exception of "A Draft of Shadows" will not develop this mode of writing. On the contrary, the poems of *East Slope* (1969) and those of *Return* (1976) will break down lines of verse, playing with the white space of the page. In this sense, *La estación violenta* is the culmination of a certain period of Paz's work; like all moments of glory, however, it has to be seen as a transitional work, already containing the seeds of a possible change into other poetic modes. One is tempted to see this collection as a series of preparatory exercises for *Sunstone,* as opening a space that "El prisionero," from 1948, could not.

"Himno entre ruinas" was written in Naples in 1948, and it carries an epigraph from the Spanish poet Luis de Góngora (1561–1627), taken from *Fábula de Polifemo y Galatea* (1613), that describes the grotto where the giant Cyclops Polifemo lives. In his exquisite and elaborate *Fabula,* Góngora aimed for baroque chiaroscuro, philosophically rendering two opposing sides of man by framing these within an antagonistic battle between Polifemo and Galatea, who signify raw power and sensual delight, all seen from within the timeless world of baroque poetry. As befits a poem so steeped in the aesthetics of the baroque, Góngora's *Fábula* is concerned not with one side or the other, but with the tenuous balance between the two, a balance that is always precarious, by virtue of the immensely complex fireworks of Góngora's verse. Paz's choice of Góngora as referent for his poem does not come about because of Góngora's style, but as a response to the very monumentality of Góngora's construction, one of the highest achievements of European poetry. What is left, then, of the ruins of Góngora's monumental construction and of his world, is the hymnic ode that Paz writes in a language that is the antithesis of

Góngora's. In the midst of a ruined postwar Europe, the poet can only rescue the fragments of previous glories.

Paz's apprehension of the concrete instance of time and of landscape is rendered in the text by means of stanza divisions that place the reader in different realms: first, and as a primordial source of origin, in the ruins of Teotihuacan, the ancient Mexican city, and then in the ruins of Europe. Both Fein and Xirau have given us excellent readings of this poem.[9] Fein sees its structure developing by means of a sequence of two parallel columns, representing points of view that are diametrically opposed. The tension derived from this separation into two is both the cause as well as the result of their being opposed. The odd-numbered stanzas, for Fein, are a celebration of life; the even stanzas manifest the obscure side of existence, as the living antiquity of the Romans is contrasted to the actual and present sterility of pre-Columbian ruins, as well as to the ruins of contemporary society. Xirau, for his part, adds that the poem reveals the dialectical struggle between solitude and communion in Paz's poetry, rendering the opposition visually transparent, by using italics in order to distinguish between one geographical referent and the other. The desire to resolve the opposition is related, for Xirau, to the poet's desire for the word as the groundwork for all liberation. Both Xirau and Fein underscore Paz's combinatory urge, his ecstatic mingling of different geographies.

"Mascaras del alba," 1948 (Masks of Dawn), the second poem of the collection, is dedicated to José Bianco, one of the editors of the Argentinean literary magazine *Sur.* Like "Himno entre ruinas," "Máscaras del alba" is a poem of ecstasy, but this time the place is Venice, the hour of day is dawn, instead of dusk, and the inhabitants are not living presences or ruins but rather shadows or masks, since Venice's insomniac inhabitants appear at night only in order to disappear at dawn. In the first and second stanzas, Paz describes the predawn hour in order to present, in the following stanzas, a surreal ensemble of beings that are like emanations of the Venetian night. The decadent, carnivalesque Venetian atmosphere is seen in terms of beings that are nowhere to be seen: shadows, names, secret taboos.

In "Fuente," 1950 (Fountain), the poet's body suffers the mutations and transformations of ecstasy, culminating in the dissolution of the body, with the head of the poet in the center of the square transformed into a fountain. It is a poem written in long stanzas and it takes place at noon, an important time of day for Paz: it is an emblem for his idea of an eternal present, where different times and spaces coalesce in one blinding instant. As in "Himno entre ruinas," one of the most important functions of this poem is the idea of the past, particularly the European past. All the objects named by the poet in the first section—towers, fortifications, city walls—that have been tied to the ground are suddenly elevated at the hour of noon, which is also the hour of the present. What the sublime instant does in Paz is raise the things most tied to earth—the constructions and edifications, the cultural registers of centuries—and allow the poet to suffer an out-of-body experience that records an authentic nonalienated estrangement. The present denies the existence of shadows, of opaque angles. But the poet's sublime instant turns into a false epiphany, as the poet only receives banishment and exile for his efforts. Paz understands the poet's perennial exile from the city, and thus shifts the central image of the poem from the roaming eye, transparent unto itself, to the head. In myth, Orpheus's body is torn apart and rendered into fragments that float down a river. As myth, the poet's body that appears in "Fuente" sings in spite of its dissolution. It is precisely because the poet sacrifices himself, that he assumes the central place in the architectural layout of the city.

"Repaso nocturno" (The Middle of the Night) belongs, if not in form, at least in theme, with the poems in prose included in *¿Aguila o sol?* It is the account of insomnia, and, like those accounts narrated in the earlier book, it is also an account of a journey. In this particular text, Paz sees insomnia as a route toward otherness: the poet cannot sleep and his experience propels him toward the other. But in the poem the experience is reversed: it begins with the poet talking about himself in the third person, moves toward the first person singular, and once again ends with the third person. If surrealism attempted to dislodge the opposition between dream and reality and thus explore their relationship as one continuous state of desire, the true and real opposition of these two terms would be insomnia: a state of infernal lucidity, the third point of a triangular structure of desire. This discourse can be seen in "Repaso nocturno"; for the poet moves towards the state of sleep only to be interrupted in the third stanza. What the poet sees in the state of insomnia are words, inscriptions, a battle of signs and times. This is the opposite of otherness: an impossibility of true access to the other.

Paz first journey to the Orient takes place in November 1951, when he arrives in Bombay. "Mutra" is placed in Delhi, 1952, and its title refers directly to a town in India, south of this city, an important center for Hindu devotion. The poem is written in long verse, in sharp contrast to the shorter line form that Paz will use in *East Slope,* the definitive poetic account of his longer stay in the Indian subcontinent during the 1960s. The distinction is important, for in many ways Paz's first poetic, personal encounter with the East has a different philosophical perspective from that of his longer sojourn. "Mutra" begins by welcoming the arrival of summer as an inmense, terrible, and invasive feminine presence. The poet appears in the poem's fifth stanza, and he sees himself in a perpetual state of fluidity, in search of an ultimate body, a pure essence. But instead of accepting this fluidity as part of a natural state of nonbeing, the poet seeks to ground himself in the ruins of the past, in the vast architecture elaborated by men and historical time. The poet adopts, in this sense, a fundamentally Western position vis-à-vis the internal, mystical stance of the East. His position is not unlike that of Neruda's at the beginning of his *Canto general* (1950), a book almost contemporaneous to the poems of *La estación violenta.* Searching for the essence of Man in "Alturas de Macchu Picchu" (The Heights of Macchu Picchu) Neruda seeks to find eternity. Neruda's search might not be so different from that of Paz, in terms of aims, although their results are dialectically opposed. Both find a kind of hidden structure from which both history and society can be explained from the point of view of an eternal recurrence, although for Paz this recurrence allows for an interplay of constant change and repetition. It should be pointed out that this interplay of similarity and change in Paz, and its absence in Neruda's "Alturas de Macchu Picchu," might be explained by the dialectical difference of geographical locale as well as of ontology: Paz visits a living site, peopled by the agonies of the quotidian, whereas Neruda visits a relic of a demolished empire. Likewise, Neruda seeks to ground American history, whereas Paz attempts to discover the meaning of "universality."

Sunstone (1957)

After Paz's return to Mexico in 1954 he became an active figure in Mexican literary circles, collaborating in the *Revista Mexicana de Literatura,* directed by Carlos Fuentes and Emmanuel Carballo. But this was a difficult period for the reception of Paz's work. According to Pacheco, Paz's *Semillas para un himno* and *¿Aguila o sol?* were not well received by critics; as mentioned earlier, "surrealism" had become anathema to many Mexican intellectuals, a "dead" movement that had little to offer the nation's literary life.[10] In fact, Paz was seen at the time as a kind of "boy wonder" who had been "corrupted" by his stay in Europe. *Sunstone,* Pacheco recalls, renewed faith in Octavio Paz. In Pacheco's own words, people thought that Paz had finally listened to a sensible inner voice and had renounced the incomprehensible and hermetic poetics of surrealism, in order to return to the mode and style of his early youth ("Descripción" 182). Paz published *Sunstone* in 1957, and has closed the poems of *Libertad bajo palabra* with that poem ever since its second edition. It is clear that he conceives this text as a kind of summing-up of his work up till then: in one of the notes added to the latter *Blanco* (1967) Paz states that *Sunstone* closes off the first period of his poetic oeuvre.

Critics that read *Sunstone* at the time correctly perceived it as a kind of "return," while they corroborated Paz's later understanding that the poem was not merely a return but also a point of closure. From the beginning *Sunstone* was seen, then, as a liminal text: a text of beginnings and endings, a poem that was placed at a threshold. As with all thresholds, it is important to examine in what manner it concludes the previous "cycle" of Paz's career, and what is it that the text initiates. Pacheco has anticipated *Sunstone* back to a number of Paz's poems: "Arcos," "Elegía interrumpida," "Cuarto de hotel," "La vida sencilla," and "Máscaras del alba." Of these, "Arcos" which appears in *Libertad bajo palabra* under "Asueto" (1939–1944) is the clearest precursor, not only in terms of form (hendecasyllables) but also in terms of content. From its first lines "Arcos" traces a journey that takes the poet out of himself in order to propitiate a self-encounter: "¿Quién canta en las orillas del papel? / Inclinado, de pechos sobre el río / de imágenes, me veo, lento y solo, de mi mismo alejarme" (*Poemas* 42). (Who sings in the margins of paper? / Inclined, chest over the river / of images, I see myself, slow and alone, distancing myself from myself.) It is clear that the poem bears little relation to the other texts from *La estación violenta*. Gone are the violent juxtapositions of "Himno entre ruinas" with its interplay of time and space in italics, or those of "Repaso nocturno," that can be traced back to *¿Aguila o Sol?* Perhaps only in "El río" or in "Mutra" might we find a suitable point of reference for the sense of flow that the reader experiences in *Sunstone,* but those two poems express an agony and despair that stands in marked contrast to the melancholic tone of *Sunstone.* "Mascaras del alba" might provide a suitable point of comparison, but only in terms of its use of hendecasyllables and, perhaps, in the idea of recurrent time displayed in the text. It is in the latter part of *The Bow and the Lyre,* as well as in some of the poems collected in *Poemas* under the section *Días hábiles* (1958–1961) where we find a style that resembles the serene transparencies that flow in *Sunstone.*

What is clear in terms of the overall construction and elaboration of Paz's work is that *Sunstone* inaugurates an enormous revisionary process in the poet's work. *Sunstone*'s fascination with form, where the poem slowly moves as if enamoured of its own reflection, is one of the threads that joins it to the other great long poem of the Mexican tradition: José Gorostiza's *Muerte sin fin* (1929). Like Gorostiza, Paz's situates the reader not in Eliot's "unreal city" but in an unreal *climate* where nature transparently reflects upon itself. But the idea of endlessness, so prevalent in Paz's precursor, is transformed in *Sunstone* into a philosophical time of creative echoes where repetition entails the possibility of creation.

It is hard to do justice to a poem as impressive as *Sunstone* (1957). It is perhaps Paz's most astounding piece, mixing eros and history, pain, solitude, and melancholy, over a broken landscape of time whose sense of plenitude is as deeply felt as one long epiphany conveyed in a cosmic dance. Its memorable lines flow with the ease with which only ageless truths can be said; its most hidden references are touched by a rare illumination, as if this truly were the poem of a being possessed by an inner clarity, who reviews a life seen as moving panoramas, and writes his text in transparent ink over a pliable surface. Tomás Segovia has justly termed it a masterpiece in the classical sense of the word, stressing an obvious truth that nevertheless accounts for the poem's essential strangeness: modern poets rarely attempt to unveil their desires for a masterpiece in so open a fashion, and then succeed.[11] And then, underlying the poetic construction, what seems like a profoundly classic attempt to fuse poetic writing with a hidden code that is nevertheless explained by the writer himself, with no attempt at hiding the writing under the veil of obscurity: *Sunstone*'s perfect 584 free verse hendecasyllabic lines correspond or repeat the revolution of the planet Venus. *Sunstone,* thus, is literally a poetic feat. If Paz during his years in Paris attempted to fuse poetics and politics, the singular life with that of his fellow human beings, in *Sunstone* the poetic revolution has come full circle: poetry repeats the movement of the planets and the stars; it is intrinsically related to the universe. This relation accounts for its apparent timelessness; the poem surprises precisely by its unreal landscape, as if it had been an archaeological form lost at some previous century and then unearthed in its full perfection.

    Sunstone is a profoundly revolutionary poem, a profoundly modern poem, but its modernity is found not in its style or in its rhetoric. Its movement is like that of a trance meditation; the tone is one of melancholia, if not regret. The poetic voice manages to undo the effect of its own perfection, and its seamless construction is so inadvertent that the poem seems to have been written in what the Romantics called the language of ordinary passion, to the extent that the poetic voice never seems insincere. Paz's rigorous sense of form is subsumed to a particular content, and Venus is never named directly in the poem; rather its movement is presented as something that incarnates within the poem itself. To Emir Rodríguez Monegal and Roberto González Echevarría, Paz mentions that "pleasure" here is one of the axes of the poetic discourse (*PC* 24). He also states, in the same interview, that *Sunstone* is a linear poem that endlessly goes back over itself (21). He succinctly recounts not only the numerical structure upon which the text is based, but also what the text meant for him:

El número de versos de *Piedra de sol* es exactamente el número de días de la revolución del planeta Venus. La conjunción entre Venus y el sol se realiza después de una carrera circular de 584 días, y la del poema consigo mismo después de 584 versos. . . . Quiero decir, sobre el tiempo circular del mito se inerta la historia irrepetible de un hombre que pertenece a una generación, a un país y a una época . . . El tiempo quizá sea cíclico, y así, inmortal. . . . Pero el hombre es finito y no se repite. Lo que sí se repite es la experiencia de la finitud: todos los hombres saben que van a morir. . . . Esas experiencias *son* históricas: nos pasan y pasan. Al mismo tiempo no son históricas: se repiten. (*PC* 34–35)

The number of lines is exactly that of the number of days of the revolution of the planet Venus. The conjunction between Venus and the Sun is realized after a circular run of 584 days, and that of the poem with itself after 584 lines. . . . What I mean to say is, that over the circular time of myth, the unrepeatable history of one man that belongs to one generation, to one country and one era is inserted . . . Time may be cyclical, and thus inmortal . . . But man is finite and unrepeatable. What is repeated is the experience of finitude: all men know they will die . . . These experiences are historical: they happen and they happen to us. At the same time, they are not historical: they are repeated.

I have quoted Paz's statements almost in their entirety as they are a succinct articulation of the poem's form. Indeed, to *Sunstone* Paz adds a long note that fundamentally explains what appears in the first paragraph of the previous quote, although in that note Paz underscored the particularly Mexican aspect of this operation, rendering both dates and times in their Aztec equivalents. Tomas Segovia, in his short but concise essay on *Sunstone,* implicitly clarifies what this form means for the author: it reveals the poem as the product of a will, while at the same time it also allows the poet to forfeit the very will responsible for its creation.[12] In other words, authorial intention also resigns itself for the sake of a higher purpose, and the form of the poem—its 584 hendecasyllables—allows the author to withdraw his self for the benefit of the text. *Sunstone* can be seen, then, not only as a poem of control but also as one that entails a surrender to an inmutable principle.

In *The Bow and the Lyre* (published in 1956, preceding *Sunstone* by a year) and in "Los signos en rotación," Paz explains that modern man has lost the idea of the natural, and that the Aristotelian notion of mimesis needs to be reexamined in the modern word. In *Sunstone,* the mimetic act of the poem vis-à-vis Venus's revolution is part of an avant-garde gesture that denied mimesis and claimed that the poet did not have to imitate external reality, but rather operate like it. *Sunstone* does not imitate rotation or revolution; Venus is not named in the poem; the repetition at the beginning and at the end are meant to correspond to cyclical time. This repetition allows for a structural relation to be posited between Venus and *Sunstone*—a relationship apprehended by works of art such as the famous pre-Columbian *Sunstone* calendar in the Museo Nacional de Antropología in Mexico that we now endow with archaeological value. Segovia, once again, implictly allows for a point of comparison to Mallarmé's *Un coup de dés,* although Paz's homage to Mallarmé's great poem is to be explored to a fuller extent in Paz's *Blanco.*[13] *Sunstone* is a throw of the dice, an immense risk for a poet to undertake. It is the precipitous act of a poet that hurls himself toward an abyss.

Paz's control of form and surrender to it is a surrealist gesture. But aside from the belief in love as a force of salvation, *Sunstone*'s much vaunted surrealism can be found in Paz's poetical attitude toward the universe. Paz opposes cyclical recurrence to the linear, unrepeatable history of a single individual. The poet and his particular discourse—his memories, his very sense of contingency—enter within the cyclical flow of time without altering or interrupting it, but giving themselves to it. The poem's sense of surrender has been commented upon by its myriad critics. What has not been sufficiently stressed is Paz's use of the descriptive term "machine" or the analogous "machinery" in order to describe it—concretely, the poem as historical and antihistorical machine. The poet, as contingent creature, enters the repetitive flow of time by virtue of the singularity of his experience. Once that singularity has been registered in writing, the act of reading the poem returns that same, singular experience into an act of reading eternally reproduced. By insisting on his very singularity, within a cycle, the poet opens up that circularity to eternal recurrence. It is in this sense that the poem becomes a machine, positing itself as a copy of the universe, in order to then turn back and deny itself as the copy that it pretended to be. In a latter essay on Marcel Duchamp's *Large Glass* Paz states:

> In the first stage of the process, he translated the mythical elements into mechanical terms, and therefore denies them; in the second, he transfers the mechanical elements into a mythical context, and denies them again. He uses the myth to deny the criticism and criticism to deny the myth. This double negation produces an affirmation which is never conclusive and which exists in perpetual equilibrium over the void. (*MD* 71–72)

Although these are later statements, they are an apt analogy to Paz's metaphysical ground in *Sunstone,* where the clarity of the universe is affirmed by its juxtaposition to the linear singularity of an individual life that is then returned to the realm of the circular by the act of reading.

Even if we did not have Paz's explanatory note linking the number of lines in the poem to Venus, *Sunstone* should still surprise us: lines seem to be there for the sheer fact of adding a number, of counting, of filling up space— "caminas como un árbol, como un río / caminas y me hablas como un río" (*Poemas* 272) ("you walk like a tree, you walk like a river, / and talk to me like the course of a river" [*CP* 25]) or, for example, in the following section, where Woman's body turns into stone:

> . . . busco el agua
> y en tus ojos no hay agua, son de piedra,
> y tus pechos, tu vientre, tus caderas
> son de piedra, tu boca sabe a polvo,
> tu boca sabe a tiempo emponzoñado,
> tu cuerpo sabe a pozo sin salida.
>
> (*Poemas* 266)

> . . . I search for water
> in your eyes there's no water, they're made of stone
> and your breasts, your belly, your hips are stone
> your mouth tastes of dust, you mouth tastes
> like a poisoned time, your body tastes
> like a well that's been sealed.
>
> (*CP* 13)

The poem's analogy to the Venusian revolution, in essence, turns the whole poem into an image of its own process of composition. It is, in this sense, pure discourse, absolute irreality: "tiempo total donde no pasa nada / sino su propio transcurrir dichoso" (*Poemas* 273) ("total time where nothing / happens but its own, easy crossing" [*CP* 25]). The equivalence of the poem's lines to the Venusian year turns the whole poem into a supplement; it empties the poem of meaning so that it becomes pure form. No line is excessive, because all lines are redundant.

Paz's note, like the one he writes for the latter *Blanco,* reveals an enigma: Does structure precede the text, or is the text an effect of its own structure? To what extent is the composition dependent upon the mutual relationship between structure and content? It is relatively well known that Paz's work in *Blanco* follows a structural system that forms an underlying layer on the text, and that Paz is interested in figures like the American composer John Cage, who used chance and the *I Ching* as a mode of surrendering the will of the poet to another, more impersonal will. Nevertheless, *Sunstone* does not seem to have been structured a priori, in order to conform its number of verses to the astronomical number: there are actually no references to the Aztec solar calendar within the poem. Venus, we should recall, is merely a cultural referent; the planet itself, regardless of its name, is a celestial fact. From the point of view of the observer, names reveal an underlying structural equivalence between myths, as Paz explains in *Claude Lévi-Strauss o el nuevo festín de Esopo* (1967). That Mexican—or, more properly, Aztec—cultural signifiers of the poem are found at the margins of the text (but also as their underlying sense of foundation) is also related to the displacement of the writer in the text; *Sunstone* speaks not only of the poet as a singular individual but also of the poet as an entity, as a principle that repeats itself over time.

Whether for the sake of making the poem fit with the Venusian revolution in the Aztec calendar, or for underscoring to what extent Man and Woman are singular but also universal principles, *Sunstone*'s major trope is that of repetition. The first lines of the poem display a number of elements that will be repeated at the end of the poem:

> un sauce de cristal, un chopo de agua,
> un alto surtidor que el viento arquea,
> un árbol bien plantado más danzante,
> un caminar de río que se curva,
> avanza, retrocede, da un rodeo
> y llega siempre:
>
> (*Poemas* 259)

> a crystal willow, a poplar of water,
> a tall fountain the wind arches over,
> a tree deep-rooted yet dancing still,
> a course of a river that turns, moves on,
> doubles back, and comes full circle,
> forever arriving:
>
> (*CP* 3)

The poem insists on the singularity of these objects, it repeats "un" as if it were a mantra, one that has the virtue of emptying the objects of their very singularity while at the same time insisting upon it. The objects are, furthermore, unreal, subject to the particular deformation of language: the willow becomes a crystal willow; it is rooted on the ground although it moves with the wind; the river's route is circuitous.

Sunstone is an ecstatic poem, one that needs to be read at one sitting. Perhaps the best account of the poem is the one offered by José Emilio Pacheco in his "Descripción de Piedra de sol."[14] That the poem invites description is interesting in itself; this belies the sense of transparency given in Paz's poetry.

For Pacheco, the first and last five lines of *Sunstone* introduce the very notion of mobility: there are no endpoints in the poem, but rather colons, semi-colons and commas, underscoring the text's fluidity. Pacheco sees a first move-ment of the poem geared toward the future, an impersonal gesture broken up by the appearance of the second person singular *tú,* which is the woman addressed in the poem, almost immediately followed by the poet's "I." Woman and World become one body that is then traversed by this "I," who abandons himself in order to undertake a search or mythical quest. This searching "I" evokes a Mexican childhood—the past tense, as Pacheco points out, is here employed for the first time—and thus begins the poem's second movement. Here, the poem speaks in the mode of remembrance, as memory awakens thoughts of love along with other historical events of the poet's life. Woman incarnates in at least five names, all of which are in turn cultural referents: Melusina, Laura, Isabel, Perséfona, María. María refers to the Catholic Virgin; Laura and Isabel are not only common names in Spanish, but may also be seen as refering to the two great sources of Western poetry: Petrarch's Laura and Garcilaso de la Vega's Isabel. Melusine is a mythic name that refers back to hermetic lore; she is also alluded to in one of the sonnets in Nerval's *Les chimères,* from which *Sunstone*'s epigraph is taken. According to Pacheco, Melusyne is a naiad married to a mor-tal (Raymondin de Poitiers) who discovered her secret: Melusyne was con-demned to turn into a serpent every Saturday, from her hips down to her feet, in penance for having jailed her father in a mountain. Finally, Persephone rules as the Queen of Hades. Pacheco brings out these names and others mentioned or at least alluded in the text (Astarté, Istar, Venus herself as well as Quetzalcóatl, who is transfigured into Venus) in order to explore the mystical background of eros that underlies *Sunstone.*

If on the one hand, the poet's quest entails recuperating the past through love, this love can only redeem a history that is always lived as an interplay between the private and the colective. Paz mentions concrete experiencies of his life, streets in New York and in Mexico; he returns to his experiences in republican Spain, when placid time is suddenly ruptured by sirens, screams, and bombs. The world is full of chimerical monsters, ruling society with an implacable grip out of which human beings' only defense is love. The experience of solitude and alienation that is part and parcel of modern man's expulsion from the garden of innocence leads to a sense of solidarity where historical figures are images, and singular men and women bond with each other in order to survive. The poet reads himself as he reads history, and finally invokes the doors of perception that will allow him to escape. But no escape is possible, and the poem ends with a sense of acquiescence or surrender. As all doors and walls are rent, the poet is hurled out of himself into the time of all beginnings, as the sun once again revives the poem's initial lines, the timeless landscape of memory, the labyrinthine meandering of the world and of individual conscience.

CHAPTER 3

The Labyrinth of Solitude

One of Octavio Paz's most ambitious and widely read works, *The Labyrinth of Solitude* was his most sustained meditation on Mexico—on its history, society, internal structures of power, particular, paradoxical modernity, and relationship to Latin America and to the European and modern world. *The Labyrinth of Solitude* culminates Paz's attempts throughout the 1930s and 1940s to blend aesthetics and politics, commitment and solitude, Marxist thought with surrealism, by focusing on a critique on Mexico and nationalism. It represents Paz's most succinct combination of poetry, aesthetics, and politics; it fashions once and for all Paz's image as an intellectual engaged in a critique of the state and of its power.

Paz works from within the cultural crisis brought about by the progressive institutionalization of the Mexican Revolution, which fossilized a revolutionary language that had become, in the late 1940s, pamphleteering, sloganistic, debased. Language as the means of social exchange is immensely important to Paz. He complains, for example, that the only poetry left to Mexicans is found in the obscene verb *chingar;* that the linguistic world of the Mexican-American *pachuco* is a mélange of Spanish and English, and so on. *The Labyrinth of Solitude* is fundamentally the work of a poet who reexamines the meaning of such words as *nation, love, society, poetry*. At times, its heightened emotion and despair (particularly in the rhetorical endings of chapters) signify Paz's attempt to communicate to his readers the state of crisis that the poet himself feels. In this sense, more than to persuade, as in a rhetorical tract, Paz wants the reader to *feel* the extent of the crisis that has provoked his discourse. Paz's constant appeals to emotion are, then, appeals that intend to invoke readers' empathy. For Paz, Mexico is a neurotic patient, and the poet fashions himself into a hero—if not a healer, at least the one who makes others aware of the patient's status. If the society is ill, language is both index and cure. One should insist then, on the therapeutic effects of Paz's poetic journey through this labyrinth: the Mexican crisis is *named* in order to find a Mexican *cure*.

As Paz's first sustained meditation on politics and nationalism, *The Labyrinth of Solitude* presents an *other* Paz. But one must resist the temptation of critics who divide Paz's work into two different modes. If in his poetry since *Entre la piedra y la flor,* he had been trying to give an account of modern man's exploitation of Man, in *The Labyrinth of Solitude* Paz brings his concerns to touch upon a hidden cultural anthropology for Mexico, one that is poetic and moral, attentive to the outer as well as to the inner history of the nation. A historical as well as a semiotic treatise, this work will be the model upon which Paz will fashion his intellectual role in Mexican political discourse after 1950, by presenting himself as the one who defines Mexico as a particular geographical entity torn by the conflicting voices of the nation and the state. This other Paz is, as he says in his poetry, also the same. In *The Labyrinth of Solitude* Paz creates a sociology and an anthropology that are based on a poetics, and poetics itself rescues his interpretation from mere pamphleteering. In other words, Paz's political critique is based on a system internal to it and that spreads out toward his poetic texts.

As poetry and politics become more interrelated, particularly during the 1960s, Paz tries to explain his own dialectical categories. For example, in an essay from *El ogro filantrópico* (The Philanthropic Ogre) he focuses on the interplay among poetry, science, and history. If repetition entails degradation in poetry, in science repetition signals a regularity that confirms a hypothesis. The historian is situated at some midpoint between the scientist and the poet. His kingdom is like that of the poet, the realm of exception and uniqueness—but also like the scientist's, operating with natural phenomena that he intends to reproduce in terms of currents and tendencies. In this sense, "Los hechos históricos no están gobernados por leyes o, al menos, esas leyes no han sido descubiertas" (*OF* 38). (Historical events are not governed by laws, or at least those laws have not been discovered.) In these later words of Paz, he gives a holistic reading to his cultural work. The words remind us that Paz is attempting to fuse disparate realms of an activity grounded in poetry, seen as part and parcel of one and the same work.

It is important to understand *The Labyrinth of Solitude* as growing out of Paz's growing disaffection with the political developments of his time. He returned from Spain in 1938 full of political conviction that he expressed in a series of articles written for *El popular,* the pro-Communist paper of the Confederación de Trabajadores Mexicanos. After the Hitler-Stalin pact of 1939 and Trotsky's assassination in Mexico, Paz stopped writing for *El popular* and two years later, in 1941, entered into a dispute with Pablo Neruda over politics. In these shifts we can see Paz more vocally expressing his dissaffection with the nationalist interpretation of Mexican reality. Paz, who had started to write about

Mexico and its reality in 1938, undertakes his first journey to the United States in 1943, and it is during this trip that he will start consolidating many of the themes found in his work.

Paz repeatedly mentioned the year 1943 and his absence from Mexico for nine years as marking an epochal change for him. During those nine years, Paz lived in the United States and, later, in France, India, Japan, and Switzerland as a member of the Mexican diplomatic corps. But the most pertinent experiences for *The Labyrinth of Solitude*'s creation take place in the United States, which is where Paz encounters the Mexican-American *pachucos* that he portrays in the first chapter. It is his encounter with the Mexican reality in the United States that gives this series of meditations their sense of urgency. As Paz himself states in his book, he was able to see and to read the fate of Mexico implicitly and explicitly described in the body of the Pachuco. However, if the United States was important for the origin of the book, the bulk of its writing took place in Paris, and this situation of exile accounts for the essay's distance from the popular currents of Mexican thought at the time.

Paris represented the beginning of a fruitful decade for Paz. It was in Paris, in 1949, where Paz consolidated the first edition of *Libertad bajo palabra,* in 1949, as well as of *The Labyrinth of Solitude,* which was published the following year. In Europe during the decade of the 1950s Paz published such seminal books of poetry as *Semillas para un himno* (1954) and *La estación violenta* (1957), and *Sunstone* (1957), the essays *The Bow and the Lyre* (1956), and his collection *Las peras del olmo* (1957). In 1959, he published a second, revised edition of *The Labyrinth of Solitude,* underscoring the closed character of colonial society, amplifying the historical narration on the period of independence and the Mexican Revolution, and recasting chapter 8 into a much more critical assessment of the revolution itself. It is at this point that he also revised the book's psychoanalysis of Mexico.

The recastings of *The Labyrinth of Solitude* would have not changed the overall thrust of the book, had it not been for the addendum written after the events that occurred on 2 October 1968, in the Plaza de las Tres Culturas, or Tlatelolco, where the police fired on protesters who demanded a more open and democratic system of government. At that time, Paz was already a well-known writer, the author of essayistic and poetic works such as *Cuadrivio* (1964), *Claude Lévi-Strauss o el nuevo festín de Esopo* (1965), *Alternating Current* (1967), *Blanco* (1967), *Conjunciones y disyunciones* (1969), and *East Slope* (1969). Paz's immediate reaction to the brutal police action was to resign from his diplomatic post in India. It was at this time, surely one of the most prolific in Paz's life, that he wrote "México: la última década" (1969), a critical assessment of the events known as "the massacre of Tlatelolco." This lecture has been published, in later editions, in *Postdata (The Other Mexico: Critique of the Pyramid)* and included as a sort of appendix or continuation of the theses that Paz had initially developed in his book. Both *Labyrinth* and its continuation in *Postdata* reflect the development of Paz's thoughts on Mexico over the course of twenty years. In this way, *Labyrinth* has become a kind of diary on twentieth-century Mexican politics. Remarkably, it is a book that remains immensely consistent over time. As we shall see, Paz has refined or nuanced his points of view, but he has never recanted the core basis of these ideas.

Like Paz's *Libertad bajo palabra*, *The Labyrinth of Solitude* is also a book that has grown and been revised over time. Paz wrote what we may now call the core of the book principally in Paris, between 1948 and 1949 (a period roughly contemporaneous to the poems of *¿Aguila o sol?*), although the text originates out of meditations that precede it at least for a decade. Thus, it can be seen as the logical conclusion to experiences that begin after Paz's journey to Mérida and his encounters with the Mexican Indian milieu of Yucatán, and after his trip to Spain, in July 1937, to the Segundo Congreso Internacional de Escritores en Defensa de la Cultura. These two experiences are important to the development of Paz's political ideas; they beckon him to search for a language free of immediately partisan concerns. Paz's indebtedness in this regard spans a wide array of figures: from the national search for a Mexican philosophy undertaken by Leopoldo Zea, to the work of Alfonso Reyes, to the essayistic model of Samuel Ramos in his *Perfil del hombre y la cultura en Mexico* (1934) or Paz's search for a poetic discourse that was Mexican without the external trappings of nationalism. But the core thinkers in Paz's pantheon at the time of his writing are two dissenting members of the surrealist enterprise whose anthropological work was nevertheless steeped in surrealist responses to alienation. One was Roger Caillois, whose fundamental *Man and the Sacred* illuminated the sacred importance of the fiesta; the other was Georges Bataille, who shed light on Mexican customs via his ideas of ritual sacrifice and expenditure in society. These two, of course, are added to a philosophical stratum that already included Friedrich Nietzsche and the Spanish Generation of '98.

The Labyrinth of Solitude then, is not so much a book on politics, as a political book. The distinction is as subtle as it is important; Paz's epic sweep, spanning centuries of Mexican history, is not meant to take sides on the petty and partisan political squabbles of the moment. Its sense of crisis is not, as in the later *Postdata,* the product of a concrete situation, but of a general sense of malaise, coupled with an awareness of changing historical times felt by a new generation of Mexican intellectuals that came of age after the revolutionary struggle had ended. The book's rhetorical "family" can be seen in its use of the work of the Spanish Generation of '98, particularly Miguel de Unamuno and José Ortega y Gasset. Unamuno sought to explain not only the visible, but also the invisible threads to Spanish culture; Ortega was the foremost Spanish philosopher of his time, as well as the editor of *Revista de Occidente,* where much of German philosophical thought was translated into Spanish. For Unamuno and Ortega, one had to search history's meaning far beyond the transparent details of a chronological narration. Unamuno, for example, read the nation as a living text. As such, the nation possessed a hidden center that the historian had to decipher, in order to read history from that hidden axis.

Unamuno's own indebtedness to German philosophy and to Nietzsche is clear, and these are also important precursors to Paz. But we should also clarify that what Paz does not take from Nietzsche is as important as what he does. Paz, for example, does not participate in the Nietzschean (and Emersonian) cult of "representative men," even if Paz defines eras according to the work of particular thinkers that define those eras. His debt to Nietzsche is found, rather, in the sweeping historical panoramas constructed by the German thinker. Counterbalanced by Nietzsche and later on by Lévi-Strauss, whose thought Paz discovers while in Paris, the Spanish "intrahistoria" can be seen to have a wide-ranging effect on Paz, from *The Labyrinth of Solitude* on.

Paz created in *The Labyrinth of Solitude* a mode of historical research that led to a method. In his writings on Mexico and the United States, as well as in his other essays on contemporary political or cultural situations, like *Los signos en rotación,* Paz used grand historical sweeping narratives. Few dates, and some individuals, incarnate given ideas that move and define particular centuries. The ideas that Paz wants to examine are not specifically or particularly conscious ones; rather, they are submerged in deeper strata of conciousness, and come up to the surface at particular historical junctures. All purely historical explanations are insufficient for Paz, because history should not be merely the accounting of facts. Historical events, he argues, are also full of humanity, by which we may understand "problematicity," and attitudes on life are not necessarily conditioned by historical events. In the introduction to the essays collected in *The Philanthropic Ogre,* Paz argues that the nation in itself is a product of not one, but of multiple pasts, and that historical narrations serve a therapeutic purpose for the nation (*OF* 11). For example, in chapter 4 of *The Labyrinth of Solitude,* "Los hijos de la Malinche" (The Sons of La Malinche), he explains how insufficient history is in accounting for the particular character of the Mexican; he pursues this idea by examining language along with history. This particular notion of a historical and philosophical critique of culture that is Paz's more immediate model was initiated in Mexico by Samuel Ramos in his *El perfil del hombre y la cultura en México*. But Paz's project was more revisionary and at the same time more ambitious.

In many ways, *The Labyrinth of Solitude* is a strange book, not only in terms of its style, but also because Mexico is looked at from a philosophical and geographical distance that is nevertheless psychologically near. Re-reading the book, one notices the particular absences that account for the fact that this is a book written by an exile. To use one example, there are many references to traditional culture, but few from popular culture, from cinema, radio, mass culture. Literature spans the space of exile; it crosses borders—but incompletely.

The Labyrinth of Solitude is divided into eight chapters and an appendix. The first, and perhaps the core essay of the book, is "El Pachuco y otros extremos" (El Pachuco and other extremes) , and it opens with the figure of the Mexican-American immigrant to California that Paz encountered on his first visit to the United States in the 1940s. In the next three chapters, Paz analyzes what he considers particularly Mexican myths: "Mascaras mexicanas" (Mexican Masks), "Todos santos, día de muertos" (The Day of the Dead), and "Los hijos de la Malinche" (The Sons of La Malinche). After this mythical coda, Paz devotes the next two chapters—"Conquista y colonia" (The Conquest and Colonialism) and "De la independencia a la Revolución" (From Independence to the Revolution) —to an analysis of Mexican history. The final two chapters in the book—"La inteligencia mexicana" (The Mexican Intelligentsia) and "Nuestros días" (The Present Day)—examine contemporary Mexico, with an appendix, added in the second edition of the book (1959) titled "La dialéctica de la soledad" (The Dialectic of Solitude). As Santí points out in the introduction to his edition, what seems like a basically straightforward account nevertheless does not give a clue as to the book's mode of structuration, its interrelated construction in terms of giant blocks of myth, history, and diagnosis of contemporary reality.[1] As he sees it, *The Labyrinth of Solitude* obeys a sense of inductive reasoning, from particulars to generalities—from myth, to Mexican history, and finally, to what Paz himself terms a kind of vital and historic rhythm. The book proceeds, then, from the immediate experience, centered on the *pachuco,* to the mythical present of Mexico, and it is only after the mythical route has been completed that he moves on to history. What gives the book a certain flexibility as an essay, is precisely its discontinuous and even disarticulate, nature. Even the relationship between the mythical and the historical part of the book is neither explicit nor emphatic. The interplay between them both is insinuated, and not necessarily stated.

The Labyrinth of Solitude can be divided into two major blocks, composed of Myth and History, but there are other possible readings, particularly in relation to the first three sections on masks, feasts, and language. The first chapter posits an implicit essence for the Mexican, one that proceeds from the particular illegibility that Paz sees in the *pachuco*. The *pachuco* is seen as a reticent being, a kind of chiaroscuro subject. He inhabits a tenuous system of checks and balances. There is an implicit analogy between the *pachuco* and the collective sense of the Mexican *fiesta,* which Paz explores in the second chapter. Death and rebirth, inscribed and celebrated within the Mexican nation, are not unlike the cultural dislocation felt between North and South as it is written on the very body of the *pachuco*—a being who exaggeratedly mimics the North American in a rebellious gesture of excess. The fourth chapter, "The Sons of La Malinche," grounded on language and on the verb *chingar,* inaugurates (by means of its filial metaphor—mother to sons) the historical section of the book. The procedure that Paz follows in the initial chapters of *The Labyrinth of Solitude* is thus aesthetic: it is grounded on poetic procedure, in that it establishes a tenuous equation between two realms, and it allows that equation (that relationship) to explode by means of metaphor. These relationships, or analogies, are then replicated in the equation between Myth and History in the two parts of the book.

The Labyrinth of Solitude is based on a series of analogies for modernity, seen as the most complex problem facing Mexico. Paz's analogy, borrowed from his experiences in the United States, as well as from the Parisian debate on Camus's and Sartre's notion of engagement, centers on the interplay between the individual and the collective life of Man. The book begins by trying to give us insight into the uniqueness of singularity, of individual life. This awareness of singularity, for Paz, is equivalent to an awareness of self: "El descubrimiento de nosotros mismos se manifiesta como un sabernos solos; entre el mundo y nosotros se abre una impalpable, transparente muralla: la de nuestra conciencia" (*LS* 143). ("Self-discovery is above all the realization that we are alone: it is the opening of an impalpable, transparent wall—that of our consciousness—between the world and ourselves" [*LSol* 9].) Children and adults, says Paz, may transcend their own solitude by immersing themselves in play or work. But the adolescent, the subject who vacillates between infancy and adulthood, remains "suspenso un instante ante la infinita riqueza del mundo" (*LS* 143). ("halting for a moment before the infinite richness of the world" [*LSol* 9].) It is precisely at the end of *The Labyrinth of Solitude*—in the ninth chapter—that Paz returns to that same vision of adolescence: "La adolescencia es ruptura con el mundo infantil y momento de pausa ante el universo de los adultos. . . . Narciso, el solitario, es la imagen misma del adolescente. En este período el hombre adquiere por primera vez conciencia de su singularidad" (*LS* 351). ("Adolescence is a break with the world of childhood and a pause on the threshold of the adult world. . . . Narcissus, the solitary, is the very image of the adolescent. It is during this period that we become aware of our singularity for the first time" [*LSol* 203].)

The central concept that underlies Paz's book is solitude and its relation to modernity. In order to introduce the reader to this concept, from the onset of *The Labyrinth,* Paz equates individual to national life—adolescence to adulthood. The adolescent's encounter with his own singularity and with his own being is equivalent to the nation's encounter with its own history. It is upon this grid, one that equates the life of Man to the life of Nations, that the particular disjunction of modernity is to be found: maturity is not the time for solitude but the time for work, for reconciling ourselves with time. Modernity, however, gives us the image of a Man permanently out of touch with time, unable to lose himself in what he does. Modernity is a disjunction, a kind of monstrous asynchronicity manifested in the chronological fabric displayed between national and individual life; ancient traditions have been submitted to a discontinuous growth that has resulted in their being ill-prepared for the historical avalanche of progress, while the individual is left pondering the state of his own solitary endeavours upon reaching maturity. Paz seems to ask, If adolescence is equated with solitude, and maturity with collective endeavor, how can Mexicans, who have already fought a revolution, still be questioning their identity? Shouldn't these questions seem superfluous, now that the country has come out of its revolutionary years? Identity is one of the enigmas that provokes Paz's historical recounting of Mexican history, but this time from the particular distance of one who seeks out the monster that lurks within the labyrinth. Paz will revise the nationalistic reading of the revolution as chief guarantor of Mexico's singularity; at the same time he will diagnose his contemporaries' nationalist preoccupations with Mexico as a sign of self-defensive immaturity. As a modern nation, Mexico's adult subjects are still immersed in their own solitude; they are ill-equipped to deal with the modern world. In historical terms, the condition of alienated Man is, by definition, modernity, since modernity is, in a sense, the expression in time of Man's alienation. But alienation is also a state that demands a resolution in utopia, seen and read as its necessary end. Labyrinths are products of a mind that sees and examines the world in its own particular terms. Paz enters the labyrinth as a modern Perseus; but in Paz's book the hero is not only Perseus but also Narcissus, and at the same time Tantalus.

The labyrinth evolves out of, and tries to resolve, the dialectics between myth and history. The prize at the end of the labyrinth, as Paz explains in the appendix to the book, is the utopia of the fulfilled human being. *The Labyrinth of Solitude* is conceived as a purgation, as medicine and cure to vacuous nationalism. The labyrinth is the imagistic link that allows Paz to narrate a series of ruptures that mark the book itself: from the disjunction of modernity and of the solitary individual, to that of a country ruptured within itself. The book seduces readers into the same labyrinth that Paz has constructed for himself, by creating and not resolving the dialectics that underlie its construction. Paz lives within this fragmented multiplicity, for history's fragmentation places the essayist within the labyrinth. These ruptures, which Paz reads as the "tradition of rupture" in *Children of the Mire* (1974) nevertheless contain within their movement a moment of precarious equilibrium; it is at this moment when the form itself can be apprehended and the figure read. If the labyrinth provides both a metaphor for Paz and his and the reader's act of textual seduction, it is only as a figure that the metaphor itself may be apprehended. In this case, however, the fragmentation of the labyrinth has once again consolidated itself (has petrified itself, to use Paz's vocabulary) into a pyramid, one that allows Paz to read, once again, a series of analogies—although in this case the analogies concern the nation as well as its geography.

It seems that merely external events separate the 1959 edition of *The Labyrinth of Solitude* from the later *Postdata* (*The Other Mexico: Critique of the Pyramid*): mainly, the previously mentioned events of 2 October 1968 in the Plaza de las Tres Culturas, or Tlatelolco, as well as the decade of the 1960s, when Paz lived in the Orient as a member of the Mexican diplomatic corps. A closer examination reveals that, for Paz, the relationship between the external events and his internal change as a poet are actually one of the important themes of this meditation. If the beginning of *The Labyrinth* takes place at the border, *The Other Mexico* is also given on the border, in 1969, as the Sackett Memorial Lecture at the University of Texas in Austin, a lecture that would be the synopsis for the book itself. The more recent meditation, however, does not concern inner and outer space, but rather space itself; the analogical series that rules *The Other Mexico* is precisely geography, the nation and the state. Paz is concerned not so much with the artificial boundaries of the modern state, but with giving a vision of Mexican history—in this case of the Pre-Columbian history of Mexico precisely from what used to be called Aztlán—before the boundaries and artificial constructions of the modern state.

One of *The Other Mexico*'s central theses is stated succinctly at the end of one of the initial sections: "La crítica de México comienza por la crítica de la pirámide" (The critique of Mexico begins by the critique of the pyramid) says

Paz. From the onset, this statement does not seem to differ from other statements made throughout the book, particularly those referring to the idea of criticism: "La 'inteligencia' mexicana, en su conjunto, no ha podido o no ha sabido utilizar las armas propias del intelectual: la crítica, el examen, el juicio" (*LS* 303). ("The Mexican intelligentsia as a whole has not been able to use the weapons of the intellectual—criticism, examination, judgment—or has not learned how to wield them effectively" [*LSol* 158].) The search for criticism in Mexico is part of a wider search, as Paz explains, of a Form that is able to express the country. Comparing intellectuals in Mexico to intellectuals in Europe or in the United States, Paz states what he will repeat from here on throughout his other writings: in Europe and the United States, the intellectual has been displaced from power; he lives in exile from power, and his work takes place outside of the parameters of the State. In Europe and the United States, the intellectual's chief mission is critique; in Mexico, it has been political action. The relationship of intellectuals to the state is also taken up in chapter 6, when Paz deals with the period from independence to revolution in Mexico. In Latin America, as Paz explains, the nation was created precisely from the parameters of the state: "las nuevas Repúblicas fueron inventadas por necesidades políticas y militares del momento, no porque expresasen una real particularidad histórica. Los 'rasgos nacionales' se fueron formando más tarde; en muchos casos, no son sino consecuencia de la prédica nacionalista de los gobiernos" (*LS* 265). ("Thus the new republics were created by the political and military necessities of the moment, not as an expression of a real historical need. 'National traits' were formed later, and in many cases they were simply the result of the nationalistic preachments of the various governments" [*LSol* 121–22].)

Paz's search for a form that is capable of expressing the particular circumstance of Mexico is taken up in this book by focusing on Mexican history, from the conquest on, as the narrative of the search for that Form. What makes this account in *Postdata* different from the one in *The Labyrinth of Solitude* is that Paz tells his readers that he has found in the pyramid the Form that expresses what Mexico is. Form lives outside and inside; it is fashioned from the state to the individual, and at the same time is internalized by all Mexicans. This revelation of Form entails a criticism that is not necessarily a critique of history but a critique of forms of power. If *The Labyrinth of Solitude* concerns history in terms of *myth,* then *Postdata* talks about history from the point of view of an analysis of *power.* The book is, above all, dedicated to the continuous lines of power that underlie the historical ruptures from Pre-Columbian to post-Columbian history, from the construction of the nation and the state, to the narratives that allow for the construction of that history. But in giving an account of what Michel Foucault would call an archaeology of power, Paz has to construct a theory of form as symbol, from the point of view of a concrete historical event that once again, crystallizes a series of analogies. These analogies, at the same time, undercut the historical singularity of the event, and place it under the guise of a Form, one that reveals itself by virtue of the event, and that the event itself gives witness to. The circular logic of this event makes it difficult to understand its origin. But Paz implicitly argues that he is not concerned, in this case (as he was in *The Labyrinth of Solitude*) with origins. Rather, analogy itself is the point of departure for his critique. The inductive method that Paz follows in the earlier book is cast aside for the mode of revelation: Mexico's geography reveals the very functioning of the state as a pyramidal structure of power: "México se levanta entre los dos mares como una enorme pirámide trunca: sus cuatro costados son los cuatro puntos cardinales, sus escaleras son los climas de todas las zonas, su alta meseta es la casa del sol y de las constelaciones" (*LS* 393). ("Mexico rises between two seas like a huge truncated pyramid: its four sides are the four points of the compass, its staircases are the climates of all the zones, and its high plateau is the house of the sun and the constellations" [*LSol* 293].)

Paz clarifies that a historical event—even the massacre of Tlatelolco—is never entirely singular: rather, its seeming singularity accounts for its profound links to the substratum it renders visible. Once again, Paz insists on his own vision of history, one that unmasks the idea of history as a series of events. Just as during the first part of the essay he insists on dismantling the definitions of development and underdevelopment, at this point he dislodges history from its standard definition as a series of events. Paz says he speaks about the "true past" and not merely about a sequence of dates. What he aims for is a constant principle that underlies historical change, a kind of perpetual, rotating present. For Paz, history contains certain invariable elements that a mere account of dates and events cannot explain. The "old habits and beliefs" that Paz talks about at the beginning of chapter 5 in *The Labyrinth of Solitude* become a much more terrible proposition at the beginning of *The Other Mexico*. The events that Paz mentions in *The Labyrinth of Solitude* reveal the hidden history of Mexico, or better still, Mexico's *other* history. The concrete event of 2 October 1968, reveals that the hidden history of Mexico is a history of power inscribed within the very landscape of the geographical entity that is now known as Mexico. The labyrinth, seen this way, becomes a prison.

Paz would not be so seductive a reader of Mexican culture if he did not take pains to dislodge the idea of determinism from his critical thinking. He allows that the true character of the Mexican changes through time, that the construction of power is mobile and flexible, and he still retains a belief that naming and exposing that hidden reality will somehow result in a cure. But the reader also leaves this book with the perception that by inscribing form within geographical space, and geographical space as analogous to a particular form of power, what necessarily follows this tight construction is dispersal: the fragmentation that will produce another labyrinth, and then again another form that collapses, and so on, like the successive layers constructed on top of a given pyramid. This is why Paz's account of the events of 2 October begin with a general consideration of the student movement in 1968, and then lead to an analysis of the power relations of the PRI, followed by his vision of the event itself. Paz reads backward, in order to uncover the present by means of a history that predates the one he examined in *The Labyrinth of Solitude*. If the previous work was concerned fundamentally with the rupture of the Conquista, and sought to explain Mexican history from the point of view of that event, the bulk of *The Other Mexico* is an analysis of the Mesoamerican world before the arrival of the Spaniards.

The revelation of Form perpetually sends the reader back to more distant historical realms. For example, Paz begins chapter 5 of *The Labyrinth* with a statement as to how, underneath the apparent Occidental forms of the Mexican people, there lurks a hidden substratum of ancient and vital beliefs. But after the massacre in Tlatelolco, that same vitality is seen in fear; once the pyramid has appeared as a symbol, what is uncovered is the immense majority of victims crushed or sacrificed beneath it. One can say that the pyramid seduces Paz into a reading of power, that the pyramid is a sickness that infects all aspects of society. Paz ends *The Other Mexico* with an account of the multiple readings arising out of this image and recalls the Museum of Anthropology in Mexico City. What can be seen in the public space is not the ruins of a particular discourse, but the very articulation of the pyramid's effects. If the labyrinth was the image for the subject lost in the narratives of history and myth, the pyramid insidiously renders society and history collectively lost and recapturing the fetishes of power. Form always uncovers a relationship to power: this is the necessary conclusion posited by the history that follows *The Labyrinth of Solitude*. But it is a history whose bases must now be uncovered in previous work.

Borderlines: The Pachuco and Other Extremes

By starting with more recent sections of *The Labyrinth of Solitude*, I repeat one of Paz's techniques: that of the retrospective reading. Indeed, it seems as if for Paz one starts reading from the present, only then to go back and examine a presumed origin that brings the reader back into the present. The later sections of what is now the complete *Labyrinth of Solitude* can be seen in this light. If one of the beginnings for the historical narration of the *original* book is the conquest, *Postdata* will go even further back, to the Mesoamerican, pre-Columbian world. The later book takes us from the youth rebellion in the 1960s back to the Toltecs, Aztecs, and Mayas, in order to bring us back, once again, to the Museum of Anthropology. *The Labyrinth of Solitude* also starts with the present, with the figure of the *pachuco,* then it goes back in history, and then proceeds back to the present, to "The Present Day."

The pachuco is the most important emblem in *The Labyrinth of Solitude:* in him and through him, Paz reads his own contradictions. The Pachuco is, broadly speaking, a border figure, installed precisely at the fissure between two cultures and two modes of life:

> El pachuco no quiere volver a su origen mexicano; tampoco—al menos en apariencia—desea fundirse a la vida norteamericana. Todo en él es un impulso que se niega a sí mismo, nudo de contradicciones, enigma. . . . Queramos o no, estos seres son mexicanos, uno de los extremos a que puede llegar el mexicano.
>
> Incapaces de asimilar una civilización que, por lo demás, los rechaza, los pachucos no han encontrado más respuesta a la hostilidad ambiente que esta exasperada afirmación de su personalidad. (*LS* 148–49)

> The pachuco does not want to become a Mexican again; at the same time he does not want to blend into the life of North America. His whole being is sheer negative impulse, a tangle of contradictions, an enigma. . . . Whether we like it or not, these persons are Mexicans, are one of the extremes at which the Mexican can arrive.
>
> Since the pachuco cannot adapt himself to a civilization which, for its part, rejects him, he finds no answer to the hostility surrounding him except this angry affirmation of his personality. (*LSol* 14)

Paz sees in the pachuco a kind of unmotivated rebellion, a "grotesque dandyism" that persists in naming and referring to itself as different purely for the sake of difference. The pachuco's dress, for example, does not outwardly manifest a culture for Paz; on the contrary, it presents a kind of rootless fashion that merely imitates and exaggerates certain aspects of the dominant culture. Contrary to the general trend in North American clothes, with their emphasis on practicality and comfort, the pachuco takes the signifiers of that culture and renders them "impractical." The aggression of the pachuco is then, for Paz, merely a vain gesture of unfocused rebellion, one that insists on seeing itself perpetually as the victim of a society that does not accept him. Within his "victimhood" the pachuco achieves his true essence, as the "son," or the product, of the excluding society. Thus, the pachuco's externalizing gesture is vain, insisting precisely on its own sense of impotence.

Paz does not see in the pachuco a particular mode of rebellious and culturally assertive behavior by means of which opressed members of society establish and insist on their own weakness as a form of power and strength. For the political ideology that Paz has at this moment, there is a direct and unbroken link between rebellion and aims. Paz negatively reads the pachuco as merely intensifying his own status as victim, without seeing in that gesture the beginnings of a revolutionary attitude. Paz's reading of the pachuco is one of the more polemical sections of the book, and countless commentators have noticed or have insisted on what Paz did not notice here: to insist on one's victimization within the society is already to strike a revolutionary gesture; by calling attention to himself, the pachuco initiates a process of *representation*. But Paz at this point, immersed in the Parisian dialectics between engagement and rebellion, cannot conceive of this kind of attitude as a display of a certain kind of impotence, one where the display itself becomes a mode of passive agression that will ultimately lead to affirmation.

Metaphor: Mexican Masks

The pachuco leads Paz to devote a whole chapter to what he calls Mexican masks, as well as to the very idea of masquing, of simulation. In Paz's poetry, masks are directly related to the notion of otherness, and to his concern with transparency and legibility. All Mexicans, says Paz, regardless of class or origin, participate in an economy of masks, and he presents this mask as the essential and constitutive form of the Mexican. The economy of the mask regulates all behavior: it allows men to be close to one another, albeit distant from each other. The very legibility of the face is implied in the mask, as every gesture masks some other gesture. By means of the mask, the Mexican "being" is allowed to be preserved and contained; the individual makes the mask itself the root of his being. Paz does not necessarily want to strip away the mask, or demolish its economy; for him, Mexican culture simply becomes *legible* once the mask is exposed as such. The mask is the language of Mexico, the mediating factor between its people. If language, as Ferdinand de Saussure pointed out in his *Cours de linguistique générale,* is a system based upon the arbitrary relationship between signified and signifier, then the mask is what mediates this relationship; it renders visible, as in writing, the particular absence that it names. Not unlike language, the mask is also a rhetoric: it allows us to understand that the very directness of expression can only be given by indirect means, even while exposing its own self in the process. What is important is not what the mask hides, but rather the means employed in order to redirect whatever it is that is being said. In this sense, the mask is a form of visibility, and the Mexican is vulnerable, precisely because he exposes this rhetorical play.

Many readers have felt that this description of the Mexican is negative, but few have noticed that Paz is also masking himself, and that within the general framework of the book, the mask is one of the central elements that allows the Mexican to be *read*. We should notice that Paz begins his chapter with the possibility of a reading: "el mexicano se me aparece" (the Mexican seems to me) in a rhetorical play where he will not use the first person pronoun, but rather will place himself as an indirect object, or as part of a collective "we" that will only come forth in the second paragraph. This chapter then, accomplishes the paradoxical function of reading an illegibility and indirectness that *makes* the reading possible. In other words, and keeping with the system of paradoxes that is a trademark of Paz's, if everything is a mask, what is not masked is the mask itself, which is, in effect, transparent. Its transparency is such that it can only be compared to a metaphor, as Paz himself does already by the third paragraph of the chapter:

> El hermetismo es un recurso de nuestro recelo y desconfianza. . . . La dureza y hostilidad del ambiente—y esa amenaza, escondida e indefinible, que siempre flota en el aire—nos obligan a cerrarnos al exterior, como esas plantas de la meseta que acumulan sus jugos tras una cáscara espinosa. (*LS* 165)

> Hermeticism is one of the several recourses of our suspicion and distrust. . . . The harshness and hostility of our environment, and the hidden, indefinable threat that is always afloat in the air, oblige us to close ourselves in, like those plants that survive by storing up liquid within their spiny exteriors. (*LSol* 30)

The metaphor that compares the individual to the natural plant anticipates Paz's later comments, in *Postdata,* on the relationship between the state and Mexican topography, as if these were part of a system of equivalences, where A equals B. In this case, the individual Mexican is as hermetic as the plant; a hard and spiny exterior hides water beneath the arid appearances. Both the plant and the individual conceal and reveal at the same time; what is important, however, is that metaphor itself is able to join them in one particular space. Like metaphor in language, the mask brings together two realities, in appearance antithetical, but that are nevertheless related by means of the metaphoric operation. If it is clear that Paz wants to apprehend and read what the economy of the mask hides and reveals, if he intends to look at the plant's outer form and at the same time glimpse inside, what is interesting in *The Labyrinth of Solitude* is the extent to which this position is a result of his inability to tear and demolish the economy of the mask. Hence, the book does not really move into the realm of action in terms of the dialectics that it reveals. One of the few times that Paz does this is precisely in what used to be the last paragraph of the first edition, which in the second (1959) has been displaced (or masked) at the end of the penultimate chapter:

> No nos queda sino la desnudez o la mentira. . . . Si nos arrancamos esas máscaras, si nos abrimos, si, en fin, nos afrontamos, empezaremos a vivir y pensar de verdad. Nos aguardan una desnudez y un desamparo. Allí, en la soledad abierta, nos espera también la trascendencia: las manos de otros solitarios. Somos, por primera vez en nuestra historia, contemporáneos de todos los hombres. (*LS* 340)

> There is nothing left except nakedness or lies. . . . If we tear off these masks, if we open ourselves up, if—in brief—we face our own selves, then we can truly begin to live and to think. Nakedness and defenselessness are awaiting us. But there, in that "open" solitude, transcendence is also waiting; the outstretched hands of other solitary beings. For the first time in our history, we are contemporaries of all mankind. (*LSol* 194)

This is, perhaps, one of the few times that Paz has come close to writing a manifesto. But it would be a terrible one: the elimination of the mask only entails salvation after understanding that the kind of authenticity that it hides covers a void. Thus Paz avoids the tone of prescriptive manifesto in the chapter on Mexican masks, limiting himself to plot its terrain.

The economy of the mask permeates all aspects of Mexican culture. Paz begins his exploration by noticing its appearance in language, insofar as the culture itself presents an ideal of a man that does not "open" himself up. After proving that the system of the mask permeates the language of Mexicans, Paz goes on to show how Mexicans use language as a mask that defines the relationships between men, relationships based on a system of formal constraints. These modes of control branch out from public life (the political system) to private life. Both in politics as well as in art (and Paz here brings the example of Juan Ruiz de Alarcón and of Rodolfo Usigli's play *El gesticulador* as paradigmatic), as well as in their quotidian exchanges with one another, Mexicans, says Paz, aspire to create closed systems and closed worlds. What is particular to this system of particularities is that, unlike North American puritans, Mexicans do not fear their bodies; they are constantly aware of their own bodies as these are read by others. Mexicans are not prudish, says Paz, but use prudishness as a defense against others.

This prudishness as self-defense colors men's attitudes toward women, as what is most valued in women is precisely that veiled attitude toward others that Paz names "recato" (modesty). Women are those most affected by Mexican masks, as the system exercises its most repressive function on them. By the same token, male homosexuality is understood according to the particular role of each of the sexual partners, with most societal opprobrium reserved for the (passive) man who allows himself to be penetrated.

The mask allows Mexicans to value what is guarded and closed to the world, not necessarily in a hermetic, but in a baroque system of simulation and dissimulation. Mexican masks turn all social beings into actors on stage—but actors who dissimulate by trying to pass unnoticed and unobserved. Paz ends his chapter with these two concepts, establishing the subject as one who lives within society as if in a theatrical realm where the actor knows that he is acting, but at the same time does not want to be noticed while acting. In dissimulation, the actor mimetically reproduces the other to the point of abolishing the self. Both simulation and dissimulation allow for a vision of social action as simulacra, one that Paz reads in its more negative vein. Since, as he confesses at the end of the book, his aim is precisely to help Mexicans break out of their masks, his chapter cannot but end with a particularly ominous vision of the social theater of masks, one that goes back to the sense of crisis that Paz feels has mired Mexican society at the present moment:

si todos somos Ninguno, no existe ninguno de nosotros. El círculo se cierra y la sombra de Ninguno se extiende sobre México, asfixia al Gesti-culador y lo cubre todo. En nuestro territorio más fuerte que las pirámides y los sacrificios, que las iglesias, los motines y los cantos populares, vuelve a imperar el silencio, anterior a la Historia. (*LS* 181)

73

And if we are all Nobody, then none of us exists. The circle is closed and the shadow of Nobody spreads out over our land, choking the Gesticulator and covering everything. Silence—the prehistoric silence, stronger than all the pyramids and sacrifices, all the churches and uprisings and popular songs—comes back to rule over Mexico. (*LSol* 46)

The notion of the mask is vital to Paz's work. It is directly pertinent to his political works, as can be seen in *El ogro filantrópico,* where he talks about bureaucracies as masks. Paz explains that if the simulator's lying actually presents his reader with a form of authenticity, an excess of sincerity, conversely, may lead to more refined forms of lying. The example that Paz brings is that of erotic or love poetry. When the lover, for example, opens himself up (Paz's examples always gender the lover as masculine), he presents himself as a spectacle: by doing so, he actually evades himself from the erotic game; he rescues his self in order to substitute himself with an image. Outwardly acting in a theater of erotic abandon, the lover is actually protecting his real being by always behaving as an image of himself, as an Other. In this way, the self's most seemingly authentic emotions are seen as filtered and defined by lies to the self and to others. But it is precisely in the realm of simulation, in the substitution of the self for an image, that the only possible authenticity lies. Paz will link this safeguarding of the self to the notion of feast and death in the next chapter, particularly by linking it with Xavier Villaurrutia's poetry. For now, one must ponder what this notion of simulation says about literature as the expression of truth. For what Paz expresses at this point as truth can only be consciousness of simulation.

Metonymies: "The Day of the Dead"

If "Mexican Masks" was concerned about the circuit, network, and economy of the mask as a metaphorical construct, in "The Day of the Dead" the feast is the metonymy. Like one of those lightning bolts that appear throughout Paz's work, the feast metonymizes the complete economy of life and the awareness and denial of death. The fiesta allows for the explosion of the social equilibrium that is maintained by means of the Mexican masks. But in the fiesta, as Paz explains, the Mexican changes one mask for another, for a "careta"—literally, a second face—in order to liberate himself. The fiesta allows subjects to go out of themselves, it heals the void within by giving the subject recourse to another face that can also hide authenticity.

Paz obviously avoids essentializing the fiesta as a moment that exposes the Mexican as he truly is. In this way, he steers clear of the folkloric, nationalist vision of the *fiesta* as that which exposes innate joy and happiness. For Paz, the violent explosion of the fiesta entails a deeper problem, one that is allowed to vent itself by means of elaborate pyrotechnics. As a symptom of a deeper malaise, the fiesta is an attempt to heal the wound of being. Nevertheless, this attempt produces, in its own way, still another wound. Although Paz implies that the wound can be explained by a combination of historical and psychological causes, he opts not to inquire directly as to its origin. Instead, Paz talks about how the *fiesta* leaves the subject with a sense of loneliness, of ontological orphanhood.

At times, Paz implies that the fiesta must be, at some level, a kind of redemptive expiation for an original notion of guilt, or sin. Because the condition of guilt produces the sensation of solitude, the fiesta is the means for transcendence. But Mexicans do not, in effect, transcend their solitude; rather, they show, by means of the fiesta's excess, a highly complex mode of behavior, one that further isolates each of them within a community of solitary beings. For Paz, the fiesta is a complex performance where outer excess can only come into being because of an inner sense of control. This is why, even in the midst of the communal atmosphere of the fiesta, Paz says that no being is more solitary than the Mexican, the one who does not transcend his solitude in the midst of revel. Only at the end of the chapter do we understand that Paz has actually implied as much from the beginning: "El solitario mexicano ama las fiestas y las reuniones públicas" (*LS* 182). ("The solitary Mexican loves fiestas and public gatherings" [*LSol* 47].) What in the chapter's first sentence seems to be a paradox is revealed at the end to be part of the very dialectics of the piece, where Paz himself is the solitary walker who meanders through plazas decked with celebratory flags.

The title of the chapter, "Todos santos día de muertos" (The Day of the Dead), refers to the one feast that is not actually named in the chapter, although references to it abound throughout: 1 November, the Day of the Dead. Thus the section in the book dedicated to the fiesta is also the one that deals with Mexicans' attitude toward death. In its opulence and excess, in its violent sense of rupture, Paz equates the fiesta with death. Like many other social forms, the fiesta entails an avoidance of self. Following a medical image that underlies Paz's analyses, the symptom is avoidance, and what the patient is avoiding is death. As avoidance of self, the fiesta is an elaborate mask whose ultimate meaning must be found in the Mexican's understanding of death: "Dime como mueres y te diré quién eres" (*LS* 190). ("Tell me how you die and I will tell you who you are" [*LSol* 54].)

For the ancient Mexicans, Paz explains, life and death were not irremediably opposed: life, death, and resurrection were all states of a given cosmic process. For the Aztec soul, as Paz explains it, all was linked in an indissoluble unity, like space and time themselves. The Western Catholicism that was imported into Mexico changes this situation at the onset: what used to be collective principles for the Aztecs—sacrifice, salvation, and death—now become incarnate in each and every human being; they become individualized principles. In spite of their apparently irreconcilable opposition, both attitudes, Paz explains, are founded upon a common principle. For modern man, as well as for modern Mexicans, death has no meaning except as an end to the natural process of life. Whereas other nations refuse to think about death, Mexicans court it; they feign indifference; they pretend that death has become as intranscendental as life. For Paz, Mexicans despise death as much as they despise life; modern Mexico is founded upon a loss, and it has been unable to give new meaning to a death that used to have it. Because there is no transcending the world that has lost meaning, Mexicans will have an intimate relationship with a death that means nothing: "La muerte mexicana es estéril, no engendra como la de aztecas y cristianos" (*LS* 195). ("Death in Mexico is sterile, not fecund like that of the Aztecs and the Christians" [*LSol* 59].) Thus Mexicans face death with uncommon fascination.

Because the Mexican subject, as well as the Mexican idea of self, are so linked to solitary apprehension of the fiesta and of death, Paz closes off his chapter with two examples from literature. By reading the work of Xavier Villaurrutia (1903–1950) and José Gorostiza (1901–1966), Paz explains that in these books Mexicans can see their own vision of death as a nostalgia, and as a continuous fascination with the Void. Paz has dedicated a long poem to Villaurrutia, "El desconocido," published in 1943 and later included, in *Libertad bajo palabra,* in "Calamidades y milagros." Paz has also written extensively on Villaurrutia in *Xavier Villaurrutia en persona y obra.* As to Gorostiza's most important poem, "Muerte sin fin" (1929) Paz has collected an extensive commentary on the poem in *Las peras del olmo* (1957). Because both of these poets write as solitary lovers of death, of the void, of nothingness, Paz feels connected to their work.

"The Sons of La Malinche"

Throughout *The Labyrinth of Solitude,* Paz alludes to a grand historical narrative in order to explain the Mexican character as seen in a series of Mexican myths. Because the book is concerned with circuits (masks, fiestas, borders) and ruptures (Mexican history) Paz examines the relationship between both within the context of a historical narrative. History becomes a wound inscribed in the nation, once this nation is conceived as a body. And the wound must heal before the nation can inhabit modernity. Paz's reading of history as a wound implies a rhetorical position, a taking of sides. But Paz positions himself both inside and outside history; he is a participant but also an observer. Paz installs himself at this juncture precisely because history is felt as a wound not only by the nation but also by the subject. Its most perfect emblem reveals itself at the moment of conquest, in the figure of La Malinche, Hernán Cortés's lover and translator. But the way in which Paz focuses on La Malinche is as interesting as the essay itself.

"The Sons of La Malinche" is one of the most tightly contructed essays in *The Labyrinth of Solitude.* Paz begins by proposing a general discussion about how subjects are hermetic to each other. Every society has a segment (class, group of people) within itself or within others that needs to be rendered as difficult to read, as obscure. For example, for metropolitan cultures, peripheral cultures are other, they are strange and full of mystery; within certain societies, women are construed as possessing "mystery." The process that endows this other with attributes not possessed by the self is one that confers a paradoxical form of individuality to the other, one that at the same time individualizes the collective. Paz clarifies that the only segment that society does not read as mysterious is the working class, as that class is difficult to individualize. In terms of the working class, the individual is always submitted to a class construct. In a trenchant critique of capitalism's effect upon individuals, Paz decries how the modern worker has been mutilated, instrumentalized; how modern society, capitalist as well as totalitarian, has emptied beings of their substance; how the worker in these societies has been figured and represented as a being with no density. The working class is "transparent," its body is not mysterious to the other. The world of terror is a world of things, and advanced capitalism has sometimes turned workers into machines. Still, because Mexico is in the process of industrialization at the moment in which Paz writes, Mexicans, he says, have not yet been turned into cogs of the capitalist machinery. The Mexican worker has not lost his mystery, that is to say, his individuality. But this is also the source of a particularly Mexican contradiction. Mexicans are still a problem to themselves and to others; they are still enigmatic beings, they have not been turned into abstractions. By the same token, Mexicans live within a premodern or precapitalist system of production; they are not yet instruments of capitalism but, rather, precapitalist serfs.

Paz explains that these complex Mexican attitudes could be seen in socioeconomic terms in light of a kind of serf mentality that is a product of history, of the Mexicans' being submitted throughout history to the position of serfs. But he immediately discards that interpretation: because the Mexicans' reserve is not distinctive of a particular class of Mexicans but is found in all classes. Most important, Paz says that this attitude of mystery, of closing off to the world, is not directly related to history. History, says Paz, is neither a cause nor an effect, but a complex sequence of indissoluble factors. It is not a false, but rather an insufficient, explanation for the particularities of Mexicans. At this point, Paz launches into a meditation of what history means for him. In delimiting the reach and the extent of the influence of history upon Mexicans, Paz denies that their character is defined passively by history. His presentation of history unfolds within the panorama of the present, as different strata of a common narrative that can be shown through language. The emblem for history is always language: part of the present, but at the same time containing the vestigial remains of the past.

Paz has started "The Sons of La Malinche" with a vision of the enigma that Mexicans are to themselves and to others. Subtly, he has pushed aside economic (servitude, serf mentality) as well as historical explanations for this enigma, in order to focus on language as it relates to history. His particular focus is on the myriad, related forms of the verb "chingar," as well as the particular inflections that Mexicans give to the word. For Paz, "chingar" is obviously more than a Mexican profanity; it is the synecdoche for a social mode of relationships. It is a word that denotes power, on the one hand, and envy, on the other; the "chingón" is the one who is never "opened" but is, on the contrary, constantly "opening" others. The Mexican's unscrupulous masculinity implied in the word consigns others to the no-man's-land of the "Chingada." Within the verb itself Paz inscribes time, history, and myth. As he says, "En cierto sentido todos somos, por el solo hecho de nacer de mujer, hijos de la Chingada, hijos de Eva" (*LS* 217). ("In a certain sense all of us, by the simple fact of being born of woman, are *hijos de la Chingada,* sons of Eve" [*LSol* 80].) Paz's obsession with "chingar" reveals an obsession with origins.

Mexicans' obsession with origins is an obsession common to all men, says Paz: in all mythologies Man is the fallen creature—fallen into an alien and hostile world. In terms of myth, Paz uncovers in all civilizations a common structure that can be seen by means of the triad of father-son-mother. What is particular to the Mexican ethos is that the father, "el gran chingón" is always an absent principle—not so much venerated as feared, and held in awe, precisely because his sense of humor entails humiliation and destruction. The son, on the contrary, is always the adored principle; he comes in the guise of Jesus Christ, as redeemer, or, as Cuauhtehmoc, the fallen eagle. The mother, the third figure in the triadic structure, is for Paz a more ambivalent figure. As a passive entity, she is venerated as the Virgin of Guadalupe, or rejected as La Malinche, the Indian woman who was Cortés's lover and translator. But the ambivalent acceptance and rejection focused on La Malinche amounts to an unresolved tension within a tradition that has condemned Mexicans to a state of ontological orphanhood. By denying La Malinche, the nation can only live history under the sign of one continuous rupture. That the figures of Cortés and La Malinche are still present in popular usage reveals for Paz the essential nonresolution of a Mexican conflict with origins that prompted the nation, as he will examine in the following chapters, to turn its back on its past.

"The Sons of La Malinche" allows Paz to locate solitude as the essential definition of nation, a solitude born out of denial, and one responsible for the strangeness that the individual feels toward himself. Once Paz has arrived at what seems to be the center of the labyrinth, he can then inaugurate his own narrative and account of the discontinuous Mexican past within a framework that, in literature, he will define as the "tradition of rupture." In this case, Paz will deploy history in order to allow the patient (Mexico) to come to terms with itself. At the beginning of the chapter, history was discarded as the totalizing explanation for Mexican behavior. After examining the problematics of rupture at the center of the Mexican self, however, Paz can now turn once again toward history with a model of knowledge:

El mexicano y la mexicanidad se definen como ruptura y negación. Y, asimismo, como búsqueda, como voluntad por trascender ese estado de exilio. En suma, como viva conciencia de la soledad, histórica y personal. La historia, que no nos podía decir nada sobre la naturaleza de nuestros sentimientos y de nuestros conflictos, sí nos puede mostrar ahora cómo se realizó la ruptura y cuáles han sido nuestras tentativas para trascender la soledad. (*LS* 226–27)

The Mexican and his Mexicanism must be defined as separation and negation. And, at the same time, as a search, a desire to transcend this state of exile. In sum, as a vivid awareness of solitude, both historical and personal. History, which could not tell us anything about the nature of our feelings and conflicts, can now show us how that break came about and how we have attempted to transcend our solitude. (*LSol* 88)

Paz has examined whole networks of symbols and emblems that uncover the different strata of the past in the present. It is time, then, to work our way out of the labyrinth and work out Mexican history as Paz sees it. The nation has been analyzed from the point of view of myth; Paz's history will be centered on culture.

Mexican History

What follows will gloss Paz's readings of Mexican history as they appear in *The Labyrinth of Solitude* without much comment; Paz's words on this point are particularly clear, and to refute them would require the work of a historian. Above all, one should recall, as Paz claims in *El ogro filantrópico,* that history is the therapeutics of the nation; when the patient is a society or a nation, however, the diagnosis is particularly difficult, given that many groups have an interest in hiding or occluding certain areas of the past.

Paz sees Mesoamerica, before the Spanish conquest, as an area where the plurality of cities and cultures nevertheless allowed for a surprising homogeneity. The historical analogy that Paz brings to the text (not without underscoring differences) is that of the Hellenic world at the onset of Roman imperial power. Paz attributes this homogeneity to the unifying function of the previous Toltecs. In this, Paz seems to follow traditional pre-Columbian historiography. Despite its homogeneity, Mesoamerica was torn by the competing claims of its many peoples. In fact, the area underwent many wars of domination and conquest, culminating in the political (although not cultural) superiority of the Aztec Empire, which had, at the time of the Spaniards, dominated most other cities in the region. This surprising combination of homogeneity within difference explains, for Paz, the total success of the Spanish conquest, which also bred on the resentment of other dominated groups in what is now Mexico. The Aztec was the collective suicide of a civilization that had become exhausted in a short period of time. For Paz, Montezuma yields and embraces the Spaniards because he feels abandoned by the gods. Not only Montezuma, but the Aztec empire itself, had lost consciousness of its own destiny.

Paz sees that same contradictory multiplicity at work in the Spanish Peninsula, for Spain was a country that had retained many medieval forms behind the trappings of modernity. Regardless of the point of view under which one examines the enterprise of conquest, Paz concludes that it was the product of a unified will. This unitary will makes it imperative for Mexicans to study the colonial world, and not consign it to a mere historical interruption between the pre-Columbian period and independence. Paz seeks to understand colonial society without necessarily justifying it, as a contradictory and living totality. Colonial art, for example, is one that recycles, that adapts and transforms. In "Nueva España: orfandad y legitimidad" (New Spain: Orphanhood and Legitimacy), he explains that "el arte de la Nueva España, como la socedad misma que lo produjo, no quiso ser *nuevo:* quiso ser *otro*" (*OF* 43) (the art of New Spain, as the society that produced it, did not want to be *new:* it wanted to be *other.*) Paz explains that art is at the same time a paradigm for other social and philosophical modes: Catholicism in New Spain, for example, did not offer a new philosophy or a new way of understanding faith, but rather a ready-made philosophy and a petrified faith. Hence, the colonial world for Paz is the root of the psychological problems of the Mexican soul; religion and tradition have been given to the people as dead, useless forms that mutilate or asphyxiate Mexican singularity.

Paz's vision of the imposed order of Catholic society in New Spain ends with his first approximation to the works of the Catholic writer and nun Sor Juana Inés de la Cruz, to whom he will dedicate the monumental *Sor Juana Inés de la Cruz or the Traps of Faith* (1982). Paz sees Sor Juana as a victim of the closed and hermetic universe of colonial times—a writer who is a product of her context, and who at the same time was crushed by it. This situation Paz will later see in terms of the pernicious effects that bureaucracy has on writers everywhere, particularly those oppressed by the intolerant ideological regimes of the twentieth century. Sor Juana's fall from grace and into silence ends Paz's assessment of the colonial world; she represents the pinnacle of artistic achievement of that time. Paz's vision of New Spain, in a latter essay collected in *El ogro filantrópico,* is of a society that was in effect founded upon the negation of its past—the Indian and the Spanish worlds—but that webbed those worlds in complex and contradictory ways, only in order to find itself negated and killed (the filial metaphor here is important) by Mexico as its offspring: "La sociedad novohispana fue un mundo que nació, creció y que, en el momento de alcanzar la madurez, se extinguió. Lo mató México" (*OF* 41). (The society of New Spain was a world that was born, developed and that, at the moment in which it was to reach maturity, was extinguished. Mexico killed it.)

The groups that brought independence to the Latin American continent were influenced by modernizing projects superimposed on a society ill equipped to handle them. The dominant elites consolidated themselves as the true heirs of the previous order, and were thus incapable of producing a truly modern society. Paz subscribes to the historical assessment that says that Latin American nations were actually creations of the state, that the sense of national consolidation is part of a process that is, in many instances, imperfect. But for Paz, Mexico represents a singular case within this Latin American panorama. If in the rest of Latin America the *criollo* (Creole) American-born landowning class asserted the prerogatives of its power to the foreign-born Spaniards and to the empire, Mexico's War of Independence was an incipient agrarian revolt, in many ways analogous to a stilled class warfare; in Mexico the people rebelled against the local aristocracy. Even in terms of its ideology, the heroes of Mexican independence were, at times, more concerned with reform than with separation. Only when a new form of constitutional monarchy was abrogated in Spain did the conservative factions launch the War of Independence, and the Mexican empire was born with Iturbide as its head. When, shortly thereafter, a rebellion dislodged Iturbide from power, the era of "pronunciamientos" (sedition) was born; the consequent result was internal dissension, manipulated primarily by the United States, with the resulting loss of almost half of Mexico.

In this series of disputes, the liberal faction in Mexico formally broke with the colonial structure of society, and its project accounts for one of the most important moments in the life of Mexico: the Reforma. For Paz "la Reforma" is the most nuanced and complex moment in Mexico's past, precisely because the Reforma itself sought to deny that past. Paz's two main arguments against the Reforma are that it turned its back on the past, and that it represented the will of one minority against others. The liberal rebellion does not bring about the much expected birth of the bourgeoisie but rather the birth of a new *latifundista* (owners of vast rural properties) class, best exemplified in the figure of the dictator Porfirio Díaz. The *porfiriato* represents the pinnacle of Mexican inauthenticity: it adopts the positivist philosophy without actually engendering it within the country.

These historical events for Paz are the symptoms of a crisis. The image of prerevolutionary Mexico is that of a nation in discord, but the revolution allows for the true revelation of the Mexican's being: "La revolución mexicana es un hecho que irrumpe en nuestra historia como una verdadera revelación de nuestro ser" (*LS* 279–80). ("The Mexican Revolution was an explosive and authentic revelation of our real nature" [*LSol* 135].) Paz gives incessant variations of this phrase. He sees the revolution as Mexico's moment of self-awareness, as a fiesta where Mexicans finally, once and for all, know and understand each other. Only after this historical narrative do we understand that Paz's narrative of history could only have been accomplished after exploring both the mask, the fiesta, and the Mexican longing for origins. This historical narrative is also fundamentally marked by three events: conquest, reform, and revolution.

If in his later *Children of the Mire* Paz will expound on revolutions and revolt, in *The Labyrinth of Solitude* he sees the revolution in the guise of an eternal return: all revolutions, says Paz, attempt to create a society where men can truly express themselves and *be,* and a revolutionary society is one that puts all hopes on the inherent possibilities of human beings. As such, revolutions are utopias that postulate a return to a previous Golden Age. Certain aspects of the Mexican Revolution confirm this model. But for Paz, the Mexican Revolution has no ideology except that of a hunger for land. Paz sees the resulting triumph of liberalism as compromise in 1917, as a result of the lack of ideas of revolutionary leaders. Paz warns that this situation could create a new *porfiriato,* where bankers and intermediary classes could take over the government. In a later interview with Paz (*PC* 112–13), Claude Fell underscores the innovative aspects of Paz's account of the Mexican Revolution, particularly his views on Emiliano Zapata, who at the time of the book's publication was considered a bandit from the south.[2] Paz explains the biographical links between himself and *zapatismo* (his father was a sympathizer and zapatista lawyer) but also that Zapata represented with utmost clarity the reality of the revolution itself, particularly in his demands for land as well as in his traditionalism. Paz's most succinct statement on the revolution, however, is found in his next chapter, on the Mexican intelligentisia.

As far as the Mexican "intelligentsia" is concerned, Paz critiques it in global terms, within the context of the end of the Mexican Revolution. For Paz, intellectuals compromised with authorities after the revolution, and became the advisers of those in positions of power; they did not exercise power themselves, with major exceptions. Among these he carefully examines José Vasconcelos, Samuel Ramos, Jorge Cuesta, and Alfonso Reyes in a chapter where he seeks to come to terms with his precursors as well as with his contemporaries. He closes the chapter with a carefully measured critique of Leopoldo Zea and his project of creating a Mexican philosophy, and warns against both the term and the concept. Mexican philosophy, he says, can be nothing but a study of the way in which Mexicans have incorporated the particular ideas that they have received from the West. Mexicanness, as Paz defines it, is neither a form nor a concrete historical tendency: it is the narrative that oscillates between different systems: "la filosofía mexicana, si de veras lo es, será simple y llanamente filosofía, a secas" (*LS* 318). ("Mexican philosophy, to be truly that, must be philosophy plain and simple" [*LSol* 171].) In this respect, his vision of a de-centered world seems to anticipate what has more recently been termed post-modernism: "hemos vivido en la periferia de la historia. Hoy el centro, el núcleo de la sociedad mundial, se ha disgregado y todos nos hemos convertido en seres periféricos, hasta los europeos y los norteamericanos. Todos estamos al margen porque ya no hay centro" (*LS* 317). ("We . . . have always lived on the periphery of history. Now the center or nucleus of world society has disintegrated and everyone—including the European and the North American—is a peripheral being. We are all living on the margin because there is no longer any center" [*LSol* 170].)

Paz ends his book with a snapshot of the revolution and the world in the 1950s. Read retrospectively, his words bear witness to the immense faith that intellectuals had at that time toward what was later called Third World solidarity or nonalignment. They also anticipate a state dominated by the banking or comprador (intermediary) class. Paz's gaze on the Mexican Revolution both in 1950 as well as in 1959 yields the following assessment: there has been in the Mexican state an excessive demographic growth coupled with insufficient economic progress, the revolution has created a capitalist state with a working class to a certain extent co-opted by the ruling class, and the particular development of the state and the society has created a bourgueoisie that is not unified. This working class should start becoming progressively more independent from the state and should align itself with the middle classes, and the state should confine itself to being the mediator in terms of social growth. The main problem facing Mexico in economic terms, as Paz sees it, is the absence of capital to render the nation more than a producer of raw materials. In the 1950s Paz already questions the function of the proletariat as the agent of change, and examines the rise of party bureaucracies as a new phenomenon in twentieth-century society. This latter part of the book amounts to a manifesto for the creation of an independent critical voice.

Politics

Although, as we have seen, Paz was concerned with politics since the 1930s and 1940s, his political thoughts are better expressed after the second edition of *Libertad bajo palabra* (1960) and his experiences during the 1960s. After his resignation from the Mexican Foreign Service, Paz achieved an independent and critical stance that was unique at the time, and his essays become the central and defining features of his work. The full extent and range of Paz's essays—even those chiefly devoted to politics—is immense. It is possible to divide these into two major groups: those concerning Mexico in particular, and the relationship between Mexico and the United States; and those concerning events in other arenas. Among the latter, it is important to mention *Pequeña crónica de grandes días,* 1990 (Small Chronicle of Great Days), *Vislumbres de la India,* 1995 (In Light of India), his partial political autobiography *Itinerario,* 1993 (Itinerary), and *Tiempo nublado,* 1983 (although the latter combines essays on Europe with others on Mexico).

Undoubtedly, Paz felt that his meditations on Mexico and on Mexico and the United States should be read as a cluster, one that gives an account of the political thinker's changes over the course of almost a lifetime. In the introduction to *El ogro filantrópico,* he separates political literature and "literatura comprometida," opting particularly for the former and not for the latter. Paz, in that sense, always defined himself not as a politically engaged writer like Mario

Vargas Llosa, Pablo Neruda, or Gabriel García Márquez, but as a writer of political thought. His essays, particularly the section on the Mexican intelligentsia in *The Labyrinth of Solitude* as well as those included in *El ogro filantrópico,* give an account not only of Mexican politics and history, but also of the conflicted relationships between intellectuals and state. Thus, Paz's work articulates a critique on intellectuals and their relationship to power that predates many of the more contemporary concerns on the role of intellectuals in the public sphere found in contemporary sociohistorical essays. Paz's principal political concerns, however, center on the interrelationship between the nation and its history (or histories, as he specifies) as well as on the relationship between the modern state and the bureaucracy as its creation. Because most of this discourse concerns Mexico as a nation that possesses a unique form of state bureaucracy, I shall focus on Mexico.

The more recent edition of *The Labyrinth of Solitude* includes three essays on Mexico that continue the latter chapters of the original book. I shall briefly comment on these essays as well as refer to some of those collected in *El ogro filantrópico.*

Paz's political essays concern the relationship between history and nation, state and bureaucracy. Paz sees the development of postrevolutionary society by examining the structures of power entailed in the PRI, the Partido Revolucionario Institucional. The PRI arose, as he explained in "La libertad como ficción," 1976 (Liberty as Fiction) (*OF* 316) as a compromise between authentic democracy and Latin American *caudillismo* (dictatorship). Paz thinks that this particularly Mexican form of political compromise has become anachronistic and inefficient. In an interview from 1971, Paz dates the origins of the crisis of the PRI as far back as 1958 (*OF* 104) although he explains that it became more and more acute in 1968, with the protests that led to Tlatelolco, which in the 1973 introduction to the American edition of Elena Poniatowska's *La noche de Tlatelolco* (The Night of Tlatelolco) he compared to the colonial insurrection of 1692. Like its predecessor, the extent of the rebellion surprised the institutions of power, which did not know how to approach it other than reacting to it with the deafness of those in power toward the legitimate needs and demands of a sector of the middle class and students. This event, more than any other, initiates Paz's most trenchant debates with the PRI, as well as his most sustained attempts to understand the Mexican system of government as a system in need of reform.

Paz's ideas, nevertheless, do change over time. By 1972 Paz is arguing for a return to *cardenismo* (the nationalist politics of the Mexican president

Cárdenas) as a point of departure for government reform (*OF* 109) although later on, when this neo-*cardenismo* actually became an important force within the Mexican political system, Paz blamed it for not articulating clearly a program of government (*LS* 496) that explained what kind of socialism it had as its aims. If Paz has been arguing throughout for the reform and reformulation of the PRI, by 1985 he explains that merely reforming the PRI is not enough, that the hour at hand demands something more than merely reform (*LS* 499). After 1988, Paz's overriding idea is that the PRI should take steps in order to become independent of government and refashion itself as a social-democratic party (*LS* 519).

Paz's criticism of the PRI is related to his criticism of bureaucracy and that of the state. The twentieth century, Paz argues, has seen the emergence of bureaucracies as a new category, a new class whose very definition and constitution as class is suspicious. In effect, for Paz the emergence of a new social class "es un fenómeno análogo al de la emergencia, en el de la naturaleza, de una nueva especie animal" (*LS* 472) (is a phenomenon analogous to that of the emergence in nature of a new animal species). It is difficult, furthermore, to catalogue bureaucracies as a class, and Paz argues that to an extent it is useless to categorize bureaucracies with the usual economic taxonomies. The bureaucracy as such, he argues, is a new historical category, one that is different from the bureaucracies of the past: the former achieved their cohesion by being powerful groups of functionaries or employees, whereas present-day bureaucracies achieve their sense of cohesion by virtue of politics (*LS* 471). In fact, Paz argues in *El ogro filantrópico* (1978) that capitalism itself has become bureaucratized, and that transnational companies already prefigure a bureaucratic form of capitalism (*OF* 86).

The key issue in examining bureaucracies seems to lie in the very form and function of the modern state. The bureaucracy, to a certain extent, replicates the state, and the modern state is a machine that endlessly reproduces itself; its economic organizations tend to imitate the corporatist model. Because Latin American societies are strange hybrids, and have always juxtaposed liberalism and counter-reformation (where haciendas coexist with industrialized zones [*OF* 86]) the notion of the state has to be examined carefully. The Mexican state represents a particular phenomenon; Mexico, Paz argues, is not a democracy, but it is also not a totalitarian ideocracy. Paz insists that Mexico is not a totalitarian state because in Mexico there is no perfect symbiosis between the party bureaucracy and the state (*LS* 491). Nevertheless, Mexican bureaucracy lives in a state of contradiction: it has been instrumental in achieving social change but it is also, at this point, the greatest obstacle for political change.

In *El ogro filantrópico,* Paz mentions that there is a contradiction within the Mexican system, where there are two ways of understanding politics, two sensiblities with distinct moralities: on the one hand, the modern technocratic bureaucracy; on the other hand, the patrimonialist state (*OF* 92). For Paz, the peculiar nature of the Mexican state contains three distinct orders or formations in a state of continuous osmosis and communication: (1) the governmental bureaucracy, composed of technocrats and administrators and functioning like other bureaucracies of democratic Western societies; (2) favorites and friends; and (3) the political bureaucracy of the PRI, formed by political professionals that are grouped, mainly, by convenient alliances. It is the persistence of the patrimonialist morality within the Mexican state that impedes modernity, and renders the Mexican state an imperfectly modern one (*OF* 99).

In a later assessment (1986) included in the essays added to *The Labyrinth of Solitude,* Paz explains that one of the more important characteristics of the contemporary Mexican political system is the presence of a social group that dominates the state, one that has control over the political, cultural, and economic life of the nation. Paz does not completely change his assessment, although in the late 1980s he will specify that the two bureaucracies within the PRI are political and governmental. The state itself, as Paz said in *El ogro filantrópico,* belongs to both (*OF* 89).

Paz continued developing and refining his analyses. His critique of both right and left has to be seen within the context of his desire that Mexico abandon one-party rule. What has happened in Mexico since the late 1980s Paz reads as a breakdown of the system of compromises that characterized the PRI throughout its history. Hence, the particularly ominous character this breakdown assumes for Paz; for better or for worse, the PRI had allowed at least a form of stability, however imperfect. Nonetheless, the return of the past, of the repressed, is also to be feared.

CHAPTER 4

Poetics

The Bow and the Lyre, Children of the Mire

The Bow and the Lyre

In terms of Mexico and politics, Paz's central book is *The Labyrinth of Solitude*. To understand Paz's poetics, one turns to *The Bow and the Lyre* (1955; 2d ed., 1967). *The Bow and the Lyre* seeks to explain a poem's origin, as well as poetry's relationship to history and to the poet; it also seeks to understand the meaning and the origins of inspiration. Not only is this where Paz gives us a narrative of his own idea of poetry, it is also where he spells out a narrative of the poet and history that leads to later books, such as *Children of the Mire* (1974) *Sor Juana Inés de la Cruz and the Traps of Faith* (1982) as well as to his more recent *La otra voz*. Like *The Labyrinth of Solitude, The Bow and the Lyre* is a book that has grown over time. The second, revised, edition includes one of Paz's most famous works, "Los signos en rotación" (Signs in Rotation), a pivotal essay in the Latin American literary canon, one in which Paz tackles the tradition of poetry in the modern world. As a book-length meditation on the art of poetry, *The Bow and the Lyre* is unparalleled in Latin America. If we think of Latin American books that are roughly contemporaneous to it and that attempt to cover the same terrain, only Alfonso Reyes's *La experiencia literaria* (1942), and José Lezama Lima's *La expresión americana* (1957) come to mind. But none of these books have the breadth of Paz's, where personal experience and theoretical reflection join to explain literature from the point of view of poetry—poetry understood as the foundation of literariness itself. Paz explores the full range of his knowledge: East and West, North and South, ancient and modern traditions. *The Bow and the Lyre* threads all of these into the fabric of the present almost rhapsodically, as Paz fuses general exposition with concrete detail.

But *The Bow and the Lyre* is also, perhaps, Paz's most difficult text: the dizzying configuration (or rotation) of events, histories, poets, traditions, evolve into what Paz would later call a "rotating system" of signs that are hard to pinpoint, precisely because there is no attempt to immobilize them into a structure. What Paz wants is to apprehend it all as a movable system, as if literature, history, and society rotated like a mobile. The title, as Paz explains in one of the latter sections of the book, comes from Heraclitus, whose acceptance of change and time Paz rescues in an attempt to go back to a pre-dialectical, pre-Socratic tradition. For Heraclitus, the universe is in a state of tension, like the strings of a bow or those of a lyre, and Man is the meeting point of a cosmic war. The bow (with its hunting, warring connotations) and the lyre (a referential emblem of poetry) are metaphors for a dialectical condition that is resolved by a metonymy that joins them: both the bow and the lyre have strings, and these strings are in both instances in a state of tension, but for opposite effects. In one, the string prepares the hunter or the warrior to shoot at the blank; in the other, the same string entertains the listener with song. The image of the bow and the lyre, thus, carries its own sense of resolution, as a meeting ground for opposition.

Faced with metaphors that lead to other metaphors, and that are always in a precarious balance, readers have silently displaced close readings of *The Bow and the Lyre* and concentrated on its concluding essay, "Signs in Rotation." But one should be wary of reading the book by just focusing on one of its parts: the question that underlies *all* of *The Bow and the Lyre* is writing, and the writing mode that Paz examines is poetry, which he defines in the most ample terms possible. Poetry for Paz is a kind of transcendental absolute that can only be defined in relation to its incarnation in time—the poem. It is this definition that accounts for Paz's reading of poetry as a genre that is beyond genres, as an absolute that can only be apprehended by means of the historical fact of its incarnation into poems.

It is important to understand that Paz's definition of poetry also incarnates and changes in time, just as poems themselves. If we compare the first pages of the two editions of *The Bow and the Lyre* we can see how Paz's notion of poetry, even as absolute, is subject to temporal change. For Paz, the absolute always brings contingency to play, and contingency is where the act of writing needs to be localized. In the first edition Paz begins by defining the adjective "poetic" as incapable of being fixed:

Nada más huidizo e indefinible que lo poético. A fuerza de acompañar a sustantivos adversarios, este adjetivo parece vacío de contenido. . . . Flota, sin que nada lo sostenga; a la deriva, no va a ninguna parte, salvo, acaso, al encuentro de sí mismo. El adjetivo lo arranca de sus referencias habituales y lo enfrenta consigo, con su propio ser, para que sea más plenamente. (11)

There is nothing more fleeting and undefinable than the poetic. Because it has had to accompany contrary nouns, this is an adjective emptied of meaning. . . . It floats, with nothing to sustain it; on its own, it goes nowhere, except, of course to an encounter with itself. The adjective tears it out of its common references and confronts him with himself, with its own being, in order for it to be more fully.[1]

Paz approaches poetry by means of an adjective, which already belies the difficulties at hand. For in this first "incarnation" of *The Bow and the Lyre,* he has chosen to immobilize an object that he himself defines as elusive. There is nothing that is poetic per se, Paz explains; rather, the urge to objectify (to turn something into an object) reveals poets' own biases: their desire to define, fix, signify, and possess what refuses possession. This tentative approach is abandoned in the second and definitive edition of the book. The direct definition of what poetry is that starts on the third paragraph of the first edition is turned into the opening paragraph of the second:

> La poesía es conocimiento, salvación, poder, abandono. Operación capaz de cambiar al mundo, la actividad poética es revolucionaria por naturaleza; ejercicio espiritual, es un método de liberación interior. La poesía revela este mundo; crea otro. . . . Aísla; une. Invitación al viaje; regreso a la tierra natal. Inspiración, respiración, ejercicio muscular. . . . Expresión histórica de razas, naciones, clases. Niega a la historia: en su seno se resuelven todos los conflictos objetivos y el hombre adquiere al fin conciencia de ser algo más que tránsito. (2d ed., 13)

> Poetry is knowledge, salvation, power, abandonment. An operation capable of changing the world, poetic activity is revolutionary by nature; a spiritual exercise, it is a means of interior liberation. Poetry reveals this world; it creates another. . . . It isolates; it unites. Invitation to the journey; return to the homeland. Inspiration, respiration, muscular exercise. . . . Historic expression of races, nations, classes. It denies history: at its core all objective conflicts are resolved and man at last acquires consciousness of being more than a transient being. (*BL* 3)

Paz's change—from an attempt to fix *the poetic* to a definition of *poetry* already shows that he has swerved from the indecisive to the concrete, that he tries to embody the experience as poetry and to allow it to contain all that the adjective "poetic" sought to contain. Poetry is beyond categories of body or soul, beyond good and evil, beyond benediction, praise, or excoriation. The first two pages of the second edition of *The Bow and the Lyre,* with their epiphanic definition of poetry, are already an attempt to push aside what poetry is in favor of the *poem* itself as the true incarnation of something that, now, is able to be defined, explored, and examined, in a way that "the poetic" was not.

Paz's focus on the poem per se allows him to frame the questions that have haunted him in the writing of the book:

> Las tres partes en que se ha dividido este libro se proponen responder a estas preguntas: ¿hay un decir poético—el poema—irreductible a todo otro decir?; ¿qué dicen los poemas?; ¿cómo se comunica el decir poético? . . . Si es cierto que en toda tentativa por comprender la poesía se introducen residuos ajenos a ella—filosóficos, morales u otros—también lo es que el carácter sospechoso de toda poética parece como redimido cuando se apoya en la revelación que, alguna vez, durante unas horas, nos otorgó un poema. (25–26)

> The three parts into which this book has been divided propose to answer these questions: Is there a poetic utterance—the poem—irreducible to any other form of expression? What do poems say? How is the poetic utterance communicated?. . . If it is true that alien residues—philosophical, moral, or others—intrude in every attempt to understand poetry, it is also true that the suspicious character of all poetics seems to be redeemed when it rests on the revelation that once, for a few hours, a poem gave us. (*BL* 15)

This statement will be the first of many that Paz will make throughout his poetic career, distinguishing his theoretical and critical writing from the exercise of literary criticism, by separating the disinterested, critical meditation on literature from what in *The Children of the Mire* he would call the "partial" or "interested" reading of poetry—a term which he borrows from Baudelaire in order to define those works of criticism written by creative authors. In this way, Paz defends the loose systematicity of a work, at the same time arguing that his work is a kind of "testimonio" (testimony), the work of a *witness* to poetry. As such, the practitioner has to ask himself what writing is, and Paz opens his warning to the first edition of *The Bow and the Lyre,* with just such a statement:

> Escribir, quizá, no tiene más justificación que tratar de contestar a esa pregunta que un día nos hicimos y que, hasta no recibir respuesta, no cesa de aguijonearnos. . . . Desde que empecé a escribir poemas me pregunté si de veras valía la pena hacerlo: ¿no sería mejor transformar la vida en

poesía que hacer poesía con la vida?; y la poesía ¿no puede tener como objeto propio, más que la creación de poemas, la de instantes poéticos? ¿Será posible una comunión universal en la poesía?

Writing, perhaps, has no other justification except that of trying to answer a question that we asked ourselves one day and that, until we have not answered it, will not cease jabbing at us. . . . Ever since I started writing poems I asked myself whether it was a truly worthwhile endeavor: wouldn't it be better to transform life into poetry rather than making poetry out of life? And as to poetry, can it not have as its object, more than the creation of poems, that of poetic instants? Will a universal communion within poetry ever be possible?

The question that haunts Paz in *The Bow and the Lyre* is permanently displaced, permanently shifting, between the being of poetry—that which poetry is—and how poetry is in society. Never quite dislodging poetry from time (Paz will conclude the introduction by stating that "la poesía no es nada sino tiempo, ritmo perpetuamente creador" (Poetry is nothing but time, perpetually creating rhythm) he nevertheless posits an ultimate question that will be resolved by recourse to writing as phenomenon and, therefore, to poetry as it is incarnated in time.

Contexts

Between 1953 and 1958, Octavio Paz received a scholarship from El Colegio de México that allowed him to publish *Semillas para un himno* (1954), and to complete poems included in *La estación violenta* (1958), translate the work of the Japanese poet Basho in *Sendas de Okú* (1957), write essays included in *Las peras del olmo* (1957) as well as complete his long meditation on poetry, *The Bow and the Lyre*.[2] The scholarship was obtained thanks to the aid of the Mexican poet and essayist Alfonso Reyes, who had been one of Paz's intellectual mentors since 1941. It was already thanks to Reyes, one of the most important presences in twentieth-century Mexican literature, that Paz had been spurred to publish *Libertad bajo palabra* in 1949, and Reyes was also crucial in publishing *Eagle or Sun?* Some of the first indications that Paz is working on a long book related to poetics are found in his correspondence with Reyes since 1951, where Paz talks about a short, sixty-page essay on the situation of poetry in the modern world.[3] Five years later, what was conceived as a short essay, became the almost three hundred pages of what we now know as *The Bow and the Lyre*.

Although Paz's initial thoughts on writing a poetics can be dated back, as we shall see, to the early 1940s, the initial wholescale planning and composition of the book takes place during the latter part of the decade, particularly while the poet lives in Paris, works in the Mexican embassy, and travels through Europe, India, and Japan. When Paz returns to Mexico in 1953, his scholarship will be firmly devoted toward completing the book on poetics. Thus, the first edition of the book reflects Paz's experiences in Europe, as well as an initial encounter with the East apprehended with the aid of British and French sources. It reveals the poet as one who has delved principally into French and Spanish literature (his more extensive comments on North and Latin American literature will be added in the second edition of the book), and who has immersed himself eclectically in Heideggerian phenomenology (as this was translated into Spanish by José Gaos, whose translation of Heidegger's *Being and Time* in 1951 culminates Gaos's crucial role in Mexican letters since the late 1930s). Paz's book reveals the poet's reading of multiple sources; its curious mélange of both phenomenology and existentialism is an attempt to understand the poetic experience itself by underscoring its essence as one that speaks of temporality. It also reveals the profound traces of surrealism as an aesthetico-philosophical account of the mysterious essence of the literary text.

The first edition of *The Bow and the Lyre* is principally grounded in the French and Hispanic tradition; the book's second edition adds sources from Mexico, France, and India.[4] The subtle changes between these two editions are revealed both in his choice of literary texts as well as in the book's poetics. In terms of literature, there is more space allotted to the work of Stéphane Mallarmé, particularly to *Un Coup de dés,* a poem fundamental to understanding Paz's experimental work in India. His readings of Joyce, Pound, and Eliot are broadened, with more space allotted to each. The Hispanic literature discussed is not almost completely Iberian Spanish literature; Paz comments on Latin American *modernistas* and *vanguardistas* like Vallejo, Huidobro, and Neruda. In terms of poetics, Paz has felt the impact of structuralist poetics, particularly because of his reading of Claude Lévi-Strauss and Roman Jakobson, as well as his understanding of the work of Lacan and Barthes, whose *Writing Degree Zero* was published in Paris in 1953. All these readings coalesced in what became, since the second edition of *The Bow and the Lyre,* its concluding chapter, "Signs in Rotation," which completely puts the book up to date, and joins structuralism with Eastern poetics, phenomenology with the tradition of modern poetry.

In the "advertencia," or "warning," to the first edition of *The Bow and the Lyre,* Paz mentions that his book originated out of a series of conferences organized by José Bergamín in order to celebrate the fourth centenary of the birth of the Spanish mystical poet San Juan de la Cruz. At that time Paz, prompted to reflect on poetry, wrote his essay "Poesía de soledad y poesía de comunión," which anticipated many of the concerns expressed in *The Bow and the Lyre*. Paz's essay is divided roughly into six parts; although it is only in the later part where he returns to read San Juan de la Cruz by juxtaposing him to Francisco de Quevedo, as if these were two sides of the Spanish soul. In San Juan de la Cruz, Paz sees a poet who cannot explain the mystical state of communion in which he finds himself; Quevedo appears on the contrary, as one whose expression always leads to lucid consciousness. These two poets are paradigmatic for the discussion that follows, where Paz does not allow us to forget that he had placed them as foundational principles. What will be clear, at the end, is that Paz seeks to establish some sort of balance between the two; that he constructs a dialectics in order to present himself as mediator.

Most of the terms Paz will use throughout his essays on poetry and poetics—not only in *The Bow and the Lyre* but also in "Signs in Rotation"—appear for the first time in "Poesía de soledad y poesía de comunión." Reality, desire, and knowledge are seen in that essay within general comments on experience as well as on poetic "technique." Paz begins reading from Spanish baroque poetry and leads to a general discussion of the hermetic tradition of Romanticism—a tradition that includes Blake, Novalis, Nerval, Lautréamont, and Poe, one that he will go back to, again and again, in later books. Paz sees in this tradition the key to the modern experience: a desire for a future reconciliation with reality that is also nostalgia for a prior, unfallen state of being. For Paz, one of the paradoxes of modernity is that to desire a future world means also to remember its prior existence. The solitary quest of these Romantic dreamers is their longing for a communal understanding with reality. Their quest Paz sees as resembling his own: the attempt for the conjunction and the reunion of opposites, such as consciousness and innocence, experience and expression, the act and the word that reveals it. It is in relating this tradition of Romanticism to the argument at hand, that Paz shows the true complexity of his thought on poetics; what underlies Paz's account is still another dialectical pair, that of poetry and philosophy. And what he seeks is nothing less than establishing the preeminence of poetry (even as an epiphanic, almost irrational act) in terms of philosophical thought.

Paz's argument flows by means of dialectical oppositions: he begins "Poesía de soledad y poesía de comunión" by isolating reality and relating it to knowledge. Reality as a whole is apprehended only partially by understanding (*conocimiento*), which tries to dominate it by means of technique (*techné*). One of the supreme forms of understanding, Paz says, is philosophical understanding, which seeks to express Man's desire for knowledge. But this thirst for knowledge leads to a process of domination and subjection—a will to power, in Nietzschean terms, whose emblem is that of the Magus or the Magician. All knowledge, states Paz, even disinterested knowledge, arises from a desire to submit nature and reality to understanding. Paz posits a second attitude as dialectical double to the desire for knowledge and power that he saw in the Magus. This second attitude has no practical use; it is not transcendent insofar as it thrives on pure experience. In this second attitude, those who contemplate nature and reality do not seek to know and dominate but, rather, to look into reality in order to forget and join that reality in contemplation. But this attitude is born out of fear, and ends up fetishizing reality and nature: "El miedo a la realidad lo lleva a divinizarla: la fascinación y el horror lo mueven a fundirse con su objeto" (*PL* 292). (Fear of reality leads to its divinization; fascination and horror lead him to fuse with his object.) Its root is love, but it is manifested in religion. Its most visible incarnations can be found in Magic (as *techné*, examined above, as a way to submit reality to power) and religion (as a mode of fusion with reality). Religious man supplicates and loves; the magus coerces and adulates ("adula o coacciona") (*PL* 293).

Having established the parameters for knowledge in this manner, Paz asks whether poetry belongs to one or the other; it is from this question that Paz frames the rest of his essay. From the point of view of the poem, poetry is neither religion nor magic. But—and this is Paz's fundamental distinction—the *spirit* that expresses poetry may come from an instinct that may partake of the magical or the religious impulse. Because of his desire to establish a dialogue with the world, the lyrical poet adopts one of two fundamental attitudes: solitude or communion. As a magician, the poet is a magus of words; he does not aim to utilize this magic but rather to possess it. And in this sense, he is closer to the mystic. But if the poet is part magus, if he participates in the spirit of the magus by using words as magic, his attitude toward religion is no less heretical, for the poet's religion is always unorthodox. Poetic expression, explains Paz, creates an order out of itself and its own laws. The poet tries to sacralize reality by creating either the poetry of solitude or that of communion as a poetry that is, at once, prayer or blasphemy. Poetry —born out of solitude or communion—becomes a reality of its own, an entity that partakes of both magic and religion. Because it bridges the dialectical oppositions that Paz has seen at play in Man's double attitude toward reality, poetry becomes the essential paradigm for all modes of communication, thus possessing all forms of authenticity. By the end of his essay, it is obvious that the tradition that Paz identifies himself with belongs neither to the poetry of solitude nor to the poetry of communion, but partakes of both to the extent that it dislodges the terms of opposition. An essay that begins as a commentary on the Spanish mystic Saint John of the Cross thus becomes an exercise in poetics that deploys terms that will continually haunt Paz. "Poesía de soledad y poesía de comunión" is one of the pivotal texts in Paz's development; indeed, it is the kernel from which his major essayistic works on poetics will germinate.

Structure and Themes

Paz divides *The Bow and the Lyre* into three major sections, with an epilogue (added after the second edition) and three appendices. The three central sections (excluding the introduction) are devoted to "El poema" (The Poem), "La revelación poética" (The Poetic Revelation), and "Poesía e historia" (Poetry and History). These major sections are in turn divided into chapters, which are also subdivided into sections. The book is organized by dividing and further subdividing matter into blocks. There is, however, a system to Paz's structure. In "La imagen" (The Image), the fourth chapter of the section devoted to "El poema," Paz defines "the image" as a verbal form that submits the plurality of the real to unity. Paz argues that the Image scandalizes and upsets dialectical principles, which then allows Paz to examine the relationship between Image and Philosophy, and devote his chapter subsections first to the philosophical thought of the West and then to that of the East. The final subsection of the three does not so much synthesize the previous two, but rather unites them in the midst of discord. If we now look at the bigger picture—from the shorter subsections to the bigger blocks—"The Poem" (whose fourth section is precisely "The Image") argues that language (first section) is related to (or is a function of) rhythm (second section), that the divisions between verse and prose (third section) are historically motivated and are defined by cultural norms. By the time readers get to the section on "The Image," they understand that poetry and history are images of each other, just as in the latter *El signo y el garabato* (The Sign and the Scrawl), poetry and technology are dialectical opposites that mediate each other. In *The Bow and the Lyre,* one term leads to another and then still to another, in a perpetual recessive movement. Dialectical opposites are presented and then allowed to remain in a perpetual present, where they reflect each other. The procedure by means of which poetry and history are mediated by a third term—the image, in this case—is repeated throughout the book.

For example, in a very complex argument regarding poetry and religion within the context of revelation, Paz distinguishes between the two terms (poetry and religion), joins them (as modalities that underscore the notion of inspiration or revelation) and distinguishes them from each other, in order to show that religion is not merely organized or "dogmatized" poetry. For Paz, poetry *reveals* our original condition, whereas religion *interprets* the same condition. The experience of the sacred, says Paz, is different in both realms because both their ontology and their aims differ. First, he asks the reader to ponder what is it that beckons Man to the experience of the sacred; he then answers his question by explaining that the sacred in Man arises out of a perceived insufficiency of being. Religion, by grounding itself in notions of expiation and sin, turns our encounter with the sacred into a kind of penance for our sense of contingency. For religion, the sacred beckons this eternal penance, this never-ending cycle of expiation and sin that will ultimately give eternal life to the subject, even if at the expense of his own liberty. Whereas religion keeps Man in chains and in control by tying the subject to a moral insufficiency, poetry reveals Man as finite and contingent, not as insufficient in a moral sense. Thus, in his dialectical account of poetry and religion, Paz reveals and progressively unveils parallel dialectical sequences, in order to allow the essayistic discourse to achieve a moment of temporary rest and balance. In this way, what separates poetry from religion is brought about by examining what joins them, and vice versa. The particular effect that the book gives its readers is that of a discourse examining accidents for the sake of uncovering some primary essence—some foundation that is, at the same time, both its origin and its conclusion.

There always seems to be a center that moves and displaces itself throughout *The Bow and the Lyre*. It is a repetitive book, in the sense that its parts mirror each other. Poetry, seen as a transcendental absolute in the book's introduction, is a metaphor for being, and it reveals the essential beingness of being over time in the form of poems. Poetry as such can only be apprehended by the dialectical relationship it sustains with time and temporality. "The Poetic Revelation" (the second part) can be read as explaining the idea of poetry, as much as "Poetry and History" (the third part) can be understood by reading back to "Verse and Prose" (section three of the first part). Paz's mode of operation in these chapters entails a kind of displacement or *relève:* myth is inseparable from the notion of time; in order to examine the idea of time, however, we must look at the cultural construction of myth. This construction of myth, conversely, defined by means of beat and rhythm, forces us to distinguish between verse and prose, which are in turn defined historically, and so on. Paz defers, in his first chapter, the study of rhythm in the poetic phrase, to the study of the distinctions between verse and prose, for beat cannot be examined in particulars without grounding this analysis in the notion of genres that we have created. But rhythm and beat are also involved in Paz's notion of the image, which in itself is also temporal.

Analogy, Otherness

The Bow and the Lyre is, in this sense, a *corsi* and *ricorsi* of poetry, language, and thought. It disavows an interpretation of poetry as a kind of transcendental signified for the sake of a historical grounding on poems as historical creations; it does so, however, by dislodging from poetry the particular historicity of the image. Once Paz has established and defined poems as historical, and also as images of history, he turns back to ahistoricity in his discussion on inspiration, in order to conclude once again with statements on society and history. Because in *The Bow and the Lyre* Paz's thought aims toward synthesis, the work of the critic is to rescue the pieces that Paz attempts to join in a totalizing whole. Although this will be more evident during the 1960s, it is already anticipated by the first edition of *The Bow and the Lyre* and fully manifested in the second, which includes Paz's attempts in India at joining poetry, culture, society, and history into a system that understands poetry and time. In this regard, it is important to anticipate what Paz says of analogy in "La nueva analogía," an essay from *El signo y el garabato* (1973), that all modes of apprehension seem to lead to the analogical process, that we are aiming closer and closer toward understanding everything as similar to everything else. In another version of the same theme, Paz says, in "Presencia y presente: Baudelaire crítico de arte" (Presence and Present: Baudelaire as Art Critic):

> La analogía es la función más alta de la imaginación, ya que conjuga el análisis y la síntesis, la traducción y la creación. Es conocimiento y, al mismo tiempo, trasmutación de la realidad. Por una parte, es un arco que une distintos períodos históricos y civilizaciones; por la otra, es un puente entre lenguajes distintos: poesía, música, pintura.

> Analogy is the highest function of imagination, because it joins analysis and synthesis, translation and creation. It is knowledge and, at the same time, transmutation of reality. On the one hand, it is an arch that joins different historical periods and civilizations; on the other, it is a bridge between different languages: poetry, music, painting.[5]

Analogy appears as operating principle after *The Bow and the Lyre,* but one can already notice how in this earlier book Paz elaborates on this idea. If in "Poesía de soledad y poesía de comunión" he places the origins of the poetic principle within a version of a will to power, in *The Bow and the Lyre,* poetry is grounded by desire or pleasure, a concept important in terms of Paz's critique on Heidegger, as well as in his discussion of the mimetic principle as one of the original clues to language. Not only does Paz here rescue the notion of mimesis from Aristotelian poetics, he allows it to spill over into his later concerns with translation in *El signo y el garabato.*

For Paz, mimesis itself is linked to time thus its elaborate incarnation into beat and rhythm. Time, says Paz, is always prior to Man, and the poet is a mimetic being who, contrary to Aristotle's belief, does *not* imitate nature (as Paz will explain in "Signs in Rotation," *nature* is a term that has lost all consistency in the modern world) but rather some other, elusive element that is grasped by means of movement, rhythm, and beat. Poetry in itself is not an imitation of nature because Man cannot imitate that which has lost all sense of consistency; rather, the poem is a mimetic act that imitates man's mode of understanding temporality.

Rhythm and beat are fundamental elements for Paz; an awareness of them is already present in childhood. Even children, he says, only learn how to isolate words slowly, but this separating of words is a function of the child's apprehension of rhythm and beat. By putting words into units of rhythmic signifiers, man is able to overcome singularity for the sake of communal experience. Rhythm, as a mode of apprehension of time, is culturally bound: every society, says Paz, possesses its own sense of rhythm, which varies from civilization to civilization. Time, therefore, can never be dislodged from culture; every culture regulates and divides time by means of calendars that distinguish between mythic and "regular" time. Poetry, in every society, is a means to go back or to have access, to a mythic time. This mythic time differs from temporality as it is generally understood; it moves back in order to move forward.

Poetry, for Paz, is to be found in all genres and forms; it is a mode of apprehending language that precedes all other culturally defined genres. Poetry bears the trace of anterior origins; it is based on rhythm and thus, on a notion of time, and both of these are, in effect, anterior to language. Throughout *The Bow and the Lyre,* Paz attaches enormous privilege to origins, although later, in *The Monkey Grammarian* he will explain that there is no original word, that all are translations of translations: "Todas son traducciones de traducciones" (*MG* 28). ("All are translations of translations.") This idea is also particularly important for *Signs in Rotation,* where Paz develops the concepts that will link *The Bow and the Lyre* to his later work.

If Paz's book seems to deal with opposites that at the same time are not, with antagonisms that end up as movable, dialectical principles, it is because perhaps the most important figure for an understanding of *The Bow and the Lyre* is Heidegger, and the book is totally informed by Paz's understanding of, and critique, of Heideggerian phenomenology.

Paz reads Heidegger as a philosopher who attempts to dislodge the dialectical oppositions that have ruled modernity. For Heidegger, as Paz says, nonbeing is not a lack, or a deficiency. Man is not an incomplete being, or one that, as Catholicism insists, constantly *lacks;* Heidegger, on the contrary, explains that death is not outside, nor separate from, life itself. Death is life, and is included in life; life contains death, just as being can only be defined by recourse to nonbeing. For Paz, Heidegger's philosophy allows for a critique of Catholic theology as well as of religion in general; he denies the mainstay of Catholicism: the antithesis of life and death, of being and nonbeing. For Paz, by means of redemption Catholic theology kills death and kills life; Heidegger, on the contrary, affirms both life and death. If Being is what emerges out of the experience of Nothingness, Man understands himself as one object among many, principally as the one that gives sense and meaning to the world—literally, the one who names nothingness and thus illuminates the All. Paz, however, as we shall see, takes issue with Heidegger, placing desire at the center of his poetics.

Paz concludes his chapter on "Inspiration" in the second part of *The Bow and the Lyre* by focusing on desire as desire for the other. For Paz, desire endows Heidegger's notion of time with a temporality that wants to fulfill itself in the image of the other. But Paz fully envelops desire within the category of the sacred; as he explains, poetry is a kind of apprehension of anteriority, a kind of machine that aims to inject mythic into historical time. Poetry is, thus, a nonrational (or better still, pararational) mode of apprehension, and it belongs to the realm of a sacred that exists without reference to institutionalized religion. As a category, the sacred is present both in "primitive" as well as in more complex societies, and it is a mode that overcomes the traditional dialectics of subject and object. The realm of the sacred allows us to go beyond our dialectical existence, but only if we understand the sacred not as an object that is "out there" but as a world of its own that is at the same time in the "here and now," and which we can apprehend by fashioning ourselves into others. Literary works, for example, are accounts of the experience of the sacred, as it is distinguished from religion proper. Religion is to culture what poetry is to the poem: modes in which historical categories are seen from the point of view of mythic time. Hence, cultural differences—like those between the United States and Mexico—can originate from an inner substratum of culture ushered in by religion.

Poetry can be seen as an experience that is analogous to religious experience. But it is one that propels the poet into new realms, a kind of trance in which all elements, while remaining in their same place, are nevertheless seen in a new light. Readers and writers participate in a text seen as a performance, where the writer is and is not what he says he is; where the actors of the rite represent their own representations. For Paz, this kind of mystical trance should not necessarily be confused with oblivion but, rather, with a kind of hyperconsciousness that has been generally seen as the province of criticism, or the essay. The experience of the sacred, like the experience of poetry, is one where consciousness represents itself as such. This is why, in *The Bow and the Lyre* Paz posits the experience of otherness as essential for understanding the sacred as paradox, for the apprehension of otherness is nothing less than an apprehension of self. The self apprehended at such instants can only be the desirous self. Being, in this way, is equated to desire.

Because being is defined as the desire-for-being Paz asks an important question and relates it to Heidegger: What kind of gash has opened internally in Man that, starting from a sensation of inauthenticity propels him to seek his true self? Here the sacred becomes the central tenet of Paz's thought. For out of the sacred, the sublime and the poetic are born. Sacred horror, says Paz, arises out of a radical sense of strangeness, which in itself is born out of a radical diminution of the I, arising out of the original situation of being born. When Man is born, he is thrown out and into the world—what Heidegger calls an abrupt feeling of being, or "thrownness," finding oneself "out there." The category of the sacred, for Paz, as an interpretation of that initial condition of existence, is a category toward which we accede by means of anguish and fear—the two parallel forms that open and close our access to the original condition, by allowing Man to understand himself only after understanding his contingence and his finitude. Poetry is born, like religion, out of thrownness and finitude as the concrete human situations of temporality. Poetry, however, does not interpret but rather, reveals our condition. It is in the nature of religion, says Paz, to interpret our condition, but it is part and parcel of the realm of *poetry* to reveal it. Poetry merely reveals; it does not take sides.

Paz says that the experience of the sacred reveals (in the sense of rendering transparent) our original condition; as an experience, however, it is also an interpretation that tends to hide from us the *sense* of that revelation. Because it is fundamentally irrational and terrifying, the sacred always beckons some kind of discourse in order for us to make sense of it. The experience of the sacred is thus born out of our condition, but it masks our condition at the same time; it forces us to come to terms with the sense of the august, while at the same time imposing obedience to that which is above us. Sin and expiation both originate out of our sense of orphanhood, which leads us to create the category (or notion) of sin.

Paz distinguishes, in this regard, between Catholic and Protestant theology. For Catholic theology, the world is not bad in itself; faced with God, all beings are less than perfect, because they are contingent beings, and contingency is expressed as the possibility of redemption or fall. For Catholicism, man is conceived as a possibility, and sin is not to be confused with this being-less but with man's preferring himself instead of God. Facing man up to his being-less vis-à-vis the plenitude of God, religion posits eternal salvation; in doing so, however, it makes of this life an eternal act of expiation and suffering. By abolishing death, religion abolishes life.

For Paz, Being is not something given but rather something that we ourselves create. Being is permanently and constantly created, and our original condition entails such a possibility. The final meaning of all poetic activity is understanding that life and death are not contrary experiences but rather experiences that contain each other. Poetry opens a wedge between the possibilities of death and life, a possibility that does not entail the eternal life of religion nor the eternal death of philosophies. Poetry uncovers this fact; it invites us to realize our condition in plenitude. Criticism is a hermeneutic operation, and thus *explains* that which is *revealed* in poetry. But criticism is closely bound with religion, as they both seek to explain what revelation leaves unexamined. In this way, Paz traces a direct link between poetry as revelation and the need to explain that revelation, the need to engage in hermeneutics.

History and Genre

In his attempt at defining poetry, Paz always seeks to dislodge what is historical from what is essential, as he wishes to articulate that which is beyond time, while understanding that Man can never quite completely separate himself from temporality. History seems to be for Paz the clearest route toward apprehension of the eternal. In this respect, he distinguishes mythic from historical time, and warns that history is but one of our modes of apprehending the temporal. Rhythm is a way of having access to that *other* time, but it is also grounded in history, although it precedes speech itself. Language may be born out of rhythm, but all rhythm already prefigures a language. One can understand Paz's concept by translating this idea into the relationship between an original and its translation. All translations are, in one sense, transpositions of the original; but, as Walter Benjamin and Jacques Derrida have explained, all originals in some sense are asking and beckoning for their being translated.[6] For Paz, language is already prefigured the moment a subject apprehends rhythm. All verbal expressions contain rhythm, but rhythm itself is only manifested, or revealed plainly, in the poem. Not only is the distinction between verse and prose ineffective as a critical tool in a world after Lautréamont, but the sheer traditional and canonical division between verse and prose veils the rhythm of language. For Paz, prose, in fact, goes *against* the grain of language.

Paz's attempts to define the poem beyond traditional and canonical oppositions leads him to interesting historico-social attempts at classification. If the
essential function of poetry is the transmutation of an instant into an archetype,
as he says in one of the latter chapters of *The Bow and the Lyre,* then the novel
may be considered the modern epic. But it is an epic that denies itself as poetic
language (because it is written in prose) and that turns the world into an ambiguous construction where humor and analysis are meant to ironize the novel's own
denial of the poetic search for the absolute. For Paz, the crisis of modern society
has manifested itself as a return to the poem, and he sees this return at work in
the texts of Proust, Joyce, and Kafka in the novel, and in Brecht, Claudel, or
García Lorca in drama. Paz's account of the cultural and historical distinctions
between verse and prose allows him to understand the tradition of modern poetry as one in which poets have rebelled against critical distinctions. When Paz
reads T. S. Eliot's *The Waste-Land,* or the poetry of Ezra Pound, Wallace Stevens,
and e. e. cummings, he focuses on these poets' rebellion against the oppositions
between verse and prose. This rebellion takes place by means of a paradigmatic
sense of opposition that will be once again explored in *Children of the Mire:*
French poets rebel against syllabic measure and go back to accented verse;
English and American poets re-Latinize the language, while Spanish and Spanish
American poets are in the crossfire, between accented versification and syllabic
measure. Throughout *The Bow and the Lyre,* as well as in *Children of the Mire,*
Paz presents Spanish and Spanish American verse as a kind of tenuous center in
the midst of what are, at times, opposing ways of understanding poetry.

Paz's cultural argument, stating that the Hispanic tradition strikes some sort
of balancé between the Anglo-American and the French, is analogous to the
poet's mediation between verse and prose, as well as that of the poem as the meeting ground between the notion of mythic and historical time. Paz is interested,
above all, in what reveals itself as the point of encounter between opposing forces
that are then disarticulated by mediators they construct. This leads to a vision
where poetry reveals all the different layers and strata of discourse, as if the poem
were a kind of tri-dimensional surface that Paz, in "La nueva analogía," compares
to the painter's canvas. In "La nueva analogía," Paz quotes from Richard
Hamilton's works as poetic events; Hamilton is a painter who explores what a
critic called "negative reversal," where signs are superimposed on slim glass
sheets, so that the viewer can pass from what we would call the front to the back.
This image could serve as the emblem for Paz's vision of poetry. In *The Bow and
the Lyre* the poem's surface reveals a continuous layering of effects.

As a poet, Paz continuously shifts the surface of representation; he
metaphorizes the poem's surface—as page, glass, and so forth. He does not

change the meaning of the page so much as its image. For Paz, an image is in the first place a verbal form, a phrase or a group of phrases that the poet says and that, all together, compose a poem. But Paz is not content merely to ascribe to the image its traditional verbal definition. For Paz, *Antigone,* or Segismundo in Calderón's *Life is a Dream,* are also images, attempts to allow the plurality of the real to coalesce at a single instant, in order to allow a metaverbal construction to say what language finds it impossible to say. Paz thus aims to isolate the image as a nonhistorical principle that is nevertheless always related to history.

The concept of revolution is central to Paz's work, as befits a poet of late modernism whose primary sense of lineage is found within the modern tradition—one that has developed fully within the context of a revolutionary age. Revolution is paramount in *The Bow and the Lyre,* not only for "Signs in Rotation" but also for Paz's relating of poetry to society and to life. Like the poetry born under the aegis of the revolutionary age, revolution manifests— brings out into the open—the occluded desires of humanity. Paz distinguishes, both in "Signs in Rotation" as well as in *Children of the Mire,* among revolution, revolt, and rebellion. Modern poetry is a product of the age of revolutions, but it sees itself also as a revolt against a society that condemns it to be an activity of no value. Faced with the growing empire of capital, where everything is measured in terms of worth, poetry proclaims itself as that which is beyond capital and value. This is why, in the modern world, poets are the true rebels: they have no place in society, they are nonpersons; they do not work and do not produce, their poems are worth nothing, and they are not products given for mercantile exchange.

The modern age, however, also defines poetry as a critical activity, as a resistance against the rational anxieties of the revolutionary age. From Coleridge and the English Romantics on, poetry proclaims itself as the rival principle to the critical spirit. Since William Blake, Romantic poets have proclaimed that truth does not come out of reason, but arises out of the poetic principle and Imagination. In this sense, Paz sees the great poems of Blake as crucial works within the history of the imaginative faculty. In German Romanticism, in the tradition of the Atheneum, of Schlegel, of the Group of Jena, in Novalis and in Hölderlin, Paz sees how modern poetry becomes an autonomous enterprise: it is not subservient to the critical spirit and it also does not find any kind of footing in the church. Paz explains that poetry is the most revolutionary of revolutions and the most conservative of revelations, as it attempts to reestablish the original world. This argument leads directly to "Signs in Rotation."

"Signs in Rotation"

"Signs in Rotation" was first published as a separate essay, and added as an appendix to *The Bow and the Lyre* after the second, revised edition of the work in 1967, a period that coincides with Paz's stay in India. One of the most important essays in Latin American intellectual thought, it can also be seen not only as a major summation of Paz's work on poetics until that point, but also as a work that joins many of Paz's concerns from the 1960s and 1970s. "Signs in Rotation" repeats (and reformulates) many of the elements already found in *The Bow and the Lyre.* Not only does it repeat many of the book's statements, however, it also adds a new metaphor to the work itself. Paz once again avoids the traditional definition of poetry: a poem is not a text that uses language in a particular manner (as, perhaps, Paz replies to Roman Jakobson) nor is it a text that affects or carries a particular affective weight toward readers. Rather, Paz says, a poem is a kind of thought *on* language, it is a particular way of thinking *about* language.

"Signs in Rotation" is, on the one hand, a kind of manifesto on poetry (although Paz has always rightly refused the term "manifesto") while it is also a demonstration of what poetry is; this can be seen particularly at those moments when Paz takes into account his own moments of aporia, his own lack of explanation for things that he wants to explain. It is at those moments that the role of the poet overcomes that of the controlled essayist, and Paz enters into a kind of sublime meditation on poetry that *reveals* without explaining (to use terms that he himself uses throughout *The Bow and the Lyre*). For Paz, once again, a poem is a kind of writing of the world, but this writing is not necessarily constrained by the page or the paper itself. Paz, in effect, tells us that there is something else, beyond the page, that uses paper as a vehicle for translating and communicating the world.

At these sublime moments, Paz himself moves from explanation to image. The first example can be seen at the end of the first paragraph of the essay, where Paz places us in a realm of disproportionate urges and absolute desires by means of two striking sentences: "La historia de la poesía moderna es la de una desmesura. Todos sus grandes protagonistas, después de trazar un signo breve y enigmático, se han estrellado contra la roca" (*AL* 253). ("The history of modern poetry is the history of an immoderation. After tracing a brief and enigmatic sign, all its great protagonists have crashed against the rock" [*BL* 233].) He then goes on to explain that all modern poetry tries to reconcile word to act, poetry to life; hence, the immense sense of defeat inherent to modern poetry. Every time poetry creates and posits a question; history responds with a different answer. This model is like a dissonant call and response pattern that Paz sees as inherent to the *problem* of poetry in the modern age. Paz only seeks, he says, a point of intersection, but this point of intersection comes by way of an image. As Paz says: "Busco en la realidad ese punto de inserción de la poesía que es también un punto de intersección, centro fijo y vibrante donde se anulan y renacen sin tregua las contradicciones. Corazón-manantial" (253). ("In reality I seek that point of insertion of poetry that is also a point of intersection, fixed and vibrant center where contradictions are constantly anulled and reborn. Wellspring-heart" [*BL* 234].) Paz still sees the image as something that manifests an act of faith.

Toward this act of faith in the poetic image, Paz is at times ambivalent— this accounts for the fact that the essay at once seeks to bury and at the same time mourn, and celebrate, the modern project; much like a believer renounces his faith but nevertheless cannot see himself totally outside of its parameters. For example, there are moments in the essay where discourse is interrupted in order to give way to an image that functions as an icon. The essay has the appearance of a piece that rescues the fragments of the demolished project of modernity, the flints and pieces of that rock on which modernity has fallen. Perhaps the most striking of these comes at the point when Paz describes his new vision of the poem as a configuration of signs moving upon an animated space. It is at this point that Paz clarifies what that surface is, and denies that the page is merely the metaphor of a nature where the words are written. On the contrary, Paz displaces the term and makes of poetry the true point of contact in a prose poem that recalls Jorge Luis Borges's ecstatic enumeration at a similar point in his short story "El Aleph." Paz proclaims:

> Al imaginar al poema como una configuración de signos sobre un espacio animado no pienso en la página del libro: pienso en las Islas Azores vistas como un archipiélago de llamas una noche de 1938, en las tiendas negras de los nómadas en los valles de Afghanistán, en los hongos de los paracaídas suspendidos sobre una ciudad dormida, en un diminuto crater de hormigas rojas en un patio urbano, en la luna que se multiplica y se anula y desaparece y reaparece sobre el pecho chorreante de la India después del monzón. Constelaciones: ideogramas. Pienso en una música nunca oída, música para los ojos, una música nunca vista. Pienso en *Un coup de dés*. (270)

When I imagine the poem as a configuration of signs on an animated space I do not think of the page in the book: I think of the Azores islands seen as an archipelago of flame one night in 1938, of the black tents of the nomads in the valleys of Afghanistan, of the mushrooms of the parachutes suspended over a sleeping city, of a diminutive crater of red ants on an urban patio, of the moon that is multiplied and extinguished and disappears and reappears over India's dripping breast after the monsoon. Constellations: ideograms. I think of a music never heard, music for the eyes, a music never seen. I think of *Un Coup de dés.* (*BL* 249)

Mallarmé is the most important presence in Paz's work in the 1960s but here Paz introduces Mallarmé within the context of a utopian will that he sees in all modern poetry. A poem is not, says Paz, a configuration of signs over an animated space that is not necessarily the page of the book; the book and the page themselves are an inert space animated by means of writing. The animated space of which Paz talks about is another surface—space itself, where words are truly written. To inscribe words in stone, in nature, or, as Paz says in *The Monkey Grammarian,* to make words into chairs or things, is part of the modernist project. Modern poetry wants to deny the space over which words are mobilized; it seeks, rather, to mobilize space itself. Because of the extraordinary utopian nature implied in this feat, modern poets, says Paz, have condemned themselves to create glorious failures. Because modern poetry desires making the word incarnate, reconciling word with act, subject with object, life with representation, it performs a critical operation on reality. As such, the modern poem works by means of a negative operation: it can only be a text by denying itself as poem, and it erects that very same negation as the fundamental point of origin for its own song. The more absolute the sense of negation is, the more is a space opened. This negation can be seen in its most absolute terms in the work of Mallarmé. "Signs in Rotation" can be seen as part of an intense meditation on the work of poets Paz will read throughout the 1960s: mainly, Mallarmé, Baudelaire, and Rimbaud.

Although in *Children of the Mire* and in *The Bow and the Lyre* Paz devotes considerable space to the work of English and German Romantics like Coleridge, or Novalis, it is obvious that for Paz the central figures in the tradition of modernity are Baudelaire and Mallarmé. Our legacy, he says in "Signs in Rotation" is the space opened by means of Mallarmé's word. Mallarmé's poem will be the central work in the modernist pantheon for Paz, and one can in fact see *Blanco* as an experiment that echoes Mallarmé. For Paz, *Un coup de dés* is one of the most ambitious undertakings of modernity, a poem that already contains its own act of reading, one of the pivotal works where Mallarmé tries to incarnate the word on the page. It is out of Mallarmé's fundamental negativity in relation to being, that the poem annuls the absurd and dissolves chance. It is virtually impossible to overemphasize what Mallarmé means for Paz. Mallarmé's poem, as well as his unrealized project for an all-encompassing Book, represent for Paz something analogous to the complete and total disappearance of the author for the sake of an impersonal principle that is none other than language speaking itself and of itself. In *Children of the Mire,* what fascinates Paz is the supreme impersonality of Mallarmé's gesture. If the universe is resolved in a Book that is but an image of nothingness because of the fact that it is an image of itself, analogy in itself is annuled. The poet becomes sheer transparency, the author sacrifices himself for the sake of discourse. Paz's commentaries are in effect signs disposed obliquely around Mallarmé's poem, as the latter's text is completely irreducible to itself: it means nothing except its own act of becoming, and thus its words are truly endowed with being. Precisely because modern poems are self-critical explorations, texts, in rigor, say nothing; their purpose is to make things transparent.

If Mallarmé stands at one side of the threshold of "Signs in Rotation," Baudelaire is at the other. As a poet that is able to join poetry and poetics, Baudelaire is an important precursor for Paz; he is an influence that Paz repeatedly mentions, particularly in all of the texts written since the 1960s. Baudelaire's account of the poet's discovery of poetics, via Wagner, entails a "going under" that Paz reads in somewhat Heideggerian terms, as the poet discovers the hidden keys to his work. This fall is akin to a moment of crisis that is also an internalizing moment for the artist. What the poet brings out of this crisis is an idea of myth that is also an image of universal truth.

In "Signs in Rotation," Paz considers the relationships between poetry and society, between the poetic and the social being. His first response to this problem follows the terms already dictated by *The Bow and the Lyre:* there is no poetry without society, but the social being of poetry is contradictory. But these terms are also inverted: society can never realize itself without poetry, and there is no society without it. For Paz, no society can survive without claiming something as its version of the absolute. If Mallarmé turns poetry into an object, and Baudelaire into a work of criticism, Rimbaud—the third figure in this pantheon—condemns not only poetry but also modern society, and chooses action over words. In historical terms, Rimbaud ushers in the realm of poetry as negation. For Rimbaud, there is to be no more division between words and society, between gestures and acts, but a silencing, a negation of the word for the sake of action. But Rimbaud's gesture, for Paz, is that of the supreme believer, the one who believed in the force of his negations to such an extraordinary degree, that he could decide never again to write poetry.

Children of the Mire

Children of the Mire belongs, with *The Bow and the Lyre* and "Signs in Rotation" to the series of long works that Paz dedicates to the tradition of poetry, and to its situation in the contemporary world. *Children of the Mire* originates out of Paz's Charles Eliot Norton Lectures at Harvard University during the period from 1971 to 1972, where he allows himself a recounting of the Western tradition. But it is clear that Paz is not only revisiting the history of modern poetry, but also elaborating on a theory of the modern literary tradition. In this sense, the book repeats the journey previously made in *The Bow and the Lyre:* it explores the relationship between poetry and religion, and among poetry, history, and society; it expounds on Paz's notion of analogy; it recounts his ideas on the radical changes in the notion of verse introduced during modernity. All in all, *Children of the Mire* might be seen as a continuation of Paz's attempt to develop a historical poetics out of concepts introduced in *The Bow and the Lyre.* But the book also tries to organize the key concepts of *The Bow and the Lyre* into a system, and then project it onto the history of modern Western poetry. In this sense, *Children of the Mire* is profoundly ambitious; it seeks to impose a poetic structure onto a linear history and a historical narrative. This search for a "poetic" narrative of modern poetry, is what gives the book its tension and accounts for its difficulty amid a misleading transparency. One is never quite sure whether to read the book as a historical survey of Western tradition, as its poetics, or as both.

The reader who has followed Paz's development will immediately notice how Paz covers familiar territory in this book. Hence, the feeling that *Children of the Mire* is a summation, a rewriting of Paz's previous essays. The general formulations of poetry's relationship to religion are similar to those expressed in *The Bow and the Lyre.* Paz's interplay between analogy and irony appears not only in "Signs in Rotation" but also in *El signo y el garabato* (1973), which contains essays written in the late 1960s and early 1970s. What is different in *Children of the Mire* is already apparent not only from "Signs in Rotation" but also from Paz's essays on Baudelaire, included in *El signo y el garabato:* his particular insistence on the anomaly or strangeness of modernity—its contradictions, its particular disruptions—within the fabric of purely Western time. This, along with Paz's analogy between social change and the tradition of Western verse, his discursive interplay in the history of poetry, between European and Spanish American verse, along with his subtle swerve from the French, to English Romantic tradition, give *Children of the Mire* its revisionary thrust.

Children of the Mire succinctly formulates what the modern means for Paz. From the onset, he delves on the contradiction that the words "modernity" and "tradition" entail; the modern began and always saw itself opposed to the conti-nuities of tradition. The modern creates its own vision of the present, as well as its own, polemical filiation with the past; it rescues the past—generally, a past that is seen as a distant, and not an immediate past—in order to bring it to the here and now, to the present. This present becomes an ever-expanding center, dissolving within itself the contradictory nature of time, of past, present, and future. All eras become coterminous within the present, while modernity re-reads the possible multiplicity of the past in unitary terms (as one tradition). In a sense, this is what makes *Children of the Mire* fundamentally modern; it enter-tains the fiction of one narrative that can be deployed in order to re-read the past, and while it does take into account the past's disputations, it sees history as a subject of knowledge that can be read in one long, continuous sweep.

The first two sections of *Children of the Mire* isolate the concept of moder-nity in order to define it in relation to its profoundly innovative, but also anom-alous background. It is a quintessentially Western tradition, born out of Western notions of time, inherited from the predominantly Judeo-Christian context. Paz will insist on this religious foundation for the modern notions of time in order to explore the difficult relationships between modern poetry and religion in his third chapter, titled "Children of the Mire." Like M. H. Abrams in *Natural Supernaturalism,* Paz sees in modern poetry the attempt to establish a religious notion of life outside of religious dogma. The first Romantics, which for Paz are truly the first critical modernists, saw poetry as a kind of heretical religious rival, aiming to create what Blake called a "natural religion." At the same time, modernity has to be seen in the context of the Reformation. Paz had already explored these ideas in relation to history in *The Labyrinth of Solitude,* when he argued for the polemical reception of the modernizing project in Mexico, but here he expounds on the Romantic ideal of poetry as a critique of rationalism that arises from the spirit of the Protestant Reformation by establishing that the literary borders of Romanticism coincide with the religious borders of Protestantism.

This grounding of Romanticism in non-Latin languages is significant. Once again, Paz joins language, religion, and history to see how the Romantic vision was sustained principally by a notion of analogy and correspondence that leaves its traces in Romantic prosody. By resurrecting the traditional meters and forms of English and German poetry, the Romantics conceived of the world as a poem—with its prosody as the mode in which both the word and the world coexist. By unearthing the traditional forms in terms of accentual versification, the Romantics, according to Paz, gave us an analogic vision of the world. If in Germany and in England analogy is resurrected by the return to traditional modes of poetic discourse, in the Romance languages analogy's appearance coincides with the rebellion against syllabic measure for the sake of a notion of discursivity that values rhythm, above all. But analogy has a deeper purpose other than merely representing one thing as another: analogical poetics conceives of the world as a communicating system and of the poet as a translator.

This idea is the crux of Paz's account of the narrative of modernity, one that more properly begins in chapter 5 of *The Children of the Mire*. The authors that Paz will examine from here on will be seen as manifestations of language. Language gives the narrative its raison d'être: it substitutes for God, Reason, or Spirit. Hence, Paz's distance from modernity's overvaluation of the poetic, creative "I" of the poet. Where the Romantic sees the poet within the idea of the cult of personality, Paz's tradition, originating from the idea of the disappearance of the author inaugurated by Mallarmé, will examine the work of these poets as projects, as attempts to balance out the double helix presented by analogy and irony on the one hand, and translation and metaphor on the other. Thus, when the reader encounters the history or the narrative of modern poetry proper, starting from chapter 5, that narrative has already begun, within the conceptual framework that Paz has traced in his book.

Paz's account of the modern tradition can be followed chronologically from here on—a chronology that was lacking in *The Bow and the Lyre*. The principal states of this chronology had also appeared scattered in many of Paz's essays: his reading of the fundamentally derivative quality of Spanish Romanticism, his underscoring of Spanish American *modernismo* as the beginning of our true Romantic, critical tradition; his account of the avant-garde, or the *vanguardia* as the heightening of a series of ruptures that were already present within the Romantic tradition. Paz seeks this tradition not only for what it rebels against but also in terms of what it attempts to rescue from the past; for Paz the rebellions of modernity have to be seen relative to the uncovering of a distant past or of a simultaneous present as an other on which the rebellion projects itself.

But *Children of the Mire,* at the same time, is a critique of the modern tradition. Hence, it is a book that inhabits a kind of impasse. After more than a century of ruptures, Paz concludes that the modern has become a ritual that repeats its own negation of the past in order to constitute itself as the here and now. Repeated rituals become simulacra that constantly refer back to more authentic ruptures that took place with uncommon violence at the beginning of the twentieth century. Paz explains that aside from its sheer repetition over time, the idea of rupture has become meaningless, because our notion of time has changed. Originating out of the desire for eternal change, the modern always sought to fulfill itself in the future. But the future has at this point no meaning for contemporary civilization. Rather, we have lost the image of the future that seemed to guide the continuous ruptures of the past.

It is in relation to that future that the modern has underscored revolutionary action; at the same time, this focus reveals modernity's desire to construct itself as part of a religious impulse. Because modernity overvalues the principle of change, Paz explains, its act of foundation has to entail a principle beyond time—an eternity seen under the guise of the here and now. Modernity's desire for what Paz, from the point of view of 1971, reads as a virtually impossible utopia, also accounts for its sense of defeat.

Because the narrative of modernity that Paz deploys is fundamentally based on a poetics of language, its teleological force, its point of closure, is harder to trace. Because it is grounded on language, the tradition of modernity can only end by *not* changing into something else; disarticulating in that manner, the principle that has propelled it throughout its history. If modernity is based on revolution and rebellion, on the desire to institute utopia within the concrete time and place of history, the contradictions that give modernity its particular raison d'être are seen not to be surmounted (that is precisely what characterizes or constitutes modernity) but rather dissolved, much in the same manner that Paz, in *Ladera este* (East Slope) and *Blanco,* argued for a dissolution of dialectical contraries. By the same token, this dissolution has to imply a redefinition of what the present means. Because Paz's narrative is based on a particular sense of identity between language and history under the principle of analogy, the narrative of modernity has to end with a redefinition of both language and history as a space of a present convergence. This definition of the present is different from that of the Romantics (one that has become a "vain ritual" as Paz explains) as it is not founded upon the principle of rupture (hence Paz's historical survey is not the history of negations). This lack of opposition, which makes Paz's present into an ample web that contains all time, is what allows Paz to postulate a present that is radically different from that of the Romantics.

Paz's notion of present, then, does not imply a return. Hence, his discoursing, in the first chapters of *Children of the Mire,* on the notion of cyclical time. Paz's time is not cyclical but, in the manner of Yeats, it assumes the form of a spiral. The re-motivation of the present is similar to, but different from, the one found at the origin of the idea of the modern. It is similar in that it seeks to ground itself on a time seen as the composite totality of all time; it is different insofar as it exists precisely after the collapse of modernity. The vain rituals of the avant-garde in their attempt to overcome the distance between the desire and the act have degenerated into uniform and failed attempts. Once again, Paz grounds the multiplicity of all events within a common identity. This identity, this structure, is given to works of art by means of language, what provides for the "invisible skeleton" of all works of art. The twilight of the avant-garde, "el ocaso de la vanguardia," is thus accompanied by the revelation of structure as essence: "La estructura es ahistórica; el texto es historia, está fechado. De la estructura al texto y del texto a la lectura: dialéctica del cambio y de la identidad" (226). ("The structure is ahistorical; the text is history, it bears a date. From the structure to the text and from the text to the reading: the dialectic of change and of identity" [*CM* 163].) This is what accounts for contemporary poetry's desire not to begin again but rather, to re-inhabit the notion of the present. It seeks "la intersección de los tiempos, el punto de convergencia" (227) ("the intersection of times, the point of convergence" [*CM* 164]). The search is not to discover the end of contingency by inaugurating a present that would end time, but rather to understand the mode of relationship between contingency and timelessness within the sphere of the present.

Paz's notion of the present time as one that will seek not to repeat the rituals of the past ends in a paradox. This paradox, this present that is fundamentally similar to, but different from, its past articulations, is what accounts for the tensions within *Children of the Mire*. But the book itself is an illustration of what it says: it repeats what Paz has said in previous books but it also varies the mode of articulation. Paz does not deny his previous work; he repeats it and at the same time varies it. Thus, his readings of himself are virtually re-readings: each reading is identical but it is also unique. It displaces the sense of the present by formulating it as eternally changing, and at the same time as eternally immutable.

CHAPTER 5

A Poetics of East and West

The first part of this chapter traces the context for Paz's explorations of the Orient, reading poems that, in his edition of *Poemas* (1979) he chronologically places before his major collection influenced by Asia, *East Slope* (1969); this latter book will be read along with *Toward the Beginning* in the second part of this chapter. The advantage of this careful and systematic exploration lies in centering Paz's most important period—the 1960s— by positing *Blanco,* in chapter 6, as its central text. *Blanco* is the axis on which much of Paz's work of this period revolves: it is a poem surrounded by words and contexts, by an archive. As such, this chapter explicitly leads to the next, where *Blanco* appears as the central icon that begins a new period in Paz's work.

Days and Occasions (1958–1961)

Days and Occasions is framed by two long poems at the beginning and the end of the collection: "Into the Matter," and "Identical Time." These are two poems on cities, and they are almost formless statements, meandering texts whose idea of form and breadth is more consistent with Paz's later explorations of space. "Into the Matter" in particular, is more related to "Wind from all compass points" or to "Return" than to Paz's previous poems. As in "Wind From All Compass Points," in "Vuelta," and "Pasado en claro," the poet of "Into the Matter" perceives sound, first of all, while he places himself at the center of the movable cacophony of the modern city. As in "El balcón" or "Nocturno de San Ildefonso" the absence of vision as the point of departure for the poem is related to its taking place at night, so that sound leads to Paz's vision of the lighted neon signs, as if these were marks upon a corporeal body that is both the city's as well as night's. The poet's "entrance upon matter," then, can only take place because of the flexibility afforded by the inner vision of night, uncorrupted by the mirages of daylight, capable of giving objects a certain kind of formlessness. Both the city and the night are seen as one shape of unclear contours: night has a body and so does the city. The poet's entrance into matter, then, allows all that is "seen" to be apprehended as corporeal shape, rendering the dichotomy of body and soul into a false distinction. The poet places himself in the position of

114

translator; he will give his testimony and repeat what body and soul say, only by "entering" into a space previously corporealized, rendered into "matter."

"Into the Matter" does not merely show the corporeality of the city and of the night, but does so by postulating words themselves as matter. Here, Paz sees that things are not in their proper place, but does not feel that he needs to rectify this. Rather, Paz seems to accept that they have no place at all, that they are ultimately beyond reach. Words (or, rather, "names" as he more adequately sees them in this poem) are also somehow debased, they are nobody's masks. To attempt an entrance into these masks in order to uncover an essence that will ultimately not be there, is like going back to a door that has already been condemned. The poet's task is, rather, religious in essence; like Mallarmé, he seeks to give "true meaning of the words of the tribe." But in this case, the "true meaning" consists less in putting things in their place, than in liberating them, allowing them the freedom given within their own sense of movement. In order to do this, the poet must recede, must question his own materiality for the sake of positing the concrete materiality of objects.

Paz's meditation upon words and things occurs within the context of a broader meditation upon the city, one that will be much more prevalent in "Return," where he reencounters his own history as well as his national and cultural context within Mexico. But the poet of "Into the Matter" already prefigures the one who will reappear in Paz's longer poems after *Blanco:* he is the solitary wanderer, an almost Wordsworthian figure lost within the city. At times, the poet seeks a return to poetry as prophecy; at other times, he is an observer who seeks a dispassionate understanding of reality. In all of these incarnations, Paz presents himself as the seeker for that other reality that he had already explored in *The Bow and the Lyre.*

"Identical Time," the poem that closes off *Days and Occasions,* returns to its point of departure by deploying Paz's version of the sublime, which entails apprehending the hidden immobility of Time within its illusory mutabilities. What starts this meditation is an old man on a bench, who speaks by himself, a man who has forgotten his identity (his past), and is conscious of the foreclosing of his future, speaking to himself in order to grasp his own reality as an other. The meaning of "transparency" here, a word that is important for Paz and that has slight variations in meaning over time, seems akin to that of identity; the moment of immobility is also the one where the poet understands the "other," essential time that is within time, while grasping that he has become aware of it by a process that entails "abstracting" the self from oneself. In this process of abstraction, eternity is seen in an instant, as in Romantic poets like Blake, or as in Baudelaire, the great nineteenth-century poet of the city. It is the confusion of the city in the twentieth century that ushers in its opposite feeling: the idea that underneath that illusion of movement lies something else, much more hidden and eternal.

Eternity is, then, seen within the space of a parenthesis that ruptures the very fabric of a constantly mutable time. This is the hidden theme of *Days and Occasions* as a whole, and many of its poems speak of a "parenthetical" moment. In "Aquí" (Here) the sound of each of the poet's steps on the street is projected onto another street where these same steps are heard. Sounds and their echoes frame the poem's central statement: the fact that otherness dissipates the concrete present to a state of unreality, where "sólo es real la niebla" (318). ("Only the mist is real" [*CP* 49].) In "Reversible" the relationship between the poet and space is seen by the continuous shifting of the poet's presence, who can only locate himself at the intersection of both spaces—outside and inside—with no distinction between both. In "Certeza" (Certainty) as in "Here" the dialectics is given as a question on the reality of the poet's lamp and his hand as it writes.

Days and Occasions refers to the poet's being able to apprehend his existence as a fluid becoming, among things whose reality only partially seems to condemn him to insist on his own sense of permanence as matter. The book progressively unveils, then, the relationship between reality and the poet, until the relationship itself acquires its own form within space and time. This slow process of becoming is analogous to the text's abandoning of punctuation for the sake of its own, progressive sense of form. This abandonment can be seen within the poems themselves; Paz at times stops the flow of discourse in order to play on words, as in "Into the Matter":

> Un reloj da la hora
>   ya es hora
> no es hora
>   ahora es ahora
> ya es hora de acabar con las horas
> ahora no es hora
>   es hora y no ahora
> la hora se come al ahora
>
> A clock strikes the time
>   now it's time
> it's not time now
>   now it's now
> now it's time to get rid of time

now it's not time
　　it's time and not now
time eats the now

(CP 41–43)

It is important to distinguish here between this kind of wordplay and that which Paz will use in other poems, as in, for example, "Petrificada petrificante" (The Petrifying Petrified). In the latter, Paz constructs neologisms in order to give the illusion of a tightly woven, almost "petrified" language. The other side of linguistic play in Paz is precisely the one seen in "Into the Matter" where the play on "time" (hora) and "it's time now" (ahora) gives the illusion of a free-flowing association of ideas based on the concrete, linguistic addition of the letter "a" —one that becomes, in one of its double meanings, a preposition, as in "a-hora" (literally, "toward the hour"). The effect underscores that there is a common identity for words and sounds, as can be seen in "La palabra escrita" (The Written Word) and "La palabra dicha" (The Spoken Word), where Paz clarifies that written words are like frozen stalactites upon the page, like frozen echoes, with the ability to petrify a language that can only be awakened by means of sound.

This juxtaposition—between the self of the poet and things, between the poet and the city, between the written and the spoken word, is echoed in "José Juan Tablada" and "Luis Cernuda," poems on poets whose work was concerned with the plays on doubles and the dialectical juxtaposition of different elements. Tablada, as Paz will later explain in one of the notes to *Blanco,* was one of the first poets to combine two different realities in a single poem: his "Nocturno alterno," a poem on which Paz also comments in 1945, when he writes his "Estela de José Juan Tablada" (collected in *Las peras del olmo,* 1971). In "Estela," Paz repeats Tablada's procedure by constructing a poem out of two distinct strands, shown by the use of italics. Tablada is also important for Paz in that he was one of the first Mexican poets to experiment with Eastern forms like the haiku, or with ideogrammatic poetry, as in his *Li-Po* (1920), revealing an experimental will that for Paz had been lacking in Mexican poetry.

Besides Tablada, the importance of Luis Cernuda to Paz's work cannot be sufficiently stressed, particularly as Cernuda forms one of the four quadrants of Paz's *Cuadrivio* (1965). As we mentioned in an earlier chapter, Cernuda's example of collecting his whole work as one book titled *La realidad y el deseo* was important for Paz's own *Libertad bajo palabra;* Cernuda's book grew out of the events of the poet's life and out of the realization that the poet was a being apart from others, who explored himself and negated, according to Paz, "the abject world that surrounds him" (*CA* 15). This denial of the world for Paz has its positive and its negative side; it makes poetry at times seem like a rhetorical monologue, but at other times it allows us to read a poet who understands and knows himself as no other. That Cernuda saw the interplay between reality and desire as the ruling dialectics for his poetry as well as for his life was important for Paz.

The Romantic interplay between the real and the ideal, between reality and the poet's desire is also explored in what perhaps is Paz's most "urban" poem at this time, "Auguries," a poem that, along with "Peatón" (Pedestrian) will show more explicitly Paz's continuing exploration on the disjunctions presented by the modern city. In "Auguries" the modern era is presented as a kind of debasement of some anterior time. This idea anticipates Paz's explorations on the Orient and the relationship between East and West.

Salamander

According to Andrés Sanchez Robayna, *Salamander* is a pivotal book in Octavio Paz's poetic journey: it shows a marked will to change the structure and form of the verse for the sake of a new thematics, where the movement of reality is reproduced on the page.[1] For Ramón Xirau, *Salamander* is a transitional book, one that will anticipate Paz's later work in *Blanco*.[2] *Salamander* is dated in Paz's 1979 *Poemas* as written between 1958 and 1961, roughly written at about the same time as *Days and Occasions*. It is a collection of twenty-five poems that begins with an account of an evening walk, titled "Sleepless Night" and ends with "Salamander," a poem that talks about the elusive nature of reality and that names the collection as a whole. As is the case with *Days and Occasions,* one can see in retrospect that *Salamander* prepares the reader for Paz's later work in the Orient. In this sense, *Salamander* is a book of desire and of change, or of desire *for* change. "Sleepless Night" is dedicated to André Breton and Benjamin Péret, two poets whose work was important for Paz during his years in Paris. In "Sleepless Night" the poet sees two lovers while he walks at night through the city with his two friends. One of the lovers has each letter of the word "love" written on the fingers of a hand. The poet is fascinated with this gesture because it shows love itself inscribed on the body—perhaps the predominant image for the beginning of the book, as Paz draws the very hand that he sees in the poem itself. By doing so, he articulates the pictorial representation of the body within the very text.

Many of the poems in *Salamander* aim precisely toward this communion, one that is based upon the body's relationship with all that surrounds it. The poems themselves are analogies to a body seen, not as a self-contained entity but as a receptive, communicating vessel for reality. They abandon all visible punctuation, and allow different elements to appear within a continuous flow. In "Un día de tantos" (One Day among Many), for example, a being is lost within a body, just as automobiles in the city seem to long for country pastures. The apparent immobility of things is not seen in a dialectical relationship to change; rather, change is also part of a relationship of identity of objects with themselves: "El cielo gira y cambia y es idéntico" (357) ("The sky turns and changes and is the same" [CP 107]), says Paz; typewriters "escriben sin descanso la misma ardiente sílaba" (357) ("tirelessly typing the same burning syllable" [CP 109]).

Salamander is written with, and toward, the body, perceived as a sign whose very definition is part of the theme of a culture exhausted by different and irreconcilable ideological disputes. This act of writing on the body is not seen as abstract rhetoric. At times, Paz renders the violence implicit in this act. In "Garabato" (Scrawl), the poet's encounter with the body is mediated by a writing implement that only allows representations of the body and of its corporeality. In his essay on Salvador Elizondo, titled "El signo y el garabato" from the collection of the same name, Paz explains that a "garabato" is a sign that is not only undeciphered but also undecipherable and, therefore, insignificant. The translation of this sign, which, like death, is the mark of our very own mortality, can never be another literal sign, but rather a metaphor. In "Scrawl," writing is the metaphor for an act that is committed on the body—metaphor allows the translation between the act of writing and an implicit violence done to the body. But they are metaphors of each other. If the metaphor tames the explicit violence of the text, for Paz violence is itself a metaphor for a mode of existence. Although the image is much more elaborate in his essay on Elizondo, we can already see how Paz's later elaborations already find their point of departure in Salamander.

Paz's moments of agony are related to the representational character of the word, to its status vis-à-vis reality itself. Even if at other points in his work Paz argues for a nondialectical mode of thinking (particularly in Blanco, and in the essays and poems written in Asia, as we shall see) there are moments where Paz's imminent desire for language to be leads to the acts of violence represented in "Scrawl," acts of violence that were already present in "Words," from Calamities and Miracles. The poet will seek to draw the name of a body onto a door, until the very door and the wall upon which he is inscribing this name will bleed, will scream, and will finally breathe as living things do. The act of writing can only be rendered as a material act contingent upon the poet's violence upon the surface of writing—until this surface becomes a body, leaving the representational character of the word intact.

It is interesting to compare the explicit violence of "Scrawl" with another version of Paz's dialectical struggle with writing: that of writing as a communion, which appears in "A través" (Across), a poem written as a journey divided into seven stages, where the poet enters into a woman's body, seen as a body without borders. In "A través," the internal landscape barely occludes the journey's center as one in which blood continually reappears. Anticipating both the title of one of Paz's pivotal essays on the Orient and on tantrism ("El pensamiento en blanco") as well as his later *Blanco,* the journey reflected in "A través" can only take place beyond discourse, in a series of instances that paradoxically reflect totality and boundlessness by means of their fragmented expression on the page. It may not be so far-fetched to see the poem itself as a blood mask (máscara de sangre) that can only render its own sublime communion by means of fragments.

If "A través" seeks to explore an instant in time by giving us fragmented epiphanies that lead to timelessness, *Salamander* presents a notion of circular movement as a response to the anxieties of temporality. In "Movimiento" (Motion) or in "Vaivén" (Sway), in "Duración" (Duration), "Rotación" (Rotation), and in "Ida y vuelta" (Coming and Going), Paz aims to undo a linear notion of existence by means of circular time. This undoing can be seen in "Motion," where Paz posits thirteen lines, or possibilities, on the object, along with an equal number of possibilities on the subject, in order to create, between them both, the sensation of something that perpetually moves as if an arc. The movement seeks to undo temporality by insisting on relationships, or analogies, where the second part of the proposition provides the ground for the first, in a perfectly reversible operation. (that is, "yo soy el camino de sangre / Si tú eres la yegua de ámbar" ("I am the road of blood / If you are the amber mare" [*CP* 113]). This notion of a time that can go foward or backward, and ultimately collapses unto itself is also present in "Coming and Going," where the poet's life is seen as a search for death. From the point of view of death as the ultimate "scrawl," notions of coming and going have no meaning in and of themselves.

The most important element in "Salamander," the central poem of this collection, is fire—increasingly for Paz a symbol of eternal change and of purification. John Fein has perceptively remarked that in "Salamander" the choice of the animal world as its point of departure is unusual for Paz, and that the constant repetition of the animal's name turns the poem into an "extended anaphora."[3] Although the poem, as others from this period, is written with Paz's notion of a space that provides for a particular mode of punctuation, the reader can notice how it is divided into different sections, where the salamander itself is metaphorized. Fire and metaphor are directly pertinent for the vision of the salamander, as well as for the salamander's changing of skin according to the different contexts in which it finds itself. In this way, Paz centers his notion of change as well as of metaphor by using the salamander as symbol. But Paz also articulates a notion of mimesis in this poem, transported precisely upon the fabric of discourse, by creating an analogy based on both the poet's and the salamander's movement. The first section apostrophizes the salamander by imitating the rapid swish of the salamander upon a surface, where one referential strata of the discourse is piled upon the next. As Paz immediately explains, the salamander was the ancient symbol or image for fire, but also the antidote to fire; thus he makes it unreachable, in a material and a linguistic sense. In its opening stanzas the text attempts to grasp the salamander (an attempt that should end in a sacrificial act of torture) but at the same time wants to give an account of its freedom and mobility. The poem is thus a circular writing around the salamander, created as if a gyrating orbit around an elusive object. The idea of a poem that moves as a spiral, around an elusive center, is furthered by the repeated comparisons of the salamander to an opaque sun, as a kind of heliotrope and moon constantly gyrating around themselves. Paz attempts, finally, to grasp the salamander by means of definitions, naming words that magically conjure the object although, as the concluding lines of the poem suggest, the poet understands that only wordplays and games that return language to its origins in mimetic play are able to capture, even fleetingly, this elusive center. The poem ends with "Salamadre Aguamadre" ("Salamander Salamater" [*CP*149]) as if the salamander could only be grasped by exhausting the referential possibilities of language.

Another interpretation is also certainly in order here, if we see the salamander as a metaphor of the subject, of Paz himself, as well as an analogy for his poetics. If the object seen, as Paz has explained, is directly related to the subject that is at the same time contemplating, Paz's association with the salamander points to a notion of his own self as one that is ultimately ungraspable. It is important to see this, in retrospect, as one of the possible avenues that lead to Paz's work in the Orient. For it is in the realm of otherness that Paz will rediscover the foundations of his own sense of self, as one that accepts the principle of eternal change.

"Solo for two voices"

In the thematic and chronological arrangement of Paz's *Poemas* of 1979, "Solo for two voices" is the poem that immediately precedes *East Slope* and the major segment of Paz's work in the East. The poem is introduced by a sentence from Corominas's *Dictionary* that warns, "En ninguna lengua occidental son tantas las palabras fantasmas" ("In no other occidental language are there so many ghost words" [*CP* 151])—although Paz does not clarify what ghost words he is referring to. Foreshadowing a kind of explicatory mode that will be seen above all in *East Slope,* the poem is accompanied by an extensive note in which Paz recurrs to philology, this time in order to explain the etymological meaning of the word mundo (world). Paz's etymologies are born out of desire, out of an attempt to rescue some kind of essential meaning from the past to the present. Parenthetically, one must say that Paz's notes increasingly become not only venues that explain obscure cultural references found in poems themselves, but also modes that continue the poetical exploration of the text. The note that accompanies "Solo for two voices" explains that in the modern world an individual must go against the grain, must reverse the perpetual forward movement of clocks. But this journey backward is done not to argue for a return to plenitude, as is the case with myth, but in order to find, or rescue, once again, the moment of convergence that Paz had named, in *The Bow and the Lyre,* as the moment where poetry is born.

This convergence is the original and originary poetic moment. Nevertheless, it is directly in opposition to the condition of modern man in the world, for the poet's words belie his unreal attempt at grasping the paradoxes of time and space. This is why in "Solo for two voices" the poet cannot innocently exclaim what Paz seeks to explain at the beginning of his notes: "En el mundo moderno: ¿qué quiere decir *hoy es solsticio de invierno en el mundo?*" (678). (In the modern world, what does it mean to say *today is the winter's solstice in the world?*)[4] The poet's statement is affirmed, and denied, at the same time, by the reality of space, which has been foreshortened and reduced in the modern world by technology. All major statements, then, become partial and tentative—undoing, to a certain extent, the reality of a line like T. S. Eliot's "April is the cruelest month." Poetry in the modern age, says Paz, can only give an account of this fissure.

"Solo for two voices" opens by problematizing the same phrase that Paz has sought to explain in his notes, although the question here is directed toward the very act of saying, toward the poetic utterance. The vision of the winter solstice leads to Paz's evoking the image of its opposite, of a world in which Ceres leads the procession of the Earth's fruits. These fruits are compared to words that the poet reads in the dictionary, in an alternate movement (or voice), against the grain of time. This backward movement entails "Desandar el camino / volver a la primera letra / en dirección inversa / al sol" (389) ("Retracing the road, / going back to the first letter / in a direction contrary / to that of the sun" [*CP* 159]). If we read the poem according to Paz's notes, we are meant to understand that the poet's backward reading is at all times counterposed to the very structure of the poem, one that like "Hymn Among the Ruins" seeks to juxtapose two distinct moments represented on the page by means of italics. In "Solo for two voices" however, the opposition is not one between two moments in time, but between the regressive aims present in one section, to a present time given by sections in italics. The two voices of the poem are not necessarily separate; the juxtaposition is not so abrupt as that of "Hymn among the Ruins." At times, the two different strands of the poem seem to create two different works; at other times, they function as interlocking calls and responses.

Solo for two voices seeks (as do the different sections of *Blanco*) to understand a principle of complementarity, not by means of opposition, but by blending elements. If we examine this poem in relation to Paz's previous poetry, we will notice how much he has ameliorated the sense of irreconcilable oppositions. The two voices in this poem can actually be divided into four, as in the time-space quadrants, or they can blend themselves into one. Identity, in this way, is permanently subdividing itself and thus understanding the roots of its own principles of unity. Paz aims toward a generalized understanding of the world by an awareness of the paradoxes of time and space. These paradoxes will be further explored in *East Slope,* especially in those poems where Paz allows for East and West to be intermittent reflections of each other.

East Slope (1969)

Paz's first encounter with Asia occurs in 1951, one year after he had published the first edition of *The Labyrinth of Solitude,* his thorough exploration of Mexican myth, history, and politics. This juxtaposition is of immense importance to understand the gaze that Paz brings into India upon his first encounter, a gaze that will be repeated in his longer sojourn in India during the 1960s.

As Paz recounted the story in interviews, he had been living in Paris, in the relative obscurity of a job in the Mexican embassy where he had started to work in December 1945, when a cable ordered his transfer to a recently opened Mexican embassy in India, a country that had acquired its independence as recently as 1947. In 1951 Paz went to Cairo, and from Port Said took a Polish ship to Bombay, a city that immediately fascinated him, as Paz recounts in *Vislumbres de la India* (1995). A week later, on a train to Delhi, Paz was astonished at the similarities between the Indian and the Mexican landscape, and remembers a trip made with his mother from Mexico to San Antonio toward the end of the Mexican Revolution. If we add to this the fact that Paz's encounter with the Indian reality is also mediated by English travelers (he mentions he carries in his first trip *Murray's Handbook of India, Pakistan, Burma, and Ceylon* along with books given to the poet as gifts from his friends in Paris (notably, Henri Michaux), we begin to understand the different cultural strata that Paz brings to Asia. Furthering the comparison to Mexico, the India that Paz sees is a recently independent country, one that had seen its share of bloody massacres between Hindus and Muslims in 1947. Part of this initial encounter is reflected in "Mutra" of *La estación violenta.* But Paz's longer sojourn in India dates from 1962 and lasts for six years.

The years in the Orient were some of the more important in Paz's life. As he expressed it in *Vislumbres de la India,* India meant a kind of "rebirth," important also for the fact that in India Paz met Marie Jose Tramini, his wife, and with her he traveled around Asia: not only most of India but also Thailand, Cambodia, Vietnam, Nepal, Afghanistan, and Pakistan. In the course of these years, he met some of the subcontinent's most important political and cultural figures. Not wanting to write a full-length memoir or biography of this period, Paz explained that what he felt and saw in India is fundamentally contained in *East Slope* and in *The Monkey Grammarian.* For Paz, a book of poems is like a diary, where the author seeks to represent certain exceptional moments. In other words, *East Slope* contains the essence of those possible memoirs, and each of the sites named in the book, as well as the moments contained in it, are for Paz talismans for different sites and moments. As we shall see, this juncture of poetry with the idea of place, with given geographical sites, is at the root of the analogies that Paz makes between the writing surface and the body. The page in this work is the double of nature: a blank space on which the sign is written in a scrawl that is at times incomprehensible for the poet himself.

Context

In his first note to *East Slope,* probably Paz's most profusely annotated book, the poet explains that with the exception of "Cuento de dos jardines" ("A Tale of Two Gardens"), composed in a maritime journey between Bombay and Palmas, most of the poems of *East Slope, Toward the Beginning,* and *Blanco* were written in India, Afghanistan, and Ceylon. This insistence on place and locale allows readers to understand that *East Slope* is fundamentally a book about space, both external (India, Asia) as well as internal (the poet's reactions to an unfamiliar locale). To this we must also add Paz's particular principle of book composition: *East Slope* is neither an itinerary nor a travelogue, its sites and locales probably not directly named in the order of lived experience. To this date, the only diary of the poet in India that we have is structured in the mode of a book of poems—which is to say, the diary has been arranged according to aesthetic concerns, and not necessarily biographical narration. Many of *East*

Slope's poems were published in different journals, and with the recent addition of the essays from *Vislumbres de la India* (1995), we may clarify some aspects of the relationship between geography and biography, between the poet's lived experience and the organization of the book of poems itself.

In terms of the book's composition, Manuel Durán has explained that *East Slope* is written in the mode of melody and counterpoint—the melody contained principally in the long poems, with the shorter, almost haiku-like compositions serving as their counterpoint.[5] Long and short poems for Durán offer both a vision of the immense complexity of India as well as of the small details within its fabric—the sacred and solemn Indian subcontinent in the longer poems, and the ironic, instantaneous gaze in the shorter ones. It is not that this opposition between long and short poems is not present in other books by Paz; indeed, as we have seen, the books that lead directly to *East Slope* are framed by long poems both at the beginning and at the end. What is different about *East Slope* is precisely what makes the book unique in terms of Paz's other books; here the effect is one of a totalizing gaze on one geographical space—a gaze that, projected onto a different cultural sphere, is able to apprehend both the infinitesimally small and the enormously immense. This unity of purpose in apprehending a given "object" was not present in Paz's previous books to the extent that it is in *East Slope*. That Paz does not hesitate to use specific Indian terms, as well as directly refer to particular sites, is meant to show that, as Manuel Durán himself states, Paz has lived India in an authentic manner, that his gaze at all times is premised on the notion of authenticity. Unlike Neruda, who as a young man also lived in Asia, and whose sojourn forms the central part of his *Residencia en la tierra* (1935), Paz arrives in India as a well-known poet and essayist. The books and poems that immediately precede the Indian period, like *Sunstone,* show a marked desire for a sense of closure that is also a new beginning—or, as in "Hymn Among the Ruins" the will to join different locales and places within a single poetic discourse. In other words, Paz arrives in India in order to explore and understand the continent from rational, philosophical, political, and historical angles, and not merely to write an internal account of the poet in his relating to a different reality.

Paz's decision to "understand" India as well as himself, allows *East Slope* to be a book of poems that is implicitly and explicitly marked by essayistic discourse. The relationship between *East Slope* and Paz's essays during the 1960s has prompted critics to read the book in relation to Paz's vision of East and West, as this is found in *Conjunctions and Disjunctions* (1969) and in *El signo y el garabato* (1973). To summarize at this point Paz's immensely complex arguments (some of which will be explored later on in this chapter and the next), I would say, initially, that they are rooted on a vision of comparative cultural anthropology. If in poetry, Paz seeks not origins but a point of convergence, in *East Slope* he is also looking for a site from which East and West can be explained. The point of contact varies throughout Paz's work: in *Conjunctions and Disjunctions,* for example, Paz seeks a movement, a flow of history's definition of the body that would account for the different articulations of art and body in both East and West. The essays included in *El signo y el garabato* are centered on translation, technology, and religion, but they seek to apprehend a hidden structure for divergent historical developments. In his *Vislumbres de la India,* Paz centers his analysis on the historico-political entity that is the Indian subcontinent, by examining India in terms reminiscent of those used for Mexico in *The Labyrinth of Solitude.* For Paz, East and West parallel each other in their similarities as well as in their differences: North and South America, as he will explain in *Children of the Mire,* are ex-centric creations of two countries—England and Spain—that have also been ex-centric to the central European tradition. Because Paz arrived in India for the first time immediately after it won its independence, he can comment on India as the product of a colonizing that was very different from that of Mexico by the Spaniards. The Indian subcontinent is thus a Babel of tongues, as well as a religious cauldron, with English as a *lingua franca*—a language that also allows India to be seen as a supranational project inherited from the British. The foreignness of the East is mediated, for Paz, by Latin America, while both Latin America and the East are mediated by the European tradition. The idea of a kind of double, rotating helix, mediated by central columns that inscribe and erase themselves, may account for the structural layout of *Blanco,* which is also conceived in terms of a central column flanked by two other columns written in red or in black ink.

Composition

The title *East Slope,* as Eliot Weinberger has explained in a note to his translation, is an homage to the Sung Dynasty poet Su Shih (1037–1101) whose pen name was precisely "East Slope" (*CP* 640). But there is another, underlying metaphor in *East Slope,* one that recalls Dante's metaphor of the world as a mountain with two slopes, East and West, that correspond to the geographical mise-en-scène of the book. Of course, *East Slope* plays between East and West in poems such as the series on "Intermitencias del oeste" (Interruptions from the West) and in "Himchal Pradesh" or "Wind from all compass points." As do those in other books examined here, the poems included in *East Slope* have changed between their first publication and their recompilation in his *Poemas* of 1979, most notably, with the separation of one book into two. In *Poemas, East*

Slope is followed by *Toward the Beginning,* a book that starts with "Wind from all compass points." These two books were conceived as one in the original edition of *East Slope.*

Because so far this discussion has focused on the relationship between *East Slope* and Paz's essayistic writings, it may seem surprising to begin reading the book with "La exclamación" (Exclamation) a text that seems to be most distant from the book's wider cultural preoccupations. But precisely this lack of overt cultural referents show to what extent Paz's own aesthetics can account for poems that seem to bear no relationship to Indian culture. There is, apparently, no difference between a poem like "Exclamation," from *East Slope,* and other poems of the same haiku-like quality collected in *Libertad bajo palabra:*

> Quieto
>> No en la rama
> En el aire
>> No en el aire
> En el instante
>> El colibrí

> Stillness
>> not on the branch
> in the air
>> Not in the air
> in the moment
>> hummingbird

(*CP* 234–35)

Readers will have no problem situating this poem within Paz's other work collected in *Libertad bajo palabra.* Once again, the aesthetic impulse implies the desire to capture an instant that leads to an aesthetics of evanescence. The poem only describes the appearance and disappearance of a hummingbird that has posed on a branch; the poet captures the instant on paper or, as Manuel Durán has explained, turns the image of the hummingbird on the tree branch into an exclamation point on a flower.[6] The image, as Durán implies, is already that of a written glyph, a fleeting sign. The poem's format, with three lines on the left margin and three indented lines, speaks not only of the hummingbird, but of the echo that the hummingbird itself has left, the instant as evanescence. The first two indented lines (2 and 4) negate lines 3 and 5, and this spiral of affirmation and negation ends up with the hummingbird as an image, as a point of rest that

127

is also the point of origin for the poem itself. It is also important to underscore, as Durán does, that the poem's typographical arrangement imitates the hummingbird's gaze, as it looks to one side and then another before fleeing. But one is also tempted, at this point, to read the poem according to Paz's vision of analogy, and say that the text moves between affirmation and negation, in a kind of dialectical movement where both terms of the dialectics are images of each other.

This dialectical impulse is mediated, or resolved, by the hummingbird as object—but it is hard to know, in this book, if the hummingbird stands as a symbol for something other than a written sign itself. Briefly put, what does the apparition of this hummingbird as a natural object—as a bird that is both familiar and alien—mean in a book of poems that is so consumed by cultural referents whose meaning has to be explained by means of the poet's notes? The question is pertinent because, as we shall see, in poems like "Cerca del Cabo Comorín" (Near Cape Comorin) Paz explains that nature can only be apprehended by means of culture, and that culture is a way of allowing nature to speak, to be understood. The comparison of the hummingbird to a written sign puts the object into a realm outside of nature. It isolates it, in a way, so that it can turn into a written sign that escapes from geography—it is, and it is not, a hummingbird, but it is also a written sign, perhaps the French poet Guillaume Apollinaire's hummingbird, that in "Zone" (1913), one of the most important avant-garde poems, arrives from America to a space that is seen as the sum total of all modern space. Taking into consideration that *East Slope* is presented as a journal of Paz's epiphanic moments in the East, it is important to note to what extent writing mediates the dichotomy between nature and culture, an aspect that belies *East Slope*'s almost total dependence on the written word. It is surely by virtue of its context that we can notice the differences between "Exclamation" and a poem of the High Romantic era. But unlike Keats's "Ode to a Nightingale," to use a common example, nature here does not speak; or, to the extent that it does, its only language is a "mute" sign, an exclamation point. Writing mediates the differences between nature and culture, but only if we see this mediation in terms of other statements by Paz, most notably in "Signs in Rotation," about the absence of meaning that "nature," as it was usually understood, has for us.

East Slope is full of the kind of silences that are evident in "Exclamation," and this is where Paz's sense of strangeness vis-à-vis India can be more visibly perceived. Nothing speaks in *East Slope,* except for particular surfaces whose meaning is given in cultural terms. The landscape is a part of a whole that is contained in each of its parts. Paz begins "Los caminos de Mysore" (On the roads of Mysore) by showing us the dryness of the landscape, and mixes Indian and Mexican elements as if they were all part of one continuous totality. As he says in *Claude Lévi-Strauss: An Introduction* (1967), geology endows a landscape that seems to be a random collection of objects with some kind of hidden meaning. The landscape becomes a juxtaposition of different forms—the meeting point of different spaces and times. Nature only has meaning when this is given within a cultural framework. The interplay of culture, seen as a system of knowledge akin to what geology meant for Lévi-Strauss, is what produces these perceptions in the first place.

The interplay of nature with the poet, nevertheless, allows for Paz's epiphanies, and these are apprehended by means of events. "Near Cape Comorin" is a good example, as the poem talks about a particular situation that is important because of its apparent insignificance: the fact that a landrover has broken down, in the middle of a landscape where it has rained. The poem begins with this statement of fact, but concludes with a kind of literal dissolving of the landrover. The reader understands that it is not the rain itself that will produce this meditation, but the spectacle of a mechanical object breaking down. One could imagine a different poem, one that uses the accident itself as a point of departure for a meditation on chance, or one that rewrites the accident in providential terms. But such a rewriting would entail a subject that reads the universe self-centeredly. Rather, the poem leads toward a question directed at the self, and not toward self-affirmation: "¿Soy alma en pena o cuerpo errante?" (Am I a troubled soul / or a wandering body? [*CP*, 200–201]). The question separates, but also joins, body and soul, for pain is what both body and soul feel—aimlessness, doubt. The spectacle of the rain does not produce the meditation; it is, rather, the rebirth of objects (to which the breaking down of the landrover as machine stands in perfect contrast) after the rain. The storm itself is as much of an accident, as meaningful or as meaningless as the landrover's breakdown. This is equivalent to what the poet observes in nature: both adorable and despicable forms joined together, referents emptied of a signified, universal indifference.

The poet's naming of these objects in "Near Cape Comorin," as well as the question that he addresses to himself, all point to a particular mode of observing reality—one that is passionate but dispassionate at the same time. For Paz, the objective and the subjective are not the referential center of the poem; rather, attention is focused on the very naming of these objects on the page. Paz writes this text as if he were painting, but his is a kind of painting that thrives on the relationship of different objects in one space. Hence, its almost surreal images and the insistence on dissolution: dissolution dissolves contraries and allows for a dispassionate observation on a reality apprehended by means of unreality.

The poet reads, but also interprets, nature's silence, even if nature may or may not speak in a language different from the poet's, or that of the (presumably) Western reader. Paz, therefore, places himself as mediator, as living translator. He frequently disappears into the text, and this evanescent subject disorients the reader; for, after all, it is Paz whom we have as a guide for his season in Asia, not only as conscious informant, but as translator. This desire for dissolution is already present in "The Balcony," the first poem in the collection. In "The Balcony," Paz immediately wants readers to see what he himself is seeing, and this vision is the guiding metaphor of the book. The poem opens with a broad, panoramic view that paradoxically (considering the balcony's possibilities for spatial depth) insists on the idea that there is nothing behind the surface of what is seen. In the balcony, the poet himself is doubled: he talks about what he, as an other, sees. In spite of its being the opening poem of *East Slope*, "The Balcony," nevertheless, refuses to be a beginning: "Si es un comienzo este comienzo / No principia conmigo / Con él comienzo / En él me perpetuo." ("If this beginning is a beginning / it does not begin with me / I begin with it / I perpetuate myself in it" [*CP* 168–69].) This refraction of the "I" is also an integral part of the longer poems of *East Slope*, such as "Perpetua encarnada," "Vrindaban," and "Felicidad en Herat" ("Happiness in Herat").

It is, however, in the shorter poems of *East Slope* where another important strain of the book's cultural argument appears: the thematics of colonialism. In "Apoteosis de Dupleix" (The Apotheosis of Dupleix) the statue that commemorates the imperial mission commands a sea without ships, in the midst of a temple that signifies a cultural world whose meaning escapes the very statue that welcomes travelers to the site. The poet-observer of "The Apotheosis of Dupleix," as well as of "Madurai" is the one who anticipates postmodern culture, insofar as he observes what is left—the ruins of empire. But unlike more recent postmodern writers, Paz does not necessarily celebrate postcolonialism as carnival, but pictures it with gentle irony. In "Madurai," an encounter in a bar juxtaposes two voices (the poet's and his interlocutor, Sri K. J. Chidambaram); the "native" refers in one gentle stroke both to the biggest temple in India as well as to the biggest garage in the Subcontinent. Paz neither celebrates this pastiche nor does he condemn it. Rather, the poem's careful sense of distance directs its irony at the mélange of East and West. In the four "Intermitencias del oeste" (Interruptions from the West) Paz addresses the relationship between East and West as a whole in terms of the history of revolutionary struggle. The third "Intermitencias" (Interruption) is particularly important; Paz wrote it as a protest against the Mexican state's suppresion of the students' uprising in Tlatelolco, and the state's decision to whitewash the massacre with the Olimpiad

130

of 1968. The fourth "Intermitencia" (Interruption) is written in French, as if to remind us that one of Paz's cultural referents throughout the book also relates to the tradition of French Orientalism. It is important to recall that behind the facade of "intermittence" lies one of the most fractious periods in recent Western history, when the youth revolt declared its dissatisfaction with the West and searched for a way out of its sense of cultural impasse. Paz's implicit response to this attempt at redemption is nuanced and complex, as befits a poet who, in the postwar Parisian period, learned to mistrust all ideologies in exchange for his own, personal, quest for understanding.

Toward the Beginning

The first edition of *East Slope* was divided in three sections: the first, *East Slope;* the second, *Toward the Beginning;* with the third section composed of the long poem *Blanco.* In his edition of *Poemas,* Paz has divided them into three separate books. This separation is not, perhaps, so arbitrary at it seems. As a collection, it could be possible to follow a hidden geographical trajectory in the poems included in *Toward the Beginning:* it starts in Afghanistan or Central Asia—the setting for the initial sections of "Wind from all compass points"—and concludes, in "Cuento de dos Jardines" ("A Tale of Two Gardens"), with the vision of an Indian Ocean where Mauritania, India, and Mexico are juxtaposed. Thus, the wind of the first poem settles in the two gardens of the latter, with Earth and Wind on one side, and Water and Earth on the latter. But there are really few pointers in the book that allow us to trace that hidden map, although the book itself seems to have a sense of route, or at least of purpose and direction, from its very title. At one point in "A Tale of Two Gardens," there is an almost direct quotation from the book's title. As the poet recounts the key moments in a life's journey, and as he explains a process of self-involvement that leads to a different time, he is forced to stop dead on his tracks:

Un día,

como si regresara,
no a mi casa,
al comienzo del Comienzo
llegué a una claridad.
•   (472)

One day

as if I had returned,
not to my house,

but to the beginning of the Beginning,
I reached a clarity.
(*CP* 295–97)

The nim tree becomes a center, a hidden axis around which time and space gyrate. It is a symbol of constancy, with a living system hidden at its roots. Underneath its visible branches the poet can feel space itself dilating, time collapse; there, he can understand the hidden relationships that link all things in nature. This realization leads, also, to a vision of otherness as one of the fundamental modes of understanding the self, as all things are interdependent, part of one vast system. The poet's reconciliation, however, is not necesarily with the self but with "con lo que me levanta, me sostiene, me deja caer" (474) ("what lifts me, what sustains me, lets me fall" [*CP* 299]) ; what supports the poet himself is his very being.

In time as well as in space, in culture as well as in nature, this reconciliation in "A Tale of Two Gardens" is one of the fundamental moments in Paz's poetry.[7] It rewrites the idea of place: as he says at the onset, a house or a garden are not necessarily places but rather moments in time as well as in space. They appear within temporality in order to usher that *other* time of which poetry has always spoken. The image of the garden that had appeared again and again in Paz's poetry since *Libertad bajo palabra* reappears as a place of reconciliation. But the garden at this point is not only a vision of unity amid plurality, of a single space of remembrance that wants to be kept outside of, and isolated from, time. Paz recounts his inhabiting the one garden of his childhood in Mexico; he also, however, recounts his exile from it. As in other poems, the garden that existed during childhood is now lost. What is different in this poem is that another, visionary garden incarnates as if doubled, in a different time and space: outside of and within time, not only as a garden in Mexico but as a vision of the nim tree in India. The two gardens are essentially the same, but also different from each other: one represents a space that is forever lost, thus only to be recaptured by its perpetual double, a concrete time and space whose sheer physicality erases all the borders that allowed it to be a self-contained unity. Paz's awareness of this lesson is seen as the literal conclusion to his time in India. As point of closure, it takes us back to the initial site of his meditation, to Mexico and childhood, but also to the original space in which poetry is born. It not only incarnates space within time, but also blooms in the midst of a present voyage at sea, where the space between one shore and the other appears. Because Paz's awareness of an eternal present under the nim tree in India is also an awareness of, as he says, the foundation for his own sustenance as a human being, the garden can be seen as an analogy for a new way of thinking about the space on which the written signs of poetry move. In Paz's previous writings, the page was a fixed entity, and poetry incarnated on a page in which words could be anchored. But at this point Paz wants us to see words moving over a surface that in itself is in perpetual movement, in continuous relationship to that which sustains it. Hence, his frequent appeals, here and in *Blanco,* to the movement of words as well to the movement of the space on which they are placed.

This utopian movement of words and space in a kind of perpetual dance is what inaugurates *Toward the Beginning* as if that movement in itself were the premise for the work that follows—the first stage of a complete rearticulation of poetry that, in Paz's discursive ordering of his books, leads to *Blanco.* "Wind from All Compass Points" can be seen as the articulation of Paz's poetics of space, his sense of closure. The one phrase repeated throughout the poem, however, refers to time: "El presente es perpetuo" (translated as "The present is motionless") although the different locales and events to which the poem refers—Kabul, Paris, India, the American invasion of Santo Domingo—allow the poem to articulate a vision that relates time to space. The perpetual present of the poem arises, from the onset, out of a vision of eternity produced by the juxtaposition of nature and culture along with the act of writing and reading. A poem, as Paz says, is the incarnation of a moment in writing, one that is perpetually repeated in its uniqueness by the act of reading. This poetics is illustrated in his image of an ageless wind being continually reborn the minute readers begin the poem, of a day that eternally repeats itself within its own sense of difference, of a time that is reversible, where history displays itself as images whose time frame is not linear.

Although "Wind from All Compass Points" names the summer solstice as its moment of articulation, the poem is within a time seen as eternal, as somehow detained for an *other* time to take place. The typographical arrangement of the verse on the page underscores Paz's notion of wind: the poem moves in space, it is roughly divided into sections that repeat the initial line on which the poem is anchored ("El presente es perpetuo" ["The present is motionless"]) with Paz's particular mode of punctuation by spatial arrangement. The wind in the poem is similar to long lines of poetry whose scansion is measured by means of human breadth. Thus, the totality of the wind is seen not in a nature permanently outside, but also relating to the poet's and the reader's body. The wind that flows from all compass points arises from a center that continually appears and reappears throughout the text: the body of a man and a woman on a blanket, a scene that reappears in another poem of the collection, "Sol sobre una manta" (Sun on a blanket). Love is the hidden center around which human life gyrates,

133

and Paz makes it clear that he is not only referring to what the West considers spiritual love, but to erotic as well. As the situation of the poet in relation to the Indian landscape, to nature and culture, was the central theme of *East Slope,* so *Toward the Beginning* traces a journey that has erotics as a guiding principle.

Paz's work during the 1960s is so interrelated to his essayistic works that it is difficult to isolate the two. They form a vast system of communicating signs whose explication can only be seen in terms of the connection that Paz himself makes among them. The poems in *Toward the Beginning,* as well as those of *East Slope,* are at times translations of ideas that Paz explores in *Conjunciones y disyunciones* (1969) in *El signo y el garabato* (1973) or in *Claude Lévi-Strauss o el nuevo festín de Esopo* (1967). The reader has the impression that Paz is pursuing similar themes in different registers. The notion of love and eros that appears in "Maithuna" is related to the series of copulating figures in *Conjunciones y disyunciones;* the notion of journey in *Toward the Beginning* has to be read along with Paz's *El mono gramático* (1974) where a reversible journey, both forward and backward, takes place as a concrete physical event. This vast system coalesces in *Blanco,* and it is by means of that poem that we shall examine Paz's poetics in India in more detail.

CHAPTER 6

Blanco

A Poetics of Space

> Blanco: white; blank; an unmarked space; emptiness; void; the white mark in the center of a target.
>
> from the introduction to *Blanco* in
> *The Collected Poems of Octavio Paz, 1957–1987*

Blanco is Paz's most ambitious poem. If *Sunstone* astounds the reader with the sheer virtuosity of the poem itself, *Blanco* is concerned with myriad philosophical, religious threads that coalesce in the written space of the text, where Paz outlines an invisible body by means of a ritual. This ritual is engineered in painstaking detail: in *Blanco* Paz has allowed himself a poetic exploration on nature and culture, on East and West, on the concept of the book and of what role typography plays within it. Moreover, *Blanco* is a love poem, where the lover contemplates the reality and unreality of the world by taking as his point of departure a philosophical ritual that undergoes various stages, clearly marked in the poem according to a particular arrangement where the author places the text in a central column at times flanked by two others. The erotic ritual allows the reader to see the various stages of a journey that the poet has allowed himself to construct. In this chapter, we shall examine the construction of the text as object, to use this as a point of departure for the many possible readings of this text. Therefore, this chapter departs from the usual conventional "analysis" that has been followed in other chapters, and offers instead an analysis of *Blanco*'s structural underpinnings.

Before we begin our reading of *Blanco,* we must note that Paz continually talked about "procedures, or "modes of construction," when he talked about this poem. These "procedures" are first evident first in a long note written in yellow paper that was included as an addendum to the first edition, titled "Aviso al lector" (Warning to the Reader):

> Entre los procedimientos de que se sirve Paz hay uno, antiguo como la poesía misma, que consiste en enfrentar dos textos distintos que, de algún modo, producen un tercer texto. Hay ejemplos de este procedimiento en

todas las literaturas. La época moderna lo ha rescatado y de mera curiousidad literaria—mencionada con escándalo en las historias académicas de la literatura—se ha convertido en una forma de creación no sólo poética sino musical (Boulez, Cage) y aún novelística (Butor, Cortázar) En México, tal vez en español, el primero que emplea esta forma es José Juan Tablada, en un corto poema que se llama *Nocturno alterno.*

Among the procedures used by Paz there is one, as old as poetry itself, that consists in confronting two different texts in order to, somehow, produce a third text. There are examples of these procedures in all literatures. The modern era has rescued it and, from mere literary curiosity—mentioned scandalously in the academic histories of literature—it has been turned into a form of creation, not only poetical but musical (Boulez, Cage) and even into a novelistic procedure (Butor, Cortázar). In Mexico, perhaps in Spanish, the first to employ this form is José Juan Tablada, in a short poem titled *Nocturno alterno.*[1]

These two texts in particular do not seem to be the *Hevajra Tantra* and Mallarmé's "Sonnet in ix"—*Blanco*'s epigraphs—but rather a discursive combination. In other words, there are not two texts but rather two discourses that mirror each other in *Blanco*. In that same "Aviso al lector," Paz's work is broadly conceived in two periods: one ends with *Sunstone,* and the other begins with *Viento entero* (1965) and *Blanco* (1966). *Blanco,* then, is a text that revises and rewrites the poet's work, one of the moments when a new fiction originates from a text. This fiction primarily refers to the life of the poet himself.

We can more or less date *Blanco*'s visible and invisible journeys from its moment of composition. According to the first edition of the poem, Paz wrote the text between 23 July and 25 September 1966. On 19 April 1967 he submitted to Emir Rodríguez Monegal a fragment of the poem for his journal *Mundo nuevo,* with precise instructions as to how the poem was to be laid out. This insistence on layout gives added meaning to Paz's project, as we shall see later on; what is important to recall at this point is that this is a period of enormous activity for Paz. In May of the same year, the corrected edition of *The Bow and the Lyre* appeared, and he writes *Claude Lévi-Strauss: An Introduction.* In May 1967, Paz wrote in Delhi "La nueva analogía: poesía y tecnología" and in December "Presencia y presente: Baudelaire crítico de arte." In 1968, he edited *Libertad bajo palabra* and finished writing the final commentary on Mallarmé's "Sonnet in ix" that he had used, two years before (in 1966) as the epigraph to *Blanco.* Finally, in 1969, Paz published *East Slope* and, in Austin, Texas, on

December 29, he finished "El pensamiento en blanco," a commentary on tantrism that is also related to *Blanco.*

These essays are profoundly revisionary in nature, as if rounding off themes and books that had accompanied Paz for a number of years. Indeed, the bibliography itself forms a figure, as the essay on the Western theme—be it Baudelaire or Mallarmé—is written in the East, while the essay on tantrism is written in the West. These texts are lateral explanations of issues that had appeared in *Blanco:* the essay on Mallarmé as well as "El pensamiento en blanco" explain both epigraphs to the poem, each of them written in the geographical locale of its opposite. The figure that arises out of this bibliography is the yin/yang or, rhetorically, the chiasmus, a figure that is also important in terms of Paz's *Conjunciones y disyunciones,* a collection of essays that explores the chiasmic system of interrelationships between East and West. The real body of the bibliography, then, remits us to a figural scheme, one that is achieved by means of the conjunction or disjunction between the theme and its geographical locale. But it also points toward a new figure in Paz's thought: whereas *Cuadrivio* and *Signs in Rotation* continue the circular metaphor of *Sunstone,* alterity as revealed in paradox, or in chiasmus, will be one of the principal themes of Paz's encounters with the Eastern tradition; it is in this tradition that Paz finds the central current that he had seen prefigured in his poetry.

Closer attention paid to these writings reveals certain repeated themes. First, these essays show Paz's interest in translation, an interest related to his concerns with the contacts and dialogues between East and West that was already present in the first edition of *The Bow and the Lyre.* Second, here we see that Paz's cultural concerns are related to a poetics of form. Although this preoccupation with form was already present in *The Labyrinth of Solitude,* after 1965, Paz obviously desires a kind of grand synthesis, already in evidence since *Signs in Rotation. Blanco* can be seen as an attempt to deal with the very nature of signs in a state of dispersal. This is one of the reasons why it is accompanied by so much archival information; this is also why it seems so many essays serve as ancillary texts to the poem. In itself, *Blanco* is an exercise in dispersal and totality, since it represents the search for a totalizing structure that nevertheless does not allow fragments to surrender their own sense of independence.

Poetics of the Text

Blanco needs to be seen in relation to at least two of Paz's concerns during his period in India: the role of translation within Paz's general poetics of analogy, and the possibilities that technology could offer for the perception of the poetic text. It is well known that at one point, Paz conceived and tried to "translate" *Blanco* into film, as can be seen in two letters to the painter Vicente Rojo, written in March and November 1968, and reproduced in the "archive" that accompanies Enrico Mario Santí's edition (102, 106). He relates that the project to turn *Blanco* into film dates at least since 1966, probably from about the time of the poem's composition. In another letter (2 May 1967), this time to Joaquín Díez Canedo, editor of the first edition of the text, Paz argues for a reading with voices and film (*Archivo* 96). Because of his interest in surface—particularly in terms of the surface on which poetry is written or, rather "imaged"—cinema offers myriad possibilities for poetry, as the surface of the screen dissolves into an image. In this manner, both technology and translation come together in a text that in many ways is conceived as a spectacle, as can also be seen in a project for a scenic performance of *Blanco,* written in 1971 (124–29). As we shall see, the idea of the text as performance had always been part of *Blanco*'s poetics.

From the mid- to the late 1960s, as can be seen in "Signs in Rotation" (Los signos en rotación), in the final section of *Alternating Current,* titled "Recapitulations" (1966, published 1967), and in "La nueva analogía: poesía y tecnología," 1967 (The New Analogy: Poetry and Technology), Paz is reconceptualizing poetry both in terms of the crisis produced by technology in the modern age, as well as in terms of the new vistas offered by structuralism. *Blanco*'s central statement, where spirit, world, and body are inventions of each other in a never-ending repetitive circle, is part of the translucid mode in which poetry illuminates the simulacras of the technical. Technology surrounds the physical and the textual world of *Blanco,* particularly because of the careful typographical and physical tamperings with the text that we shall examine shortly. But technology is also present within the fabric of the poem. *Blanco,* to a certain extent, is a poem that faces up to a posttechnological image of the body, one that Paz finds within the (apparently) pretechnological world of tantrism.

In this sense, innovation and technology bring about a return: for Paz, technology will alter poems and poetry, but this change will always take the genre back to its origins, just as modernity itself engages in a critique of the world under the guise of a rectification and a return.

In "La nueva analogía: poesía y tecnología" and in "Baudelaire, crítico de arte" written between May and December 1967, Paz defines poems as formless verbal objects in a state of continuous change. Nevertheless, as he mentions in "Signs in Rotation," modern poetry's ontological crisis has had to face a "loss" of the image of the world, its signs condemned to dispersal. Because Man has always read temporality as an intentional process, as a process with *meaning,* technology is now entrusted with the representation of our idea of temporality to ourselves. As he did in "Signs in Rotation," Paz explains that, in spite of our desires, technology has emptied our constructions of a meaning they previously possesed, rendering things into functions, substituting an image of the destruction of the world for our previous images. Because technology is responsible for our loss of world-image, this loss, in "Signs in Rotation," has to be faced by poetry.

Paz's arguments on technology may be summarized even if we run the risk of simplifying them. Poetry, in principle, denied and opposed the technical world, but this denial needs to be seen as part of a process of complementarity and disjunction: poetry will now use any technical means at its disposal in order to exist, while at the same time opposing itself to the world of the technical by reaffirming its own sense of singularity and exception outside of the world of mere functions. Paz says that a computer can create a poem; what it cannot create is a deviation from a norm. If poetry is defined, in essence, always as a deviation from a particular norm, hence it follows that the technical can only reproduce form and not its essence. The space (or gash) that is opened by means of the technical is one of simulacra; now, in the world of mechanical reproduction, "authenticity" can be apprehended with much more clarity. Authenticity, in this case, entails the possibility of error, of change, whereas simulacra will merely entail repetition. The technical, moreover, will return poetry to its roots by underscoring, once again, the genre's oral foundations. By the same token, technological arts such as the cinema will reshape and rearticulate the page as a movable surface over which poems are written. The written sign, says Paz, does not repose on a fixed space but over a surface that develops (*transcurre*) because it has become an image of time. As such, and because of its very awareness as image, it becomes corporeal. Paz reminds us, for example, that Mallarmé always conceived of poetry as a corporeal language, as a language of gesture and movement. All written lines are metaphors for speech, and the page is the silence that allows that speech to be heard.

Analogy, the other concept important for Paz at this point, appears again and again in *The Bow and the Lyre* and in *Children of the Mire,* along with irony. In "La nueva analogía," Paz examines the combination of analogy and irony by grounding analogy in an allegorical vision of the world. All allegory, says Paz, proceeds from an analogical vision of the world, since it is based upon an identity between one thing and the other. Paz says that "la estructura lingüística es una alegoría de la estructura sub-atómica y ambas se reflejan en el código genético" (22) (linguistic structure is an allegory of subatomic structure and both are reflected in the genetic code) . Because in modernity one term cannot be isolated from the other, analogy is part of a system of correspondences, where irony signals the interruption, the abyss between the real and the imaginary. Irony problematizes people and things: because it is the sign of the rupture of the analogical principle, it defines the modern subject. When Man enters into the analogical house of being, he dislodges divinity and is faced with the world. In the modern era, where things have stopped *being* language, they possess only the trace of their silence for the poet to decipher. For Paz, negativity and negation define modern philosophy, understood as a critique of modernity's being the critical, rational age. Technology allows for a possible mediation by ushering an erotic reconciliation with the world.

Paz's ideas on the relationship between technology and poetry spill over into his concerns on translation. As he says at the onset of "Presencia y presente: Baudelaire crítico de arte": "La idea de lenguaje contiene la de traducción: pintor es aquel que traduce la palabra en imágenes plásticas; el crítico es un poeta que traduce en palabras las líneas y los colores. El artista es el traductor universal," (*SG* 31). (The idea of language contains that of translation: the painter is the one who translates the word in plastic images: the critic is a poet that translates in words, lines and colors. The artist is the universal translator.) He goes further, in "Literatura y literalidad" (Literature and Literalness), stating that "aprender a hablar es aprender a traducir; cuando el niño pregunta a su madre por el significado de esta o aquella palabra, lo que realmente le pide es que traduzca a su lenguaje el término desconocido" (*SG* 57). (To learn how to speak is to learn how to translate; when the child asks his mother for the meaning of this or that word, what he really is asking for is a translation in his tongue, of an unknown term.) This translation of different modes of art into each other is important in *Blanco,* as the poem works on a surface that is painted with different colors—the surface itself enacted by a possible relationship between different artforms. Translation is also an important part of "El pensamiento en Blanco," an extended meditation on tantric art and its relationships with European abstraction. His later poetry, particularly *Vuelta* and *A Tree Within,* is preeminently concerned with the relationships between poetry and painting. It is not that these concerns had not appeared before in Paz's work, but they are brought onto the foreground around the time when Paz conceptualizes his text.

In *Blanco,* Paz yields to a combination of signifiers that trace a journey in a space displayed over the surface of paper. But these signifiers, surrounded by the very meaningful space in which they appear, trace an act of faith in which words aim to create their own nature, and not a copy, metaphor, or supplement to an empirical reality that is beyond the page in which these words themselves are to be found. However, the very acritical act that seems to underlie a "religious" (tantric) reading of the poem, forces us to understand the poem's more "ironic" opposition to analogy. Doesn't modern poetry, according to "Signs in Rotation," face the consciousness of its own defeat in the open space left over from the division between real nature and paper? Words in the modern age do not have the status that religious icons once possessed; a poem cannot validate the acritical gesture of faith and belief, except as a belief in its own act of criticism. Paz builds *Blanco* like a cathedral of words, a sacred place whose building blocks are words. Nevertheless, Paz is aware of his own contradictions in creating for himself such a structure: the acritical temptation that underlies it is precisely based on the denial of the very narrative of modern poetry that he is constructing at the time. This is why *Blanco* finally aims toward postulating criticism (understood in the most ample terms possible) as the true religion of modernity—an idea that is also found in "Signs in Rotation" as well as in the later *Children of the Mire* (1974).

As Paz explains in *The Monkey Grammarian* (another writing of *Blanco,* a kind or ritual pilgrimage), criticism deconstructs. In a mode that is different from that of poetry, criticism is forced to begin in the center of the labyrinth and from then on find Ariadne's thread. As opposed to the consciousness of advance that Paz explains in *The Monkey Grammarian,* criticism is not written forward but, rather, backward; it is a route in reverse. It is in this sense that *Blanco* forces us to deal with certain, particular figures of modernity. One of the first figures that Paz is concerned with here entails the very act of narration upon which modernity is articulated: the idea of the internal voyage, of the Orphic initiation in order to discover a certain sense of timelessness that yields to the elaboration of "myth." This elaboration of myth can only be the result of a crisis. Because it is a poem about a journey—an internal journey—*Blanco* is the expression of a crisis. Baudelaire explained that the Romantic poet goes through a crisis that is like an internal voyage, a "going inside" in order to discover the laws or the precepts of creation.[2] Baudelaire implies that this crisis results from a feeling of anxiety, out of the exhaustion faced with an art that has turned repetitive; the artist feels that everything has been said before. The discovery of the myth, of the hidden law of creation, perpetually originates the incessant project of modernity in an analogic poet like Baudelaire—one who consistently and continually looks for the relationship between different elements. Myth allows the poet to see systems that are beyond logic (postlogical systems) created by means of a conjunction between analysis and synthesis, between the union and separation of subject and object—systems that go beyond opposition, mediation and dialectics, and that narrate themselves. Myth is related to poetics, to a sense of narrativity that looks, beyond logic, for its own foundations.

Blanco deals with a journey that is, at times, not for myth but for poetics—the hidden keys or laws, even beyond reason—of all poetical texts. It is this sense of narrativity that Paz names "myth," and this is the sense in which poetics, or the search for a poetics, creates the myth of modern poetry. The poem is the account of an internal experience, of a "going under" in order for Paz to renew himself as a poet-critic. His new status implies a denial of previous oppositions and a new act of synthesis that sees history as a means to an absolute. The particular problem for the critic is that Paz's poem is already supremely aware of its own critical bases, and that these lead to a postlogical account of myth and history in *Blanco*. Thus *Blanco* presents itself as the culmination of a process of modern poetry. In this sense it is not unusual that Paz would dedicate himself in the work that follows *Blanco* to the deconstruction of the Western tradition of poetry; the subsequent work ultimately desires to create its own nature: an artificial paradise that underscores, as we shall see, its own artifice.

Blanco is a poem born out of tantrism, the heretical, erotic belief in the possibility of having access to Buddhism's ultimate truths not by means of conceptual meditations but by corporeal, sexual acts.[3] Tantrism is chronologically a "late" manifestation of Buddhism, and the tantric texts (such as the *Hevajra Tantra,* one of the epigraphs to this poem) are, within the Tibetan canon, texts that talk about specific and concrete rituals that have at times been classified as degenerate and depraved manifestations of late Indian and early Tibetan Buddhism. As such, *Blanco* is a lover's discourse, a philosophical text that sees the physical body as a means to ultimate enlightenment. Because of its underpinnings in tantrism, however, *Blanco* is meant to be a heretical poem, going against the grain of poetry as an activity solely concerned with the subject. The tradition of the "critical poems" that are *Blanco*'s precursors all imply a heresy: attempts at understanding the world and nature by means of poetics as a mode that anticipates secrets unveiled by science. A global interpretation of the poem yields meanings that are simply contexts for a text whose philosophical sense of independence is meant to recall, for the Western reader, Mallarmé's poetic constructions. Whereas Mallarmé wants to create a Book that is the double of the universe, however, Paz in India has allowed the opposition between Book and World to inhabit the space of a paradox: both Book and World are analogical terms for each other. The Universe is always conceived as a Book and as a Body, and the Body has always been conceived as Book and as an image of the world. Starting from this premise, the letters in *Blanco* are like aids to a meditation, like the tantric drawings that Paz examines in "El pensamiento en Blanco." As readers progressively become aware of the far-reaching implications of this text, they realize that in *Blanco* the weight of all its significations experiments with a radical negation of the world. In *Blanco,* reading is conceived as a ritual on a page that would aim toward tri-dimensionality and thus, toward self-sufficiency. That is, as if writing were not an image based on another image, revealing that the illusory nature of reality is reality itself.

Blanco seduces the critic with an allegorical theater in which figures are resolved in paradoxes. Writing here is theater; and as theater, it is physical. *Blanco* is not a meditation, so much as it is a representation, a *mise-en-scène,* of tantrism. This *mise-en-scène* is part of the poem's design. It is as if Paz meditates as he writes, as if the text were a diagram. Faced with the symbolic charge of this poem, author and critic end up being translators of other bodies, of other representations. In this universe of texts, the author and the critic are always mediators. It is in this sense that the poem is a *garabato* or a hieroglyph, as Paz defines it in *El signo y el garabato:* the poem in itself is a body (*garabato*) and at the same time its translation (sign). In an essay on Salvador Elizondo, Paz talks about an eroticism that is a metaphor of itself: "No hay una realidad eróti-ca propiamente dicha porque el erotismo es, por su naturaleza misma, repre-sentación imaginaria" (203). (There is no erotic reality in the proper sense of the term because eroticism is, because of its nature, imaginary representation.) The only response to pleasure is precisely the *garabato,* a sign that is only translat-able to the extent that it is not literal, as it carries its own response within its signifier. "Al extirpar el significado," Paz says at the end of his essay, "el signo se vuelve *garabato*" (emphasis in original, 205–6). (When the signified is extir-pated. . . . the sign becomes a *scrawl.*) This *garabato* is, like *Blanco,* a metaphorical negation and a metaphor within itself: an originary and nonrefer-ential writing, one that can not be so much read as translated. For Paz, transla-tion repeats the wedge between the sign and the scrawl, between language and its irreducible form.

Reading the Text

Generally, critical readings on *Blanco* begin by descriptions based on the long note at the end of the first edition of the poem, a note that in other editions appears as the preamble to the work. In this note, Paz talks about the different "possibilities" offered by his "composition"—he does *not* use the word "poem." According to Paz, *Blanco* can be read as one poem, or as two poems that may also fragment themselves into four, six, or eight. Paz tells us that *Blanco* is con-structed and deconstructed at the same time, that the text disperses and forms itself, or that it forms itself precisely at the moment of dispersal. This insistence on explaining the structuring of *Blanco* in a series of notes begins our reading of the text.

The idea of annotating a poetic text has two important precedents in modern poetry: the introduction to Mallarmé's *Un coup de dés* (1897) and the notes to Eliot's *The Waste-Land*. Unlike the notes of these two precursors, Paz's *describes* the poem, it is presented as an a posteriori note (at the end of the text) that nevertheless tells us something about an a priori, about a manner of organizing and constructing its fragments. But what readers needed in *Blanco* was not the de-composition of the text in the notes, but an indication as to how, and with what materials, the text has been fabricated. Paz tells us, on the contrary, how it should be read.

Remember that the note is presented as a guide to a labyrinth; thus it gives us a sense of direction, a route. In the central poem, as Paz says in this note, one can already see the route of the word, "from silence to silence." This route implies an organic genealogy of the Word, as if language were "born," its origin analogous to that of a plant or a body. But this organicity is given in a poem that is presented, in fact, as a kind of engineering feat, a construction of already made things, a synthesis of disparate elements. It seems as if the content of the poem denies what the poem is. The poem itself is not born, like a plant is born, but is constructed as an artifact. *Blanco* offers an idealized image and vision of the word as body and of the poem as world, but the poem's construction gives a contrary image: not creation but rather construction, not the organicity of the text, born as a plant, but rather the impersonal nature of the machine.

In spite of, or because of, his deliberate questioning of modernity's demise, Paz situates his text within a Romantic poetics. In a second note that Paz adds to the later editions (the 1979 edition of his *Poemas* and the Brazilian edition of *Transblanco*) he explains:

Como no ha sido posible reproducir aquí todas las características de la edición original de *Blanco* (México, 1967), señalo que este poema debería leerse como una sucesión de signos sobre una página única; a medida que avanza la lectura, la página se desdobla: un espacio que en su movimiento deja aparecer el texto y que, en cierto modo, lo produce. (*Poemas* 1967)

As it is not possible to reproduce here all of the characteristics of the original edition of the poem, it should be said that *Blanco* was meant to be read as a succession of signs on a single page. As the reading progresses, the page unfolds vertically: a space which, as it opens out, allows the text to appear and, in a certain sense, creates it. (*CP* 311)

144

What is interesting about this note is the apparently innocuous "As it is," or "since" (*como*) that introduces it; the poem can be read outside of the original edition, Paz says, if one always has the other text present. Readers are reminded that they are in front of a text whose reproduction has been impossible. And readers of the present edition of *Blanco* are reminded that they can read the colorless text while preserving, in their minds, the constructed existence of the other, imaginary, and invisible text. This note is not the invitation to a re-reading: it becomes, rather, the melancholic invitation to an act of remembrance.

The space produced by the poem seems an echo of the revolutionary *Un coup de dés* (1897) by Mallarmé and of Blaise Cendrars's *La Prose du Transibérien et de la Petite Jehanne de France* (1913)—an account of a journey published as a long page written in different colors, and illustrated by a whirlwind-like painting by Sonia Delaunay.[4] Nevertheless, whereas Cendrars invites us to read *La Prose du Transiberien* in any edition, *Blanco*'s apparently innocuous introductory injunction offers us another possibility: the poem can be read outside of its original edition as long as one has the other text always present. In order to read the poem, readers must go back to *Blanco*'s originary note.

Critics have remarked that this note introduces the theme of the reader's freedom. Critical readings of *Blanco* first stipulate a sense of total freedom, but then read the poem according to the constraints of linear rigor. But just as the poem implicitly argues against its own organicity, it also argues against the supposed liberty that Paz wants readers to see in the text. Throughout Paz's work, freedom is found precisely within the most exacting sense of rigor. As a modern writer, particularly one that follows the surrealist model, Paz constructs for himself a shape or form, a linguistic constraint that allows the artist, paradoxically, to feel free. Paz has done this in sonnets (*Homage and Profanations*), poetic forms (*Renga*), or calendars (*Sunstone*). It is evident that *Blanco* is a poem open to different interpretations and different combinations, one must not think, however, that it lacks the same rigorous principles that can be found throughout Paz's work. In this sense, the procedure that needs to be followed is at odds with the one proposed by criticism: on the one hand, readers must first exhaust the keys that confer some kind of rigor to the text in order to understand precisely and in what way the text is in itself a kind of machine.

Why divide Blanco into four, six, or eight poems, as opposed to, for example, a composition in three or in nine? In "El pensamiento en blanco," Paz examines the points of contact between tantric and modern art, and underscores how tantrism is a system that explains reality: "La visión del cuerpo humano como el doble del universo," he says, "es central en el tantrismo y se desdobla en una fisiología mágica y en una alquimia erótica" (*SG* 47). (The vision of the human body as the double of the universe . . . is central in tantrism and doubles itself into a magic physiology and an erotic alchemy.) According to Snellgrove, the translator and editor of the version that Paz uses of the *Hevajra tantra,* tantrism conceives of existence in the knowledge of its nonexistence.[5] The sadhaka or yogini creates an idealized representation of the process of emanation of existence, called *samsara* (a concept that includes all that is constituted by personality and perception). The supreme mystical realization is then expressed in negative terms. Mystical realization (nirvana) is essentially equivalent to daily existence (samsara). There is no nirvana other than samsara; there is no other samsara than nirvana, according to tantrism. If samsara is equivalent to nirvana, then all men are, or may be Buddhas, a long as they let go of the illusion that nirvana can be found outside of samsara, outside of real, temporal existence.[6] In order to reach this level of knowledge, tantrism recommends the use of a series of diagrams called yantra.[7] These diagrams can be figural representations or, as is generally the case, abstract drawings, aids to meditation. The beginning and the end of *Blanco* are contained in the diagram (the yantra) on its cover, a diagram that Paz, in one of his first letters to Joaquín Díez Canedo (12 October 1966), insisted should not be figurative but, on the contrary, rather "severe" (*Archivo* 86). The poem is a kind of wave that originates in this diagram; literally, the poem displays itself within this yantra, it is its own beginning and its conclusion.

The abstract drawing joins two opposing orders (black and white) to a third (yellow). The three colors correspond to three figures: box, cover, and text. In order to reach the text one has to empty the box in order to find another copy of the box in the cover of the poem—although this time, as Paz also advised Díez Canedo in a letter (25 January 1968), the cover of the book inversely reflects (in black) the box's white cover (*Archivo* 101). The poem is written in three columns, using two colors (black and red) over the white color (it is actually yellowish, or it yellows with time) of the page. The text itself is completely organized according to a principle of three columns, and this system is replicated, or at least follows, the scheme reproduced below:

Tantra	Blanco	Mallarmé
East	Paz	West
Element	Word	Sensation

Here the third term, that of the central column, is the mediation or conjunction of the other two, situated at the extreme left or right. Each of these terms, read in vertical fashion, represents principles used by Paz. Read in horizontal fashion, they are chains of opposition that the poem establishes and annuls. Neither

Mallarmé nor the tantra is within an oppositional system, but rather as texts mediated by *Blanco.* Within the text, East and West, tantrism and Mallarmé, may be found in one point.[8] According to Paz, the left column is based on elements, and the right column on perceptions. The poem in itself is the representation of another, invisible tantric body, one that is composed of a system of canals or veins (*nadis*) distributed around the body as veins are in leaves. In human veins, these currents distribute energy to all the faculties of sense.

Blanco paints itself according to the internal circulation of the *chakras.* Each of the parts of the poem corresponds to one of the chakras of the tantric tradition, and these have been reflected within the text in a supremely programmed manner: the chakras are points for a meditation that represent a pilgrimage, a ritual that traverses the body of the yogi. Each of these points is not only ruled by different principles, they *symbolize* according to a series of links of a chain, so that each of them possesses a color, an attribute, and a number in particular. In the tantric system they are displayed in the following manner:

nirvana	white	ether
head	blue	water
throat	green	air
navel	red	fire

The different texts that compose *Blanco* can be read as places of meditation, as chakras. The verses would be analogous to the lotus petals or to the numbers that are associated with each chakra in particular:

ether	white	ether
water	blue	understanding
air	green	imagination
fire	red	perception
earth	yellow	sensation

Visually this outline, as in Paz's poem, is misleading. Reading transposes the text much as a photographic negative does, so that the text inverts the order. When it is displayed, it appears in the following manner:

earth	yellow	sensation
fire	red	perception
air	green	imagination
water	blue	understanding
ether	white	ether

Visually expressed, in the yogi's body, from head to toe, the order of the principles follows the former order. Earth should be displayed at the end of the pages, as foundation, so that the map of the poem may coincide with the diagram of the body. Between reading and vision there is in *Blanco* an inversion. In order for the system to be perfectly equivalent to the tantric drawing, one would have to write the poem from the ground up, or inversely to the manner in which the poem is actually displayed. If, as Paz seems to say, writing is a body, it appears in this text as the inversion of the body, a camera that offers images in reverse.

The organizational will that Paz manifested in his correspondence on *Blanco* underscores that every aspect of the text has a meaning beyond that of its words. Viewing *Blanco* as a total, signifying poem, we note that the sections of the poem begin where they do, not at the top of the page, but rather at the middle of the sheet of paper, precisely as the poem moves from one page to the other. By valuing the vertical, over the horizontal form of reading, the text presents itself as a kind of *relay,* a process that Paz has examined in relation to the work of Marcel Duchamp. In other words, *Blanco's* central column never appears next to the other two, but rather offers a musical relay with the others. The singularity of the word is a discourse that in itself is permanently being developed.

In that first edition that Paz never allows us to forget, the poem is written on the surface of a long, folded sheet of paper. Although Paz had initially conceived the poem as a cylindrical scroll, in the Chinese manner, he soon discarded the idea because of its typographical difficulties and the difficulties in reading the poem. In reconceptualizing the book as a kind of long, folded page, the first "page" (to speak of a "page" in this context is almost meaningless) is adhered to the cover of the book while the following pages unfold from this one. While the text itself is read, the fold between one page and the other marks its rhythm, in a manner already presaged by Mallarmé in *Un coup de dés.* Once the text is displayed in its entirety, the fissures that detain, that mark the rhythm between one page and the next are erased, so that readers are exposed to one long, single page. When that page is unfolded, readers notice a central column, written in different typographies: from the almost transparent lettering of the beginning, passing through the darker typographies of the central sections, until a kind of return, to the more transparent one that both inaugurates and closes the text.

Although Paz numbers the sequence of pages in the drafts reproduced in the *Archivo,* the first edition purposely avoids numbering the pages of this text. This avoidance is more striking considering the poem's sense of rhythm—that it is precisely every four "pages" that the poem is divided into two columns: one, on the right, in italics and with red letters, and a column on the left, also italiciced but written in very dark ink, and that each of these "pages" or sections is followed precisely by another page that contains a poem of exactly eleven lines. In this fashion, page 5 has 11 lines, and so does page 9 and page 13. Only between pages 16 and 17, can we find an interruption in this system: here there is a break in the sequence that demands that colored pages appear in multiples of four and that each page that follows that has a poem of eleven lines.

This movement of time in words is still more curious when we notice that in the last page of the first edition Paz remarks that he has written the poem between 23 July and 25 September. If one date, as Paz says in *Alternating Current,* implies a distance from time, "that moment when primitive man, suddenly aware that he is outside of natural or animal time, realizes that he is a stranger, a creature who has fallen into a literally fathomless *now*" (24), then a progression in dates implies a space. In terms of *Blanco,* however, this sequence of dates give a sense of linear writing that the author tries to undo (or break away from) when he mentions the different forms in which the text itself can be read. Once again, the text is a heretical construction, one that means something other than what it says. This illusion of linear time needs to be seen by means of surrealism, which defines chance within the constraints of rigor, and necessity as the only door that gives us access to freedom. If we count according to the body of the poem itself, from the first page of the poem (1), the page where Paz's final note is found would be page 25, and it is precisely at the end of page 25 where Paz tells us that his poem was written precisely on 25 September 1966. This coincidence—the number of the page that finishes a poem that was finished on the same cypher (cypher in the Arabic sense of number and emptiness—one of the possible titles for an English translation of *Blanco,* as Paz tells Charles Tomlinson [*Archivo* 151])—does not seem arbitrary. That it is not arbitrary can be proved if we continue counting within the poem and within the text, bearing in mind that, as Paz says in *Blanco,* "La irrealidad de lo mirado / Da realidad a la mirada" ("The unreality of the seen / brings reality to seeing" [*CP* 325])—two lines of five words each. Cyphers indeed form part of the hidden, cryptic messages that turn *Blanco* into an "open" text.

One could then proceed to a different reading of *Blanco,* one not based on freedom but on total control. *Blanco's* total universe, from the initial page adhered to the cover until the last, free page, consists of 31 unnumbered pages, or 32 if we count the abverse of the last.[9] This global number will appear from now on in this essay in parentheses, signaling the number of pages in the book, with the purpose of establishing the correspondence between this numeration and the other one of the poem, based on the text itself, from beginning to end.

149

Therefore, the first page of the text, where the poem itself names "the beginning" would be page 1(5). The first number corresponds to the poem and the second to the sum of the first four, that contain the title, the place of publication (*pie de imprenta*) the name of the editorial house and two epigraphs, that of the *Hevajra Tantra* and of Mallarmé's sonnet.

These two sequences complement and correspond each other. For example, one can allow the poem a first round or re-read (*vuelta* or *revuelta*) precisely in the numbers we have just mentioned, as the final number of pages (32) adds up to 5 (3 + 2 = 5), the number of pages with which the book begins. The decomposition of the final number re-composes the number of the beginning: the totality of the poem is created on the one hand, and divided and begun anew on the other. If this correspondence occurs here within the same numerological sequence (that of the book) it is also possible to find it within one numeration and the other. In this way, the poem ends on page 23 (27) a number that also adds up to 5 and that reflects the 32 found at the beginning of the text.

Blanco as a whole is divided into two possibilities (that of the book and that of the text) and ultimately denies the difference between them both, as the poem also has two centers that communicate with each other. Pages 16 and 17 would be the center of the poem if we count according to another mode of numbering, as we used in order to count the 32 pages of the poem in total. The 28 pages of the text would find its center on pages 14 (18) and 15 (19) the ones that begin with "Los reflejos, los pensamientos veo. / Las precipitaciones de la música, / El número cristalizado. / Un archipiélago de signos" ("the reflections, the thoughts I see. / Precipitations of music, / crystallized number. / An archipielago of signs" [*CP* 323]) up until "Mis pasos / Se disuelven / En un espacio que se desvanece / En pensamientos que no pienso" ("my steps / dissolving / in a space that evaporates / into thoughts I don't think" [*CP* 325]).

Numbers mean progression and at the same time recurrence, an indispensable element in the concept that Paz has of the long poem, as he says in his essay "Contar y cantar."[10] As one advances in time, time itself is remembered, it presents us with its echoes. Paz has commented that the virtue of the long poem is found in particular in this combination between the concision of the image and, at the same time, its extension in time. "El poema extenso," Paz writes, "debe satisfacer una doble exigencia: la de la variedad dentro de la unidad y la de la combinación entre recurrencia y sorpresa. (The long poem . . . must satisfy a double imperative: that of variety within unity and that of the combination between recurrence and surprise.") *Blanco* in this sense, is a poem that moves. This movement may be reversible within the meaning of the poem, but never in terms of its signifiers. This movement is given starting from the second poem, that of page 2(6):

Sube y baja,
Escalera de escapulario,
El lenguaje deshabitado.
Bajo la piel de la penumbra
Late una lámpara.
             Superviviente
Entre las confusiones taciturnas,
                     Asciende
En un tallo de cobre
          Resuelto
En un follaje de claridad:
             Amparo
De caídas realidades.
          O dormido
O extinto

It climbs and descends,
the spine of the mineshaft ladder,
abandoned language.
A lamp beats beneath
penumbra skin.
             Survivor
in the melancholic confusion,
                  it rises
in a copper stalk,
          breaks
into leaves of clarity:
             shelter
for fallen realities.
          Asleep
or extinct
                           (*CP* 315)

This "page" in the original edition is composed of fifteen lines. Five of these lines appear as a defined group (from "Sube y baja"[It climbs and descends] to "lámpara" [lamp]) while the other ten occupy different spaces on the page, spaces that link, according to positionality: "Superviviente" (Survivor), "Resuelto" (breaks—or resolves), "O dormido" (Asleep); while "Asciende" (it rises) occupies the more distant space to the right; and "Amparo" (shelter) remains in its own place, unprotected, from the other words. These lines are the exact half or are at the exact midpoint of a poem of thirty lines, divided symmetrically between one fold of the page and the other. The pages are linked by the conjunction of "O extinto / Alto en su vara" (or extinct, / high on its pole), with the latter line in the next page, after the fold, that at the same time divides the route between, in Spanish, the sound of the *o* and the opened vowel *a*.

One can observe how the poem says and does at the same time, in the reversible movement of the lines and in their grammatical displacements (for example, lines 4 and 5 may be reordered as "una lámpara late bajo la piel de la penumbra" (a lamp beats under the skin of penumbra)). It is also possible to go "up and down" along the first three lines, their center precisely that "escalera de escapulario" (mineshaft ladder) as complement and subject at the same time. This "mineshaft ladder" that has mystified and confused *Blanco*'s readers and translators, with its obvious musical resonance (*escalera de escapulario*), has to be seen not only in terms of language but also in terms of love. As Paz says in *The Double Flame* (1993), "The image of the ladder figures in almost all cults. It embraces two ideas: ascent and initiation" (104). Between the subject and the complement, between the world and the poem, the "escalera de escapulario" is offered as mediation, as a complement that can be a subject. The fall of reality, the concept that appears in the poems written in red and black ("caes de tu cuerpo a tu sombra" [you fall from your body to your shadow], in particular) is manifested in reverse: in an ascending line, the poem could be read as "las caídas realidades se amparan en un follaje de claridad que se resuelve en un tallo de cobre que asciende entre las confusiones taciturnas que sobreviven (a las caídas realidades o a las caídas de las realidades)" (the fallen realities are sheltered in a foliage of clarity that resolves itself in a copper stalk that ascends between the taciturn confusions surviving [either fallen realities or the fall of realities]). These realities are in turn sheltered (*amparadas*) in another paradoxical nature in which the foliage (*follaje*) is a clarity that is resolved in a supernatural world where natural reality acts in unusual ways.

Correspondences are not limited to the text but are inscribed within its composition. If we proceed according to a different mode of counting, the pages with eleven lines of poetry (that in turn follow the sequence of poems appearing every four pages or folds) are echoed by the fact that the joined pages of the text precisely add up to 11—the first one limping, in a sense, joined to the binary epigraph of two texts, the *Hevajra Tantra* and Mallarmé. If we count differently, we would notice that the joined pages add up to 13; that is, the number of the weeks within the lunar Aztec calendar, where time is divided according to cycles of 52 years—Paz's age at the time.

152

Given the series of coincidences here mentioned, it would not be surprising if most of *Blanco* were fixed in space according to a personal code that also remits to a game of chance and to a program. Suffice it to say that these examples allow us to see a different text from the one criticism has been reading thus far, one whose absolute sense of rigor and planning turns it into a construction not unlike the Aztec calendar that served as the foundation for *Sunstone,* where a series of dates gyrate around each other. But readers should not presume that these indications add different meanings onto the text. On the contrary, they reveal that *Blanco* is a poem that, in rigor, says nothing, that does not remit to any place except to a series of signs over a piece of paper. Hence, the poem's sense of irony, one in which time becomes space, and its letters an architecture of air. Its sense of analogy is a product of an act of negation: pages themselves are synecdoches of nature, paper earth, and lettered sky. For Paz, to write is to hit the ground and the sky of the page, the sky and the earth of the letter. *Blanco* constantly remits to a nature that is present on the page: "En un muro rosado / tres buitres ahítos" ("Three satiated vultures / on a red wall" [*CP* 321]). But there is no oracle and no reality except for a mental image, one that is analogous to our perception of the world.

The revisionary nature of a poem like *Blanco* allows it to be not merely one of a sequence of long poems by means of which Paz has divided and re-organized his poetic oeuvre, but actually its most important figuration, one that goes beyond the sense of classic achievement found in *Sunstone. Blanco* is truly Paz's poem of crisis, where he enters into the labyrinth of modernity and time in order to rescue another myth where poetry performs the modern age. Paz turns his poem into a figure, and this figure into a myth, in a way not unrelated to his exposition of myth in his studies of Claude Lévi-Strauss. But in this case, the myth that Paz sees as the foundation for all others is the myth of language as well as of creation. In *Claude Lévi-Strauss* Paz asked for the myth that contained all other myths; in *Blanco* the response is the myth of language's origin, articulating itself both as organic entity and as construction. And any time the myth of language is invoked, as Baudelaire understood, poets have to refer back to the myth of Orpheus, the poet whose song is able to affect nature, but also the poet who goes to the underworld in order to find his lover Eurydice, and who in other versions of the myth is destroyed by the Maenads and floats down the river. To look for the myth of myths, and to present the deracinated, fragmented Orpheus as the point of origin for a new beginning is the equivalent of looking for a sense of totality that is outside, but also inside history, just as Buddhism advises us to look for nirvana in samsara. In his paper nature, the poet becomes Orpheus. Like Orpheus, he is capable of submitting nature to the laws of its creation. As

Orpheus, the poet presents another image of Buddha. And both, Orpheus and Buddha, represent a rhetoric that subverts logic, the extended trope represented by the letters of the alphabet, the figure of language, nature in *Blanco* and nature in blank.

Table 1. *Blanco:* Calendar

Book		Poem	
	1		
	2		
	3		
	4		
	5	1	the poem begins
	6	2	
	7	3	
red	8	4	red and black page in multiples of four
	9	5	(11 lines)
	10	6	
	11	7	
red	12	8	red and black page in multiples of four
	13	9	(11 lines)
	14	10	(15 lines)
	15	11	(10 lines) joined pages 25 lines (poem's center)
red	16	12	red and black page in multiples of four
	17	13	(11 lines)
	18	14	
	19	15	
red	20	16	poem's center. Two pages counted
red	21	17	as one. Number of lines = 29 (9 + 2 = 11 = 2)
	22	18	
	23	19	
	24	20	
	25	21	
	26	22	
	27	23	poem ends (2 + 3 = 5). Count remits to the beginning
	28	24	
	29	25	date of poem's end, 25 September 1966.
	30	26	
	31	27	
	32	28	

Vuelta, A Draft of Shadows, A Tree Within

Paz's writing after his return from Asia takes him back not only to his personal but also his literary origins. In personal terms, this reversion explains the continuous reference to the "return" or *vuelta,* as if a circle were closing in upon itself; in literary terms it explains his return to the avant-garde, particularly its sense of relationship among the poetic text, visual art, and architecture. For example, Paz's notion of the poetic line, principally in *East Slope, Blanco,* and *Salamandra,* is one that plays with the space of the page. But already in *Salamandra* as well as in *Vuelta,* this mode of writing gives Paz's poems a unique visual register (unique, at least in Latin America). In other words, his "signature" as style is related to the notion of space as seen in his poetry. Paz breaks the phrase into line components that appear at different points of a page, while keeping the left margins, against which the verses are indented. The following example is from "Totalidad y fragmento" (Totality and Fragment), a poem from the collection *Vuelta:*

> En hojas sueltas
> arrancadas cada hora
> hoja suelta cada hora
> José Luis
> traza un pueblo de líneas
> iconografías del sismo
> grieta vértigo tremedal
>
> *(Poemas* 613)

> In loose leaves
> torn each hour
> loose leaf each hour
> José Luis
> etches a nation of lines
> iconographies of the tremor
> breach, vertigo, quagmire

The example is picked at random although, as a fragment, it offers a number of points of entry from which one can examine the "totalities" mentioned in the title, as well as its relationship to "fragments." Note that the poem is anchored on a left margin that it continually disrupts. This disruption is related to what Paz does to the written phrase itself: Paz's poetry is not "poetic" in the common sense of the word, but also definitely not "oral"—as oral or popular poetry has been understood in Latin America. Paz's poetic "style" is the result of his writing in a mode that resembles speech, but this ressemblance of speech is at the same time based on a certain "transparency" of discourse, one that avoids, particularly in the later poetry, obvious "rhetorical" effects. This transparency is doubly signaled by a deliberate will to turn the poetry into a description and, at times, into a statement. Indeed, the poem is one continuous phrase that could be read as follows: "En hojas sueltas arrancadas cada hora José Luis traza un pueblo de líneas" (In loose leaves plucked each hour Jose Luis etches a nation of lines). Because the poem is dedicated to the Mexican painter José Luis Cuevas, Paz is forced to put in writing some sense of what Cuevas, as a visual artist, does. Instead of describing one painting, Paz choses to give an image of the painter himself as he paints.

Presenting the work itself, as well as the painter behind the work, is what is interesting about Paz's approach; it forces him to look "behind" the painting in order to convey the idea that the painter wants to communicate. This brings the poem closer to the act of criticism—in this case, art criticism, as in "Objetos y apariciones" (Objects and Apparitions) dedicated to Joseph Cornell. There is an enormous risk in this kind of writing:in dedicating a poem to another work of art, Paz apparently turns his poem into a secondary object vis-à-vis the object at hand. The poem becomes an apostrophe, as in the case of Joseph Cornell, or it becomes a description of an image, as in the more direct mention of José Luis Cuevas. And it is this very particular placing of the poem in relation to the work that is being discussed that gives the poem its unique register—one between orality and writing, between critique and pure expressiveness, and that allows Paz to avoid making the poetic self the center of the text. The poet, in his mature phase, turns to the objects produced by others in order to create his own work.

While it is important to explain Paz's texts as ones at the threshold between two texts—visual and verbal—it is important to recall the work that Paz does with the very language of the text. In "Totalidad y fragmento," Paz initially places us in a timeless time, where the poet rips apart pages that become the equivalent of time, of hours, as they themselves are repeated in the text. What is important for Paz in the work of Cuevas is that it illustrates a particularly Mexican "wound": "cada día / José Luis dibuja nuestra herida" (*Poemas* 614) (each day / José Luis paints our wound). This wound, which is linked to the act of ripping apart the pages of a notebook, is not healed but rather painted; in painting the wound, as Paz sees it, Cuevas understands that painting is also related to something else—to a wound that he, in a sense, paints again and again, turning his work into a kind of action painting, one that implicates the page itself on which he paints. The wound (which only appears at the last line) is also related to the lines themselves that Cuevas paints, what Paz calls "un pueblo de líneas" (a nation of lines) or "una tribu de líneas" (a tribe of lines). These lines (which are also related to the poet's own lines on the page) allow Cuevas's paintings to be a synecdoche of the nation—as if the nation itself were contained within those lines. And here is the root of Cuevas's art: by rendering the nation, or its wounds, on a piece of paper, the act of abstraction becomes a paradigmatic, concrete gesture, one that tears the surface of paper and descends to the furthest reaches of painting in a process that, transformed into language, Paz renders as a version of the despair for meaning. In lines, says Paz, Cuevas represents "la filfa el fimo el figo / el hipo el hilo el filo / desfile baboso de bobos bubosos" (*Vuelta* 30). This glossolaliac exercise in sense and nonsense which challenges translation is meant to be the linguistic equivalent to what Cuevas does by hand and with paint, a linguistic equivalent to abstraction.

Paz's poetry after the time spent in Asia becomes less a discovery and more of a rewriting, in the conceptual sense of the word. The 1960s were for Paz the period where he rediscovered the spatial properties of words by creating a geography of the page that corresponded to the yin and yang of his lived geographies; in the 1970s the referent of space became linked to the idea of painting, and the poem itself turns into an idea, or an image. This change needs to be seen in relation to Paz's thinking of the origins of the avant-garde, in texts like *Children of the Mire,* or *El signo y el garabato.* At the end of the nineteenth century, for Mallarmé, the placing of signifiers on the page was related to music and to dance; the corporeal element of language was akin to a corporeal body moving in space. Since the early twentieth century, the image became the central locus of experimental change, with the emphasis in the arts changing, from music to painting. The first avant-garde writers—Apollinaire, Reverdy and, in Latin America, Huidobro—intended to give the written text the same plastic properties that they saw in cubism: a representation not of an object but of an idea. With its geometrical utopias, cubist poetry was always subservient to the radical experimentation of painting; at the same time, however, it sacrificed song, chant, and rhythm. It was possible for cubist painters to give a sense of rhythm to the paintbrush, but such rhythm was elusive in terms of the radical constructions of poets who presented in essence two radically different texts:

one that was seen, and thus, could be appreciated for its plasticity; and another that, when heard, did not give an account of the sense of plasticity underlying it.

Paz chooses a radically different method for approximating poetry to painting. He is not interested in imitating the painting, but rather uncovers the *idea* behind painting. If there is a mimetic urge, it takes place by means of rhythm, as if poetic rhythm were a transposition of action painting on the page. This rhythm, given in "Totalidad y fragmento" is a kind of modular writing, at times even a kind of "speaking in tongues," abandoning itself to a rhythm in writing that attempts to reproduce a trance experience. In a sense, Paz's poems at times seem closer to those of the Argentinean Oliverio Girondo in *En la másmedula.* But the more direct influence for Paz's experimentation with "visual" writing in books such as *Topoemas,* 1968 (*Topoems*) is the work of the Brazilian concrete poets, particularly Haroldo de Campos (also translator of Paz's *Blanco* into Portuguese). The *Topoems* are Paz's most sustained attempt at creating a spatial, as opposed to a discursive, mode of writing. As he himself says in notes to the 1979 edition, they are a recourse against discourse ("Recurso contra el discurso"). Paz did not continue to experiment in this manner, even though in *Vuelta* one can find his "3 anotaciones / rotaciones," related to the *Topoemas.*

Vuelta 1969–1975

Vuelta (*Return*) as the poet himself stated, is the account of the poet's return to Mexico City after a decade mostly spent in Asia. *Vuelta* implies return, but also "repaso" or rewriting. The title itself, as Andrés Sanchez Robayna has explained, proposes an idea of "route," of orderly succession in Paz's poetry.[1] This route has to be seen as a displacement, one that does not in itself follow a chronological order, as many of the poems in the book are in fact written before *The Monkey Grammarian* and, in some cases, are contemporaneous with Paz's *Pasado en claro* (*A Draft of Shadows*). The book offers a paradigmatic image: it marks Paz's "return" to Mexico City; at the same time, it rejects strict chronology. Again, as in *Libertad bajo palabra,* the book constructs another image for time. In this case, the image is that of a poet who will not uncover new territory but who will return to the same themes in order to clarify them. These meditations, centered upon Paz's "return," insist upon the present while also denying history's lineal notions of time, opting for a certain circularity of time proposed by poetry, one that exists in terms of verbal creations that are tied to history but nevertheless are also, in a certain way, suprahistorical, beyond history, in a perpetual present.

In the 1979 edition of his *Poemas,* Paz divided the book into four sections: "Configuraciones" (Configurations), "Ciudad de México" (Mexico City), Confluencias" (Confluences), and "Nocturno de San Ildefonso" (San Ildefonso Nocturne), the latter a long poem in four sections and along with *Sunstone* and *Blanco,* one of Paz's major poems of his later years. As a collection, *Return* is important for two axes that lead from its central section, which carries the same title as the book itself, and is composed of three poems: "Vuelta" (Return), "A la mitad de esta frase" (In the Middle of This Phrase), and "Petrificada petrificante" (The Petrifying Petrified). The second axis of the poem is composed of "San Ildefonso Nocturne." These are the poems that we will study in this section.

"Vuelta"

In "Vuelta" (Return), Paz abandons rhyme and meter and de-composes the elements of a line in order to create phrases that appear at different points upon the white space of the page. There is no punctuation, even if capital letters announce where sentences begin—although we should not speak of sentences but of phrases, instants of a time that is, according to Paz, petrified into voices on the page. According to Claudia Albarrán, this visual arrangement allows the phrases to seem like waves, whose end is in a sense their beginning; they also reinforce the notion of cycle, repetition, and return of which the poem speaks.[2] The effect is not, however, continuous throughout the poem; it is interrupted in a second movement that will be examined below. The cyclical mode of the poem is also demonstrated by the fact that it begins temporally in the morning and concludes at dawn of the next morning; in between, it passes through noon, afternoon, and night. The poem ends, according to this temporal and structural arrangement, with a new dissolving of shapes into the dissolved forms that they had at the beginning of the poem.

The poet hears voices that place him in Mixcoac, in the midst of a backward journey toward a moment where both poet and city abandoned each other. These echoes make the poet feel at a loss in the city. He feels shapeless, form-less, without body; he looks back and does not see himself. The poem's second section describes a point of convergence: Paz will reveal the hidden "catacombs" of the city—where money is incessantly produced and destroyed. This point of convergence also implies a point of desire that corresponds to the outlines of the second section, where the poem enumerates corporeal images that will lead, in the next, to a reincarnation of images of both the collective (Mexican) and the personal past. Return and re-volution (in its sense of movement), describe the structural properties of the poem. But the overwhelming image of the city that the poem gives, as Albarrán explains, is one of a city that is contaminated, infested, putrefying.

Paz's return to the native land, both in body and spirit, is underscored by the quote from Ramón López Velarde that is the poem's epigraph, which talks about a man who fears the differences that he will find upon his return to his native town. What Paz finds in his return to Mexico is an abandoned, dejected city. This return to his native land also implies a reencounter with his own past as well as with the poet's singular and collective sense of identity. Paz superimposes upon this myth of the hero's return his idea of circular time, of an eternal return that is also a cycle of beginnings and endings. This is why the poem ends with the idea of an untouchable present; it is the present itself which is most evanescent in the cycle of repetitions.

"A la mitad de esta frase"

The place of the poet is, as Paz explains, at the center of his own phrase, in a phrase that he has constructed, and by means of which he constructs himself. The poet finds himself within words; these circle around the poet, while he in turn twists and changes them, de-composes and re-composes words in order to find himself within them. This relationship of the poet with his words recalls the main argument in Vicente Huidobro's *Altazor* (1931) one of the major poems of the Spanish American literary tradition. In *Altazor*, Huidobro has his alter ego, a poet whose name is a compound word in itself (composed of "alto" and "azor" [goshawk]), fall into a void that turns out to be language itself. Throughout the seven cantos of the poem, Huidobro composes and de-composes language, he destroys the normal associations between words and creates new words and new associations. As in Paz's third section of "Return," "The Petrifying Petrified," Huidobro at one point composes portmanteau words. For Huidobro, language ends up being as transparent as crystal or as opaque as a rock. In Huidobro's poem, the poet places himself within language in order to defy nature and thus show both nature and the poet as constructions of language. Huidobro argued that the poet had to be, above all, a creator, and that the objects that he created (poems, images within poems) possessed the kind of internal logic, coherence, and independence that was particular to all created objects in nature. The poet, then, does not hold himself at bay; he is a being composed of words, a supreme fiction.

The three sections of "Return" bear a closer comparison to *Altazor*. Not only for the ecstatic language of "The Petrifying Petrified" but also, in "In the Middle of This Phrase" for Paz's naming of his particular, personal route a "nacicaída" (birthfall) (*Poemas* 603). But Paz presents to us the poet in the midst of a nature that is as illusory as he is, thus radically re-reading Huidobro's insistence on the created fact of nature on the page. For Paz, nature is what is written on the page, and the poem is always, in a sense, a rewriting, but these ideas both prove illusory. There is no sense of agonic struggle in Paz's poem, just as Paz does not entertain the sense of directionality that is found in Huidobro, who does structure his poem according to a series of cantos with a certain (albeit interrupted) idea of progression. Paz's notion of an endless cycle of repetitions allows him, as a subject, to join into a general flow. Origins are distant, but endings are perpetually banishing, dissolving themselves into air. In this sense, Huidobro's progressive idea of destruction and creation corresponded to the individual life of the poet as creator, who wanted to discover the rules of nature's way of creating. Paz reads the individual life as part of a vaster cycle where history is a game without rules: one that, in effect, has no rules, because it is a perpetual coming and going without beginning or end.

"Petrificada petrificante"

From its title, "Petrificada petrificante," Paz already posits a certain kind of duality, one that is not necessarily based on opposition but on different ways of apprehending reality. "Petrificada," signals an effect or a result, while "petrificante" suggests a cause. With this image, Paz traces an idea and notion of cause and effect that is at odds with temporality, as if in his world causes seem to be the result of effects. The poem begins with a series of composite or portmanteau words. These initial neologisms have the effect of "petrifying" language, turning words into stones, compressing them in order to form rocks. The meaning of these neologisms (most of them, with some exceptions, are fairly recognizable combinations of words) are mostly negative: "Terramuerta / terrisombra nopaltorio temezquible / lodosa cenipolva pedrósea" (607) ("Deadland / shadowland cactideous nopalopolis / rockboned mudded ashdust" [CP 379]). Because these are words built upon combinations of other words, they refer back to an end process of language; Vicente Huidobro in *Altazor,* or Oliverio Girondo in *En la másmedula* used the same procedure. But by the same token, and because they are ecstatic or sublime exclamations, they seem to be at the beginning of language, as if they were huge continental masses that need to be fragmented. Here, Paz builds a landscape of petrified reality and dryness in order to give an account of a revelation that did not come as expected, of a certain sensation of loss that accompanied an immense historical breakdown, seen in geological terms.

In the second part of the poem, Paz clarifies that he is speaking of Mexico City and of its central place in Mexican history. The poem becomes an invocation to the Valley of Mexico as a demolished ruin—capable of petrifying its inhabitants or its poets even while it is itself petrified in terms of history. Paz's lament on Mexico does not speak of the nostalgia for an irretrievable past. Even while, or because, it is a ruin, the Valley of Mexico (still in its present tense) is like the Medusa's head, capable of petrifying the one who allows himself the enormous risk of gazing into its eyes. Because fragments have an enormous weight in Paz's poetry, the fragments of reality in "Petrificada petrificante" have lost none of their original powers.

Paz sees the Valley of Mexico as a zone where present and past collapse into one. The degeneration of the present is seen at one point as part and parcel of the bloody past that condemns all of the inhabitants of the city, as they all have disinterred Anger. This anger (or, more appropriately Ire) allows Paz to officiate as if he were a priestly shaman, one who condemns the zone itself, its present and its past. Ire dances like the goddess Ishtar over the body of Mexico, while its inhabitants, including the poet himself, seek not the water that prolongs thirst, but another water that quenches Ire and thirst, a water that cannot be seen.

"Nocturno de San Ildefonso"

"Nocturno de San Ildefonso" is a long poem in four sections. The first section describes the position of the speaking subject, in front of a window. As the poet sees the space that surrounds him, this space turns into an *Other.* The image of the window here bears some relationship to the image of the balcony in the poems of *East Slope.* But if in "El balcón" the poet was a silent witness to the millenial history of India, in "Nocturno" the poet begins by tracing a relationship between two spaces: one of the night, outside, and the other, in the page where he is writing, both spaces communicating by means of a metaphorical open window. The window itself, as the space where two realities communicate, becomes a signifying fissure. In the first section, the window metamorphoses into a tunnel, as the page turns into an anthill. The poet falls, and sees himself falling, while the nature that surrounds him disappears, leaving him with an insistent question, posed by night itself, who beckons to the poet. Night propels the poet into the past, allowing him to take leave from temporality. The first section of the poem ends with the fallen poet, seeking to answer a question that is never uttered as such, but that leads to another.

The second section threads the poet's past with the city's. It opens with a splendid image: "Calles vacías, luces tuertas" ("Empty streets, squinting lights" [*CP* 413]) and the shadow or shape of a dog that searches the garbage for a phantom bone. Paz's cinematic procedure apprehends a Mexican scene from around 1931. It is a scene of loneliness, of an abandoned and forlorn urban landscape in the midst of which San Ildefonso, the national preparatory school, appears. The architectural structure itself beckons Paz's meditations on history;

the old city reappears in the poet's memory as a surface that is barely concealed within the school's walls. It is surface itself, "los muros rojos de San Ildefonso" (the red walls of San Ildefonso) that uncovers the idea of space, just as the wind, as it passes on the walls, indifferently rips apart the advertisements that are pasted on it. At this point the singular poet recedes and becomes a collective voice, and the poem yields to the sense of melancholia that the poet saw in the abandoned and empty streets at the beginning. The wide vistas, the near collapse of the poet's own gaze, as sweeping as that of the wind at the beginning of the section, turns him into a sentimental observer of a past unreality. The poet's adolescent reverie takes him back to a time of ideas, whose very surprising, animated speed is given by the mechanical objects—cars, tramways—that partake of the illusions of a century where ideas seemed to be as plentiful as mechanical inventions. At this point, in the past or in the present, the poet is awakened by time, the clocktower pounds twelve times on a doubled space: inciting the dispersal of both the past and the present, as well as of an external but illusory reality reflected on the page.

The second section of "Nocturno de San Ildefonso" ends by positing those four quadrants that are so important for Paz: past, present, external reality, and the page as a surface. This leads to the third section of the poem, where the reverie yields to the lucid discourse of the mature poet. Paz begins the section by explaining the common identity of adolescent and mature poet, and then glosses over the history of his generation, one that participated in history and then became either silent witnesses or willing participants in the century's most infamous events. Paz recounts intellectuals' position in the utopian dreams of socialism and communism since the Spanish civil war. The third section of the poem, then, has to be seen as a discourse of rejection, in the midst of what Paz classifies as an inmense historical error. The intellectual's collaboration with regimes of terror has soiled the very concept and notion of intellectual freedom. In a world that became the representation of infamy ("el 'Gran Teatro del Inmundo'" ("Grand Theater of Filth" [*CP*] 421]) intellectuals had their own specific roles as "jueces, verdugos, víctimas, testigos" (*Poemas* 635) ("judge, executioner, victim, witness" [*CP* 421]). This leads to a central question, the relationship between history and error: "mi historia / ¿son las historias de un error?" (*Poemas* 635) ("my history. / Are they the histories of an error?" [*CP* 421]) as Paz concludes that history itself is an error, that truth is found somewhere else, beyond the narratives that humankind imposes upon time. The question of history as a discourse of nontruth leads Paz at the same time to a defense of poetry. Words uncover truth because poetry is not teleological: it does not think of its ends at its moment of beginnings, but is a road that goes nowhere—or that, at least, has no sense of its ending. Poetry allows for the true essence of time to come to the surface: a perpetual discourse that leads to an awareness of its own passing.

For Paz, poetry allows for a version of history that is closer to our own awareness of time as a fluid "passing"; the poetic experience is a state of being suspended within the hands of time, a perpetual flow that acquires a sense of structure only a posteriori, after the poet's abandoning of himself to the fluidities of time. The poem argues that, in the same manner, history is a structure imposed upon the lived experience; it can never be an a priori awareness of an end that already guides the flow of time. Paz sees the relationship between the poem and time in terms similar to those that he explored in his early poetry; when he talked about waves, for example, where the form arises out of formlessness for an instant and then recedes, goes back, is dispersed into the all. After stating an idea of history, and expressing the poet's act of faith in poetry, the fourth section of "Nocturno de San Ildefonso" dissipates all opposition in order to allow the poet to become One with the All. The poet returns to the window, but this time what he sees are the luminous advertisements of the present, the formlessness of the contemporary city. Beneath or behind it, Paz sees the eternal night sky upon which the present is written, just as the moon writes itself upon the movable surface of the stars.

The poet returns, in the fourth section, to the point of origin, to the room where he is writing and from which he has looked out into the night. The errant poet, who has joined the space of the past with that of the present, by also coalescing the city to the page as it is being written, concludes by positing another vision of eternity within contingency, this time by expressing the contingent and quotidian scene of his wife's sleeping in bed and projecting it toward eternity. The couple is a modern-day Adam and Eve, but this time seeking their own paradise within the boundless walls of a room where the poet looks out into the night. As in Paz's early poetry, the body of the woman is confused, collapsed with the body of nature, and is thus seen as presence, as evidence of the kind of attitude toward writing at the center of Paz's desires. The poem concludes with the poet's wanting to give himself over to the calmed fluidity whose emblem is the body of the sleeping woman.

As Pere Gimferrer has stated in his lucid commentary on "Nocturno de San Ildefonso," the text is similar to *Sunstone* and *Blanco*.[3] As in *Blanco,* its central scene allows for the representation of the poet writing while the woman is sleeping; and his meditations follow, chromatically, the same gamut of colors as those seen in *Blanco* ("del amarillo al verde al rojo" [from yellow to green to red]). As in *Sunstone,* the poem detains itself on a particular epiphanic instant. It also concerns the story of the poet who, from pure contemplation, allows himself to fall, while his fall incarnates the concrete past of a generation. As Gimferrer clarifies, the general question as to the nature of evil in the world is here answered concretely: evil in this case concerns the abandoning of the concrete man or woman for the sake of abstract ideas of good and evil. The past that serves as the point of departure for Paz's meditation lies in the old school of San Ildefonso; what it rescues is the vision and the image of the city as Cortés and Bernal Díaz del Castillo saw it when, full of ideals and ideas, they launched the conquest of Mexico. But the splendor of the past lies in ruins within the structure that used to house the academy of ideas. The combination of this "didactic" imperative on personal and collective history, joined to the "poetic" imperative that is at the root of the poem, shows that Paz has been able to coalesce, in his writing, two spheres of thought that lie at the origins of the modern age: the relationship between history and poetry, as well as that between the poet and writing. In Paz's work these are all different axes that meet on the space of the text, and in "Nocturno de San Ildefonso," they are the signs that gyrate around the poet, who is himself an image, one sign among others.

A Draft of Shadows (1974)

The title *A Draft of Shadows* refers to something written once again; this rewriting, however, also entails an act of clarification upon the past. In both cases, the poem speaks of the route of the poet and the relationship between past and present. In "Nocturno de San Ildefonso," the words allowed the poet himself to follow the route of language, manifested in the poem; *Blanco* is the poem of moving from one space to the other, of allowing words themselves to move upon a space that is movable. In *A Draft of Shadows* the poet mentions a kind of route, a *reverie,* but its idea of journey is more conceptual.

As befits a poem written after *Blanco, A Draft of Shadows* refers to the transforming of nature into signifiers on a page seen as a kind of transparent surface. For Paz, writing itself consists of a route, of a journey; metaphor itself entails apprehending properties that are moved, displaced, from one site to another in space. The route of the poem, then, consists of allowing the text to be the point of intersection, where nature becomes words and words assume the properties of a reality that is never entirely outside the page. The poem slowly configures this route from its beginning. The route consists, as the poem begins, of "pasos mentales más que sombras" [mental footsteps more than shadows]. This second verse allows us to see a relationship where steps and shadows are always held in a state of communicative tension. That steps would be heard over a route composed of echoes gives an elusive quality to that which is being transformed, brought onto the page in the seventh line of the poem, which identifies the present moment not with words as these appear on the page, but rather with the spaces, the silences, the invisible bridges between one letter and the next. All that the poet attempts to grasp turns into air, into nothingness, while an opaque sun, perpetually in the process of dawn, is brought into words that are seen as ruins of a previous expression.

One cannot call what appears in "A Draft of Shadows" a landscape in any proper sense of the term, but rather a site that is inside and outside, at the same time. It is, in the fashion of the English Romantics, a "landscape of the mind." The poet follows the meanderings of language conceived as a river, a source, in a tensionless flow where the more the poet distances himself from himself, the more he encounters himself. This encounter takes the poet toward the garden, one of Paz's emblematic places, which he enters by means of a fall occuring in an interval, between one instant and the next. This instant leads the poet into the abandoned garden whence he propels himself to another, physical fall into a well that is also seen as an eye—an internal eye where the poet's shadow has been eternally falling, in a timeless, all-encompassing fall. Shadows in this poem are memories, but they also represent figures that are incorporeal before they are brought into the page. Hence the particular disruption of elements that may go up or down: "el pozo de la cuenta de mi cuento / por donde sube el agua y baja / mi sombra" ("the well of the account of my account / where the water rises / and my shadow falls" [*CP* 434–35]). The act of translating from a reality that is nowhere onto the space of the page, demands this kind of inversion, the point of contact precisely marked by this exchange between water and shadows.

On one level, "A Draft of Shadows" is about translation. The poem breaks itself in different spaces, but what is marked between one section and the next are different scenes that arise in order to disappear once again. The poet reads a book that seems to talk about Tenochtitlán and ancient Mexico; a solitary *piragua* (canoe) resembles the horizontal comma of a book. By focusing on translation, the poet becomes a mere conduit, and the poem the copy of another book that, by virtue of rewriting, has become more real, turning its pages into embers that the sun fires up. Letters are seen as leaves of a tree; but the real leaves of the tree disappear, and memory becomes not the lagoon that illuminates the pages of the book read and copied by the poet, but a mere "charco," a puddle. In this poetic route, memory is the result of the fact that the poet feels spied upon, looked upon by words that are leaves, but are also the doors for perception, the eyes of the poet. Just like those steps / shadows at the beginning of the poem were heard with the soul and not with the ears, at this point words become the poet's eyes. Eyes and words are seen as the concrete traces of things that existed in some some previous time.

"A Draft of Shadows" is a poem of re-reading, not of rewriting. Here Paz looks into the past and sees that words provide an essence that proves the corporeality of an existence. Words become objects in this landscape, as was also the case with the project that underlied the experimental urge of *Blanco.* If this was the utopian dream and the possibility of language present in Paz's other long poems, in *A Draft of Shadows* the past only carries the weight of its own syllables. The repeated mention of books, along with a descriptive, meditative tone born out of the poet's vision of timelessness allows "A Draft of Shadows" to be a poem of internal spaces, of discourse that flows unto itself. The solipsistic poet is the one that reads and sees himself reading. From here on, Paz's work will delve with increasing frequency into this internal space.

A Tree Within (1987)

Paz's poetry always named a particular scene or landcape by means of one or two elements that metonymically render the whole. In *East Slope,* the poet aims for a sense of natural grandeur by simply focusing on two crows on top of a wall, or the outline of jagged peaks. Only when Paz approaches the city, does the poetry imitate the confusion of the urban milieu. Nature precludes chaos, which always seems to be a human creation. Nature is ordered and orderly—and the subject's agony precisely arises out of the inescrutability of that order, whose hidden keys are always beyond the poet's reach. Paz's vision of nature is metonymical, he apprehends by means of synecdoche, thus giving the idea that the totality of nature (of a nature to which Man belongs) is always beyond reach except through intimations of fragments—this is not so in the case of human creations, which Man endows with meaning, even within multiplicity.

In his previous books, as well as in *A Tree Within,* Paz allowed the reader to understand that this gesture in relation to nature entailed a poetics, a way of conceiving poetry in relation to itself and to the world. This poetics saw poems as fragmented totalities that invoked the absolute by their own act of negation, by their refraction of reality. The poetics of the text reflected the poet's own facing of reality; the poet is also a refractory being who negates his self while illuminating those natural fragments that appear on the page. In both cases, Paz highlights nature as if by a poetic thunderbolt; the poem is a collection of distinct flashes of lightning.

A Tree Within is a collection that sums up previous work. What we have come to expect from Paz at least since *Salamandra* are not abrupt changes in terms of form or content but rather revisions and variations, swerves, as well as a desire to piece together the different aspects of an already vast work—if not into a system, at least into a coherent, all-encompassing figure. This refusal to engage in sudden and abrupt changes is what allows us to see that in Paz's poetry ideas become clearer in repetition. It is within repetition and sameness that the new occurs in Paz's work, the discrete revision that every new poetic text entails.

In *A Tree Within,* Paz repeats a discourse of the self that the reader has already encountered; his beliefs, his memories of childhood, his vision of eros as a primordial mover of the world—all these appear in this collection along with some of Paz's more poignant intimations of death. Because death seems to be so close, *A Tree Within* becomes a preparation, as can be seen in "Ejercicio preparatorio" (Preparatory Exercise) a tryptich—the third part a kind of votive tablet in which the poet stoically prepares himself for death. This poem is not so much a lamentation of loss as a preparatory "deprecation" (in his own words) of ego in terms that correspond to a kind of Buddhist contemplation of emptiness.

Death, love, and friendship are the fundamental themes in *A Tree Within.* Many of its texts are dedicated to friends, to important people that were crucial in the latter period of Paz's life—intellectuals, academics, painters and writers. The private act of remembering in verse is linked to the preparation for an impending death; both, at the same time, are joined to a poetics. The poet here is a friend who remembers, who tries to bridge the distance between, on the one hand, the pleasures of friendship, and on the other, the exchange between reader and text. It is in order to bring the reader closer to the text that Paz also allows himself to explore his links with others. These two links explain not only the nature of the text, but also the poet's meditations on death. "A Tree Within," the poem that gives title to the collection, invites the reader to partake in the poet's inner landscape:

> Amanece
> en la noche del cuerpo.
> Allá adentro, en mi frente,
> el árbol habla.
>
> Acércate, ¿lo oyes?
>
> (*AA* 137)

> Day breaks
> in the body's night.
> There, within, inside my head,
> the tree speaks.
>
> Come closer—can you hear it?
>
> (*CP* 595)

The poem plays with distance and immediacy, by presenting first of all a tree that has become another body within the poet. But this inner tree yields its fruits only by means of another's gaze, one that is responsible not only for its "frutos de sombras" (fruits of shade) but also for a particular distancing produced within the poet's self, who then curiously abstracts himself from his body. This separation from the self allows the poet not only to portray himself on paper, but also to beckon the reader to the open space of his inner self. The text's notion of "internal" growth paradoxically turns the poet's inner thoughts into transparent meditations. This transparency, where nothing is hidden but everything is "inside," allows Paz to think openly about death as a veil that will be neither more tragic or meaningful than life.

That many of the poems in *A Tree Within* are dedicated to people that Paz has known throws light on Paz's self-awareness as a public figure; the poems themselves become a diary of lived experience. But these texts also make explicit a poetics that Paz has explored at least since *The Bow and the Lyre:* poems are irrepeatable instances of time, lightning bolts that illuminate specific moments. This is why many of the texts written in homage to others are not really about a particular "narrative"—history of the friendship, say—but rather about an image of the person to whom the poem is addressed. The narrative is found, however, in the section of notes appended to the book as a whole. For example, "Decir: hacer" ("Between What I See and What I Say," titled changed in English [*CP* 485]) the second poem of the collection, is dedicated to the eminent linguist Roman Jakobson. It is a poem where Paz uses linguistics as a point of departure for his own thoughts on poetics. Paz explains that if for Jakobson language was a system where the axis of selection was joined to the axis of combination, allowing poetry to mobilize metaphor and metonymy, then for the poet the double axis is resolved into one, where poetry becomes a *saying* that is akin to a *doing*. For Paz, poetry literalizes metaphor and metonymy, while it is at the same time, a metaphor for something else. Paz had already commented on Jakobson in sections of *The Bow and the Lyre,* and in *Claude Lévi-Strauss: An Introduction.* The difference between those comments and the poem in *A Tree Within* is not simply one of genre. In the poems Paz joins Jakobson to linguistics, in order to create a theory of the poetic act that is also illustrated by the poem itself—not an exposition of Jakobson's linguistics, as much as another version of it.

What makes "Decir: hacer" paradigmatic of many of the poems that Paz dedicates to others in *A Tree Within* is that in the section of notes appended at the conclusion of the book, Paz reproduces a conference from 1982, where he renders homage to Jakobson's words, and at the same time narrates part of his encounters in Cambridge with Jakobson. Thus, within the same book, we find a poem dedicated to Jakobson, a minor essay, and a reminiscence. What strikes the reader is not only the relationship between these three different modes of apprehending Jakobson, but the tripartite function of the writer as poet, essayist, and autobiographer. Paz's attempts to join these three modes at the same time ensures that the boundaries between the three genres are distinct but porous. This is in marked and almost exact contrast to, for example, "The Prisoner" (the poem that Paz dedicated to the marquis de Sade in *Libertad bajo palabra*) which is written in an almost essayistic manner. The poems that can be compared to "The Prisoner" in this collection are "Refutación de los espejos" (Refutation of Mirrors) which is dedicated to, and includes fragments of poems by, José Lezama Lima, as well as "Fábula de Joan Miró" (A fable of Joan Miró), "Kosta," and, particularly, "La casa de la mirada" (The House of Glances). The latter two, particularly "The House of Glances," are accompanied by essays that are also personal reminiscences. In one of his notes, Paz explains how blurred the lines are between poetry and prose, although his examples are not particularly poems like "Refutation of Mirrors" but rather "Proema" (Proem), "Hablo de la ciudad" (I Speak of the City) and "Esto y esto y esto" (This and This and This).

The link between notes and poems is part of the wider poetics of *A Tree Within,* one whose open intention is that of bringing the text closer to the reader but whose ultimate aim is to represent the poet preparing himself for death. This aim can be seen in Paz's introductory statements (not translated in the English edition of his work) to these notes, where he creates a poetics of circumstantiality in order to explain the texts. Paz rightly claims that the notes explain neither the poetic act, nor the poems themselves. In that sense, the reader may agree with Paz that they are unnecessary, or at least that they add nothing to the understanding of the poem as such. These claims (a kind of *excusatio*) Paz had also made in his edition of *Poemas.* Both in this latter book as well as in *A Tree Within,* Paz insists that what is *accidentally* born is precisely the poem and not the note: that the poem is a result of circumstance, whereas the note seeks to explain the event. But the reader that goes to the notes in order to seek an explanation of the circumstance (that is, the concrete instance that provoked a poem on Jakobson, or on Miró, along with what Paz was thinking at the moment, and so forth) will not find such an *explication du texte* but rather a sweeping narrative, in most cases, one excluded from the poems themselves.

Paz argues that the relationship between poetry and prose has differed among poets. Certain poets, like Dante or Basho, who transform circumstance into context, give us a clue as to how a poem is to be read (allegorically, for example, in the case of Dante). Paz does not object to that impulse but also explains that it is not his own: his notes, as he implicitly says, are not meant to fix the poem within a particular mode of reading; what he aims to do is to bridge the distance between the poem and the reader: "acercar el texto al lector" (*AA* 178) (place the text closer to the reader). The possible distance or closeness between text and reader in *A Tree Within* is mediated, then, by the poet; particularly, by the poet's public life, in his relations with other artists who are also his contemporaries, a relation that had already appeared in *Salamandra* as well as in *Vuelta*. But Paz's use of biographical discourse establishes the particular circuit for these texts: from poetry, to biography, and then back to the poem, which is then understood, or replayed, in a second reading; that is, in a "closer" fashion. The relationship between act and context (or between "decir" and "hacer" in the poem on Jakobson) forecloses, to a certain extent, the poem's creation of its own context, particularly when other public figures appear. As long as the poem is about the poet himself or about his life, poetry is able to create the contextual situation of its own reading. But as soon as the poem deals with other figures (Kostas) or with their art (Matta) or system of thought (as in Jakobson) the poem demands a double reading (a meta-narrative) whose keys need to be found within the context that Paz narratively performs.

The reader could imagine that the obligatory question in these cases is, To what extent is the poem intelligible without the narrative that Paz provides? This question could be explored in two cases. The first, for example, would be the poem dedicated to Antoni Tàpies, which follows texts included in *Vuelta* or in *Salamandra,* where Paz aims to translate, in words, what the painter seeks to do in the canvas; the other, "La casa giratoria" to Ivar and Astrid, friends in Oklahoma, is given without biographical information. In both of these cases it is clear that circumstantiality works in different ways; at some points the referent is a given work and in others, a particular instance whose context the poem in itself explains. Paz does not provide an explanatory note for these poems as he does in "Kostas" and in "La casa de la mirada." In the former, the poem is not meant to be seen as the supplement of lived experience or of a work; the notes appended to the latter poems, however, establish the texts as somehow supplementary to lived experience. Paz's desire for reader and text to embrace, mediated by his own person, aims for a fusion of the two. And it is within this fusion, related as well to the notion of accident and circumstance, that Paz will explore the concrete meaning of death within his own life.

Because all of the themes included in *A Tree Within* seem to speak of a poet still in the midst of a very active life, the theme of death comes as a surprise to the reader. But this "surprise" is one of Paz's themes in this collection; life, understood as human exchange, as friendship, needs to be seen in conjunction with death. This is particularly the case in "Ejercicio preparatorio (díptico con tablilla votiva)" (Preparatory Exercise—Diptych with Votive Tablet) divided, as explained in the subtitle, into two parts or "tableros" (diptych) titled "Meditación" (Meditation) and "Rememoración" (Remembrance) and a votive tablet, titled "Deprecación" (Deprecation). The exercise is intended to be religious in nature, as can be seen by Paz's mention of a diptych, with its reminiscence to icons or prayer tablets.

The first "Meditación" opens with a quote from Michel de Montaigne, from the essay titled "That to philosophize is to learn to die."[4] The fragment that Paz quotes says, in its entirety: "It is uncertain where death awaits us; let us await it everywhere. Premeditation of death is premeditation of freedom. He who has learned how to die has unlearned how to be a slave. Knowing how to die frees us from all subjection and constraint" (60). The gist of Montaigne's stoic argument in this essay is that death must not be feared but rather accepted, or at least, death "must be rid of its strangeness" (60) and all beings must be continually prepared for death as it is as much a part of nature as birth is: "What stupidity to torment ourselves about passing into exemption from all torment! As our birth brought us the birth of all things, so will our death bring us the death of all things. . . . Death is the origin of another life. Just so did we weep, just so did we struggle against entering this life, just so did we strip off our former veil when we entered it" (64). At the conclusion to this essay, Montaigne ponders why is it that in wars "the face of death, whether we see it in ourselves or in others, seems to us incomparably less terrifying that in our houses" (67–68). He concludes that it is the trappings of the death scene at home that mask death. A masked death, Montaigne explains, is more terrifying than death itself: "We must strip the mask from things as well as from persons; when it is off, we shall find beneath only that same death which a valet or a mere chambermaid passed through not long ago without fear. Happy the death that leaves no leisure for preparing such ceremonies!" (68).

Montaigne's concluding scene in his essay is the point of departure for Paz's "Ejercicio preparatorio," not only because throughout Paz's poem there is continuous mention of faces and masks, but also because Paz creates this exercise as the prelude to a stoic acceptance of death, in order ultimately to deny the terrifying aspects of death in its last "Deprecación." At the beginning of his essay Montaigne quotes and questions Cicero's statement that to philosophize is to prepare ourselves for death, since "study and contemplation draw our soul out of us to some extent and keep it busy outside the body" (56). Paz's poem begins precisely with a book that the poet abruptly closes while he suspects another's presence "spying" his thoughts behind a door. This nameless, faceless being will reappear throughout this first section of the poem, which is a mediation between the irrefutable reality of things—the poet's writing table, his book, the window—and the poet's apprehension of his self as a being that "thinks that he is not thinking." This mode of perceiving oneself as an Other, one who cannot think except by being aware that he is not thinking, is not the sign of death itself, but rather a way of conceptualizing death. Death, as the absolute instant, is only conceivable for Paz in terms of a displacement, as the absolute is in itself impossible to perceive. One can only be closer to death as an "imminencia que se desvanece / en un aquí mismo / más allá siempre." (*AA* 92) ("an imminence that vanishes / in a here / forever beyond, out there" [*CP* 553]). Following Montaigne's meditation, Paz insists that he wants to die knowing that he is dying: he refuses a death "outside" and prefers a death shorn of its masks. Following Montaigne, the poet declares himself to be at some point the master of his death, the one who creates and is created by an intimate, personal death: "Es mi creación y soy su criatura" (*AA* 93) ("It is my creation and I am its creature" [*CP* 555]).

The preparatory exercise is, then, merely the preparation for what will be. But it is also a *delusion* as to what will be. Montaigne's refusal to allow philosophy as an exercise for death is a double-edged sword. For Montaigne writes a philosophical essay that denies the idea it exposes: that the mere fact of preparing oneself to die entails a certain kind of fear of death. Similarly, Paz understands that no preparation for death can ever reveal one's face as that of death; it can only reveal the illusion and the mask that is faceless, as its face is composed of the self. This is why "Rememoración," the second "panel" of the poem, opens with a sentence from Cervantes's *Don Quijote* whose subject, "la muerte" (death) has been erased from the fragment that Paz quotes. This fragment is from *Don Quijote*'s last chapter, the first speech made by an Alonso Quijano that rejects his previous self as the errant knight and wants to prepare for death accordingly—by allowing himself the lucidity of a final instance, one that will rewrite his life as an act of folly from which death is a new beginning. Don Quijote's words underscore death as an instant where the true self of man is revealed from among the delusions of a past where life was lived according to the dictates of books of chivalry.

Paz includes the book that he is reading and quoting within the fabric of the poem, as he did in the first section. If "Meditación" puts the reader at the moment where the book is abandoned, "Rememoración" signals a return to the book, in a movement diametrically opposed to that of Don Quijote (who at the moment of death abandons all book knowledge) in order to remember the poet's life. The poet's memory is preceded by a meditation on a time that undermines itself; in Paz's words, time becomes a mask without a face. This insistence on faceless, maskless time can be traced back to Paz's "Máscaras del alba" on the Venetian carnival, included in *La estación ardiente*. The masks there were ripped apart in order to reflect, at dawn, desire's mechanical circuit of abandon. Here, if time is a mask with no face, death is what gives us both a face and a name that will dissipate into a nameless, faceless void. The poet tries to place himself at the moment of death, but all preparation seems to be part of a fiction of desire—a way of putting yet another mask, of creating another fiction. This awareness sends him toward a past where the poet is a reader within a space where nature is read as a book, and where the book mediates between ever-changing, violent nature, and the poet's desire for permanence. Reading is a fragile armistice placed between the poet and nature; it allows him to understand the other life that is lived within books, one that helps him to distinguish between what is lived and what is read: "Páginas más vividas que leídas / en las tardes fluviales" (*AA* 97) ("Pages more lived than read / in the fluvial after-noons" [*CP* 559]).

Memory, like reading, creates another present. Reading is the only analogy we have for understanding life; the irony of death is that one abandons the book that is read in order to read the book of one's life with closed eyes. What the knight sees upon the moment of death is a face that is his own and that allows him the moment of lucidity where no other masks can be seen, and where Man can no longer allow himself to play hide-and-seek with his soul. No Other takes the place of the one whose face is sheer, concrete substance. The gaze of the self returns an image of time and space dissolving into a liquid nothingness.

To meditate, or to prepare oneself for death by means of poetry, has to be, for Paz, a paradoxical act. Poetry is the realm of imminence, it is also the site where the poet as Other becomes aware of his mask and deploys it on the page. The idea of otherness, for Paz, is related to the writing of poetry, as poetry invents the other that is oneself. But poetry also returns the true face of the poet; it is an expression that the poet creates in order to define himself. Like that death, which in the first part of this text is both the poet's creator as well as his invention, poetry will also invent the poet. Like *Blanco,* "Ejercicio preparatorio" seems to be a kind of prayer-poem, and like the former text, its third section, "Deprecación" begins with a circuit that resolves itself in a moment where the soul becomes transparent lucidity. This is not to be understood as an "illumina-tion" but as an instantaneous awareness and consciousness of time. Philosophy, according to Montaigne, deludes the subject into fear of death. Paz's apparent impatience with Montaigne's book in the first part of his "Ejercicio preparatorio" revises his precursor by projecting his insights into death by means of poetry, an experience where the soul always creates an Other that is the self. Unlike prose, poetry writes the poet, and words in liberty allow for the soul's liberation. But poetry cannot take the poet to the instant of death without engaging in illusion and fallacy. What poetry *can* provide is something akin to a prayer: it can speak for desire but not for a moment where desire ceases to be. Thus, to prepare oneself for death via poetry can only imply a desire for a kind of death that is a reconciliation with both the fictions as well as the perceived realities of the self. This reconciliation is akin to the act of reading; our only metaphor for life still takes the form of a book. The impatience with the book that Paz shows at the beginning of his text is also an impatience with life, as well as a desire for death—for a knowledge that is beyond that which can be offered by a book. There are times when bookish knowledge does not offer a mediation, and at such points the book needs to be closed; its reality is but a vain consolation for the sake of another desire.

"Ejercicio preparatorio" with its references to book knowledge (Montaigne, Cervantes, Horace) is at the center of a book of poems that treats the poet's life as a text. Hence, the implicit tension alluded to before, where a meditation, or a preparation for death, is found amid poems that talk about very public friendships that Paz has sustained in his life. But *A Tree Within* is concerned with these two aspects of the poet's circumstance: if in other books Paz joined eros and death, in this book Paz is more concerned with friendship and death—friendship seen as one of the possible translations of love, as he goes on to explain in *The Double Flame.* Others are also part of the specificity of life and it is for the sake of the memory of those others that Paz wants to narrow the distance between reader and text.

At the same time, one notices in *A Tree Within* a certain impatience with a life that increasingly resembles a public and open book; this impatience, however, is seen chiefly by Paz's ironic quoting of classical modes, as in "Dístico y variaciones," where one sentence is repeated in pantheistic, Christian, hermetic, gnostic and dialectical modes, and the main focus of change between the different philosophical doctrines is found in the adjective used to describe the rhythmic conjunctions between speech and the universe. Thus, the pantheist would say, "La lengua y sus sagradas conjunciones: / riman constelaciones y escorpiones" (*AA* 24) ("Language and its sacred conjunctions: / constellations and crustaceans rhyme" [*CP* 497]) while the Christian will vary and repeat, "La lengua y sus perversas conjunciones: / riman constelaciones y escorpiones" (*AA* 24) ("Language and its perverse conjunctions: constellations and crustaceans rhyme" [*CP* 497]). The never-ending conjunctions between the different philosophies themselves lead to a rhythmic void that after a series of mutations conclude with an "Etcétera" that perhaps represents the poet's postphilosophical disenchantment, one that levels the playing field, that exhausts all philosophies as mechanical operations. In "Ejemplo," Paz goes back to the ancient Chinese riddle of Chuang-Tzu, but instead of repeating that Chuang-Tzu does not know if he dreams of a butterfly or if the butterfly dreams of Chuang-Tzu (instead of seeing it as paradox and undecipherability), he sees doubt as the province of the philosopher: "La mariposa no dudaba: volaba" (*AA* 16) ("The butterfly never wondered: it flew" [*CP* 489]). What this poem shows is an impatience with paradox; the assertion that insists on the butterfly's sheer motion as a way of eliminating paradox and doubt is of the same nature as that which makes the poet close the book impatiently at the beginning of "Ejercicio preparatorio."

In "Carta de creencia" (Letter of Testimony), the final text from this book, Paz has written a poem structured in the mode of a cantata, with three sections closed off by a coda. Once again, as in his previous poetry, love allows for the final reconciliation between loneliness and the company of others. The poet returns to the site of the original myth, to the Garden and its sense of protection and bliss. Love, finally, plants the tree within the garden and with this image, the poet once again returns to his beginnings:

> Tu mirada es sembradora.
> Plantó un árbol.
>> Yo hablo
> porque tu meces los follajes.

>>>> (*AA* 174)

> Your glance scatters seeds.
> It planted a tree
>> I talk
> because you shake its leaves

>>>> (*CP* 635)

CHAPTER 8

Conclusion

Octavio Paz has dedicated "Contar y cantar (sobre el poema extenso)" to the question of what a long poem is.[1] For Paz, each culture has a different idea of length when it comes to poetry; what for the Hindu may be a short fragment, could be a long poem for the Japanese. After stressing that culture defines the external criteria by means of which a work of art is classified or read, Paz argues for a more structural definition of the category "long poem." A long poem is defined according to a balance between unity of purpose and variety of means; a principle of difference is always related to an equivalent principle of unity. If by means of the interplay between one and the other, Paz measures the relative structural complexity of poems, then this interplay is the best criterion to use in order to understand Paz's work.

In terms of the poetics that underlies the verse, Paz is always a poet of epiphanies. He initially perceives the poetic instant and then develops it into a comprehensive system, born out of a series of contradictory, dialectical steps. Formed as part of the generation that created the literary magazine *Taller* in 1938 both his poetry and his thought arise out of a sequence of contrary elements: an ambiguous relationship to his immediate precursors (the *Contemporáneos* generation) allows poets like Paz to try to bridge the distance between aesthetics and politics, between social demands and the demands of art. This attempt can be seen in Paz's initial poetic texts: they validate the poetic instant as a sublime moment of truth, but this truth is always followed by the inevitable encounter with a reality that offers the consolation and hope that the poet will be visited, once again, by that instant of time which allows him to perceive the unity of the self. Paz conceived his work as mediation between contraries, and thus developed a vision of poetry that insisted on seeing it as a moment of conjunction between two opposite, but increasingly complementary, poles. At the risk of allowing the poet's biography to overdetermine a reading of the work, we can say that Paz's poetics arises and develops out of a series of dialectical principles that in great measure are a function of the time and place in which he lived.

In later accounts of his poetic beginnings, most notably in the long essay that he dedicates to the journal *Taller* (included in *Sombras de obras*) Paz states that his generation considered itself heir to more than thirty years of artistic and aesthetic experimentation (*SO* 103). But what at one point is an attempt to unify the tradition under a common rubric (experimentation) was also (and Paz insisted on this) the opposing of fields that artists needed to reconcile. Thus, Paz's work always operates between two terms of a given dialectic, where the terms of the dialectics themselves evolve over time. From "Poesía de soledad y poesía de comunión" (one of the first attempts to frame the two sides of a debate), to his last texts, Paz moves in a dialectical realm whose terms are invariably substituted one for the other: politics and aesthetics, nature and culture, East and West, poetry and prose. Even the titles of his works give an account of the system: *The Bow and the Lyre, Libertad bajo palabra, Conjunctions and Disjunctions*. All of the terms of the dialectic form what Paz later called a sy-tem of rotating signs, where the terms themselves are the illusory incarnation, in time, of a dialectical sequence that, in the long count, appeared in different guises at different times. It is hard not to see this work within its historical context from the initial turmoil of the civil war in Spain, through the Second World War and the division of the world into the two opposing camps of the cold war. As if to entertain an analogy between history and work that Paz would not necessarily have objected to, one could see in Paz's dialectical bent a reflection of his times.

Paz's essays seem to have been conceived to explain questions beckoned by the poetry itself, as in "Poesía de soledad, poesía de comunión," or as attempts to sketch what would later be found in poems such as "Entre la piedra y la flor." After Paz's departure from Mexico to the United States, on a Guggenheim Fellowship, the essay becomes prominent in Paz's oeuvre. In this sense, we can say that the realm of poetry—of the instant, or of the epiphany in time—is marked and bounded off by an essayistic prose. If poetry is the realm of the instant, of the concrete political condemnation or complaint (as in "Entre la piedra y la flor"), or of the lyrical expression of the poet, the essay becomes an exercise in cultural—not just poetical—interpretation. Paz's first forays into an organized and coherent poetics are generally about culture, and the essay is to culture what poetry is to nature.

The boundaries between essayistic and poetic texts will be more porous after *The Labyrinth of Solitude* and *The Bow and the Lyre.* We have explored the relationship between these two fundamental essays and Paz's poetry, and seen to what extent essayistic concerns spill over onto the poetry. But we must not lose sight of the immense reorganization of Paz's existing work that accompanies the publication of these two books. Indeed, the first edition of *Libertad bajo palabra* is roughly contemporary to *The Labyrinth of Solitude* and to *The Bow and the Lyre*. What these gestures belie is that reorganization is part and parcel of a process of rewriting whose model is the essayistic text. Paz, as we have seen, is not a poet of radical shifts; his changes are more subtle. However, the subtleness of his changes cloaks a progressive transformation of the relationship between poetry and essay. This relationship is altered, particularly since *The Labyrinth of Solitude,* so that at times the poetry seems to be the hermeneutic translation for the essay itself. Particularly in *The Bow and the Lyre,* Paz distinguishes between the two genres, but only to the extent that poetry is endowed with imminent signifiers, with an expression irreducible to any other. The book of poems will also mask as essay and as diary, as in *East Slope.*

Both the essayistic and the poetic genre show moments of change that may be plotted with relative certainty, according to the changes in Paz's life. The relationship between the poet's biography and his work is, in this sense, relatively clear: the narrative of the poet's life is always at the background, even if, in *Libertad bajo palabra,* there has been a subtle rearrangement of those periods, as we saw in chapter 2. The points of change that have been concretely examined in *Libertad bajo palabra* fall roughly around the time of *Calamidades y milagros* and before *La estación ardiente,* one of the most important books of Paz's early period. Both of these periods fall roughly around the late 1940s to mid-1950s, and also coincide with the publication of *The Labyrinth of Solitude,* of *The Bow and the Lyre,* as well as with the initial publication of *Libertad bajo palabra.*

During the late 1950s and early 1960s Paz prepares the most important work of his career. Between the first and the second edition of *The Bow and the Lyre* (1956, 1967) Paz read Roman Jakobson and Claude Lévi-Strauss, and this structuralist filiation will be important for his work both in poetry and essay during the 1960s in India. Around the mid- to late 1960s, Paz greatly restructures his work, culminating in *Blanco,* conceived as a kind of middle period, when the poet enters the fifth decade of his life. Although critics have generally seen *Salamandra* as the point of origin for a new idea of verse, *Blanco* should not be underestimated. If Paz before the 1960s was concerned with the relationships between poetry and essay, after this decade Paz was more concerned with poetry as translation.

As Jorge Castañeda has remarked in his recent *Utopia Unarmed,* Latin American intellectuals are a particular class unto themselves, mediators or intermediaries between the internal political situation of their countries of origin and these countries' relationships to the outside world. In their aesthetic shifts, in

179

their sometimes polemical relations with authority, in their critical stance toward ideology, Latin American intellectuals have sustained a dialogue with the very history that was going on around them, regardless of whether this dialogue assumed the form of a monologue, of a retrenchment, or a contestation.

Octavio Paz was the marginalized intellectual at a time of nationalist fervor ("Vigilias, Diario de un Soñador," 1930s) (Diary of a Dreamer), the explicator of national myths (*The Labyrinth of Solitude,* 1940), the rebellious voice of the cosmopolitanism of the 1960s (*Ladera este,* 1968), the follower of the Third World's increasing importance during the same time; the polemical and intractable voice during the Central American crisis of the 1980s; the chronicler of the collapse of the Soviet Union and the Eastern Bloc. All of these have found a place in a work so intertwined with Mexico that in 1989 the Nobel Prize committee seemed to be conferring its prize for literature not only to Paz himself but to Mexico as a whole—a nation that in a sense Paz invented as a tapestry made out of disparate threads, re-formed as different plateaus engaged in a collective and individual struggle with modernity.

Paz consistently argued for the reader to collapse two texts, to see the singular in reference to the collective, the poetic in relation to the political, solitude in terms of the community, the singular life as an allegorical figure of modernity. These two texts are actually a combination, an interplay of what Paz would call conjunctions or disjunctions, where there is always dialectics, and not merely opposition, between the individual and the collective, East to West, subject and nation. Paz understood that Latin American poets and writers are always in the position of representing something other than their own individuality—the life of the nation, the movement of history, the voice of the multitudes—and he made of this curse an ambiguous blessing. He defined his voice as that of Mexico's, but his definition of Mexico goes beyond the polemics of Hispanists or anti-Hispanists. It is rather, the voice of an ex-centric, suburban emanation of the West. One could say that Paz wrote and rewrote his own life in almost transparent ink, and held himself as the key to some hidden structure whose very existence is always, constantly, put into question.

Notes

Chapter One: Overview

1. "Etica del artista," in *Primeras letras,* 113. Page numbers appear in parenthesis.

2. Jason Wilson, *Octavio Paz: A Study of His Poetics* (Cambridge: Cambridge University Press, 1979), 22.

3. "El surrealismo" in *Las peras del olmo* (Barcelona: Seix Barral, 1971), 150–151.

4. See Emir Rodríguez Monegal, *Pablo Neruda: El viajero inmóvil* (Buenos Aires: Losada, 1966).

Chapter Two: *Libertad bajo palabra* [1935–1957]

1. *Libertad bajo palabra,* 1960 ed., 7. Cited in Santí, ed. *Libertad bajo palabra* (Madrid: Cátedra, 1988), 13.

2. Anthony Stanton, "Genealogía de un libro: Libertad bajo palabra" (Interview with Octavio Paz), *El Paseante,* 15–16 (1990), 36–45.

3. Santí, *Libertad bajo palabra,* 38–39.

4. Judith Goetzinger, "Thematic Divisions in *Libertad bajo palabra* (1986)," *Romance Notes* 1, no. 2 (1971), 73.

5. See Jason Wilson, *Octavio Paz* (Boston: Twayne, 1986), 27.

6. Ibid., 30.

7. "Al comentar un pasaje de la Nouvelle Justine—el espisodio en que uno de los personajes mezcla su esperma a la lava del Etna—Breton observa que el acto es un homenaje de amor a la naturaleza, "une façon, des plus folles, des plus indiscutables de l'aimer" (*CA* 62–63).

8. Jason Wilson, *Octavio Paz: A Study of His Poetics* (Cambridge: Cambridge University Press, 1979.

9. See Angel Flores, *Aproximaciones a Octavio Paz* (Mexico City: Joaquín Mortíz, 1974) for Fein's essay "Himno entre ruinas," 165–70 as well as Ramón Xirau's "Himno entre ruinas: La Palabra, fuente de toda liberación," 159–64.

10. José Emilio Pacheco, "Descripción de Piedra de sol," in Octavio Paz, ed. Alfredo Roggiano (Madrid: Editorial Fundamentos, 1979), 111–24, 121.

11. Tomas Segovia, "Una Obra maestra: Piedra de sol" in Aproximaciones a Octavio Paz, ed. Angel Flores (Mexico City: Joaquín Mortíz, 1974), 171.

12. Ibid., 171–72.

13. Ibid., 171.

14. Pacheco, "Descripción de Piedra de sol," 111–24.

Chapter Three: *The Labyrinth of Solitude*

1. Enrico Mario Santí, ed., *El laberinto de la soledad* (Madrid: Catédra, 1993), 67.
2. Claude Fell, "Vuelta a El laberinto de la soledad" (interview with Octavio Paz) in *Pasión crítica,* ed. Hugo J. Verani (Barcelona: Seix Barral, 1985), 104–28.

Chapter Four: Poetics

1. For the first edition I am using *El arco y la lira: El poema. La revelación poética. Poesía e historia* (Mexico City: Fondo de Cultura Económica, 1956). Translations are my own and page numbers appear in parenthesis in the text. For the general discussion of *El arco y la lira* I am using the revised edition (Buenos Aires: Sur, 1965) and the English translation *The Bow and the Lyre,* tr. Ruth L. C. Simms (Austin: University of Texas Press, 1973).
2. In this section I have been aided by Anthony Stanton's indispensable "Octavio Paz, Alfonso Reyes y el análisis del fenómeno poético," *Hispanic Review* 61, no. 3 (1993): 363–78.
3. Ibid., 364–66.
4. Emir Rodríguez Monegal concisely enumerates the differences between one edition and the next in his "Relectura de *El arco y la lira,*" *Revista Iberoamericana* 74 (January-February 1971): 35–46.
5. *El signo y el garabato* (Mexico City: Joaquín Mortíz, 1973), 39.
6. See Walter Benjamin, "The Task of the Translator" in *Illuminations,* ed. Hannah Arendt, tr. Harry Zohn (New York: Schocken Books, 1969), 69–83. Also Jacques Derrida, *The Ear of the Other: Otobiography, Transference, Translation,* ed. Christie McDonald, tr. Peggy Kamuf (Lincoln: University of Nebraska Press, 1985).

Chapter Five: A Poetics of East and West

1. Andrés Sánchez Robayna, "Regreso y fundación" in *Octavio Paz,* ed. Alfredo Roggiano (Madrid: Editorial Fundamentos, 1979), pp.361–69.
2. Ramón Xirau, *Octavio Paz: El sentido de la palabra* (Mexico City: Joaquín Mortíz, 1970).
3. John Fein, *Toward Octavio Paz: A Reading of his Major Poems 1957–1976,* (Lexington: University of Kentucky Press, 1986), 55.
4. Fragments of the note have been eliminated, probably by Paz himself, in the English *Collected Poems.*
5. Manuel Durán, "El impacto del Oriente en la obra de Octavio Paz: poesía y ensayo" in *Octavio Paz,* ed. Alfredo Roggiano, (Madrid: Editorial Fundamentos, 1979), 173–203.
6. Ibid., 183.
7. See Julia Kushigian's perceptive commentary on this poem as well as on Paz's gardens in her *Orientalism in the Hispanic Literary Tradition: In Dialogue with Borges, Paz, and Sarduy* (Albuquerque: University of New Mexico Press, 1991), 44–49.

Chapter Six: *Blanco*

1. This "Warning to the Reader" has generally been discarded in many library copies of *Blanco*. It is written in a yellow page and has been reproduced in the more recent facsimile edition of *Blanco* (1995). All of the quotes from *Blanco* and *Archivo* are from this edition, unless otherwise noted.

2. "Richard Wagner et Tannhäuser à Paris," in *Oeuvres Completes,* ed. Claude Pichois (Paris: Gallimard, Pléiade, 1976), 2:793.

3. The full text from which Paz takes his initial quote follows: "Just as water entered in the ear is drawn out again by water, so also the notion of existing things is purified by appearances (49). Just as those who have been burned by fire must suffer again by fire, so those who have been burned by the fire of passion must suffer the fire of passion (50). Those things by which men of evil conduct are bound, others turn into means and gain thereby release from the bonds of existence (51). By passion the world is bound, by passion too it is released, but by the heretical buddhists this practice of reversals is not known"; *The Hevajra Tantra,* ed. D. L. Snellgrove, 2 vols. (London: Oxford University Press, 1959), 2:ii f. (93).

4. See, for example, Marjorie Perloff's excellent reading in *The Futurist Moment,* (Chicago: University of Chicago Press, 1986).

5. *The Hevajra Tantra,* 1:22.

6. "Samsara consists in form and sound and so on, in feeling and the other constituents of personality, in the faculties of sense, in wrath, delusion, and the rest. But all these elements are really nirvana, and only from delusion do they appear as samsara (22). Paz also talks about Tantrism in *Conjunciones y disyunciones* (Mexico City: Joaquín Mortíz, 1969), 63–92. It is possible that Paz's project in this book comes out of one of Snellgrove's commentaries in his translation of the *Hevajra Tantra*: "In many ways the civilization developed in Tibet is analogous to that of our Middle Ages in the west, and just as here Christianity provided the inspiration and Greece and Rome the model, so there Buddhism was the inspiration and the arts and sciences of India their model" (9). Also in relation to samsara and nirvana, see Paz's "Lectura de John Cage," en *Ladera este* (*Poemas,* 435–38) ("Reading John Cage," *CP* 234–41) and Paz's note: "Samsara and Nirvana are equivalent because both are aspects of the void (sunyata), and the true sage transcends their apparent duality. But the poem says something slightly different" (*CP* 646). ("Samsara y Nirvana son equivalente porque ambos son modos de la vacuidad y el verdadero sabio trasciende su aparente dualidad. Pero el poema dice algo ligeramente distinto" [689].)

7. On yantras, see Ajit Mookerjee, *Tantra Art: Its Philosophy and Physics* Basel: Ravi Kumar, 1971), 13.

8. See, for example, Eliot Weinberger's reading of Blanco as a tri-dimensional stupa, seen from above; in "Paz en la India," in *Archivo,* ed. Enrico Mario Santí (Mexico City: Ediciones del Equilibrista, 1995), 189–202.

9. This will also be important for Paz's collective, translinguistic *Renga,* written in 1969. In his introduction, included in *El signo y el garabato,* Paz explains: "El poema

clásico japonés (*tanka*) está compuesto por dos estrofas, la primera de tres líneas y la segunda de dos. Nada más fácil que partir un tanka: 3/2, palabra/eco, pregunta/respuesta. Una vez dividido, el tanka se multiplica. Prolifera por partenogénesis: 3/2 3/2 3/2 3/2. . . . Fisiparidad verbal, fragmentos que se separan y encadenan: la figura que dibuja el *renga* participa de la esbeltez de la serpiente y de la fluidez de la flauta japonesa" (142–43). (The classical Japanese poem [*tanka*] is composed of two stanzas, the first contains three lines and the second two. There is nothing easier than dividing a tanka 3/2, word/echo, question/answer. Once divided the tanka multiplies. It proliferates by parthenogenesis: 3/2 3/2 3/2 3/2. . . . verbal physical sameness, fragments that divide and chain themselves; the figure traced by the *renga* involves the slimness of the serpent and the fluidity of the Japanese flute.)

10. Octavio Paz, "Contar y cantar: sobre el poema extenso," *Vuelta* (June 1986), 12–17. The quote that follows is also from this source.

Chapter Seven: *Vuelta, A Draft of Shadows, A Tree Within*

1. Andrés Sanchez Robayna, "Regreso y fundación" in *Octavio Paz,* ed. Alfredo Roggiano (Madrid: Editorial Fundamentos, 1979).

2. Clauda Albarrán, "Vuelta," *Revista Canadiense de Estudios Hispánicos* 16, no. 3 (1992):535–50.

3. Pere Gimferrer, *Lecturas de Octavio Paz* (Barcelona: Editorial Anagrama, 1980).

4. In *The Complete Essays of Montaigne,* tr. Donald M. Frame (Stanford: Stanford University Press, 1958 [1975]), 56–68. All quotes are taken from this edition.

Chapter Eight: Conclusion

1. In *La otra voz* (Barcelona: Seix Barral, 1990).

Selected Bibliography

Primary Sources

Poetry

Libertad bajo palabra (1935–1957). (1949, 1960, 1968, 1979). Ed. Enrico Mario Santí. Madrid: Cátedra, 1988.

Blanco. Mexico City: Joaquín Mortíz, 1969.

Ladera este. (1962–1968). Mexico City: Joaquín Mortíz, 1969

El mono gramático. Barcelona: Seix Barral, 1974.

Poemas (1935–1975). Barcelona: Seix Barral, 1979.

Arbol adentro. Barcelona: Seix Barral, 1987.

Prose

El arco y la lira: El poema. La revelación poética. Poesía e historia. Mexico City: Fondo de Cultura Económica, 1956. (2d ed., Buenos Aires: Sur, 1965.)

Las peras del olmo. Mexico City: Imprenta Universitaria, UNAM, 1957. (2d ed., 1965.)

El laberinto de la soledad. (1950, 1959.) Ed. Enrico Mario Santí. Madrid: Cátedra, 1993.

Puertas al campo. Mexico City: Universidad Nacional Autónoma de México, 1966. (2d ed., 1967; 1st Spanish ed., Barcelona: Seix Barral, 1972.)

Corriente alterna. Mexico City, Siglo XXI, 1967. (2d ed., 1968.)

Claude Lévi-Strauss o el nuevo festín de Esopo. Mexico City: Joaquín Mortíz, 1967. (3d ed., 1972.)

Conjunciones y disyunciones. Mexico City: Joaquín Mortíz, 1969.

Posdata. Mexico City: Siglo XXI, 1970.

Traducción: literatura y literalidad. Barcelona: Tusquets, 1971.

Los signos en rotación y otros ensayos. Ed. Carlos Fuentes. Madrid: Alianza Editorial, 1971.

El signo y el garabato. Mexico City: Joaquín Mortíz, 1973.

Apariencia desnuda: La obra de Marcel Duchamp. Mexico City: Era, 1973.

Los hijos del limo. Barcelona: Seix Barral, 1974.

El ogro filantrópico. Mexico City: Joaquín Mortíz, 1979.

Sor Juana Inés de la Cruz o las trampas de la fé. Barcelona: Seix Barral, 1982.

Sombras de obras: Arte y literatura. Barcelona, Seix Barral, 1983.

Tiempo nublado. Barcelona: Seix Barral, 1983.

Pasión crítica. Barcelona: Seix Barral, 1985.

Primeras letras (1931–1943). Ed. Enrico Mario Santí. Barcelona: Seix Barral, 1988.

La otra voz. Barcelona: Seix Barral, 1990.

Pequeña crónica de grandes días. Mexico City: Fondo de Cultura Económica, 1990.

La llama doble. Barcelona: Seix Barral, 1993.
Itinerario. Barcelona: Seix Barral, 1994.
Vislumbres de la India. Barcelona: Seix Barral, 1995.

English Translations: Poetry

Selected Poetry of Octavio Paz. Tr. Muriel Rukeyser. Bloomington: Indiana University Press, 1963.
Configurations. (various translators.) New York: New Directions, 1971.
Early Poems, 1935–1955. Tr. Muriel Rukeyser et al. Bloomington: Indiana University Press, 1973.
¿Aguila o sol? Eagle or Sun? Tr. Eliot Weinberger. New York: New Directions, 1976.
The Monkey Grammarian. Tr. Helen Lane. New York: Seaver Books, 1981.
Collected Poems of Octavio Paz. Tr. Eliot Weinberger et al. New York: New Directions, 1987.

English Translations: Prose

Claude Lévi-Strauss: An Introduction. Tr. J. S. Bernstein and Maxine Bernstein. Ithaca: Cornell University Press, 1970.
The Other Mexico: Critique of the Pyramid. Tr. Lysander Kemp. New York: Grove, 1972.
Alternating Current. Tr. Helen Lane. New York: Viking, 1973.
The Bow and the Lyre. Tr. Ruth L. C. Simms. Austin: University of Texas Press, 1973.
Children of the Mire: Poetry from Romanticism to the Avant-Garde. Tr. Rachel Phillips. Cambridge: Harvard University Press, 1974.
Conjunctions and Disjunctions. Tr. Helen Lane. New York: Viking, 1974.
The Siren and the Seashell and Other Essays on Poets and Poetry. Tr. Lysander Kemp and Margaret Sayers Peden. Austin: University of Texas Press, 1976.
Marcel Duchamp: Appearance Stripped Bare. Tr. Rachel Phillips and Donald Gardner. New York: Viking, 1978.
The Labyrinth of Solitude. Tr. Lysander Kemp, Yara Milos and Rachel Phillips Belash. New York: Grove, 1985.
One Earth, Four or Five Worlds: Reflections on Contemporary History. Tr. Helen Lane. New York: Harcourt Brace Jovanovich, 1985.
The Double Flame:. Love and Eroticism. Tr. Helen Lane. New York: Harcourt Brace, 1995.

Secondary Sources

Books and Sections of Books

Aguilar Mora, Jorge. *La divina pareja: Historia y mito en Octavio Paz.* Mexico City: Ediciones Era, 1978. One of the most important and trenchant critiques of Paz's poetics.

Chiles, Frances. *Octavio Paz: The Mythic Dimension.* New York: Peter Lang, 1987. Good overall study of Paz's work.

Cuadernos Hispanoamericanos, nos. 343–45 (January–March 1979). Special issue dedicated to the work of Octavio Paz. Includes many important essays.

Fein, John. *Toward Octavio Paz: A Reading of His Major Poems, 1957–1976.* Lexington: University Press of Kentucky, 1986. An indispensable study of Paz's major poetic works, Fein's readings are the obligatory point of departure for scholars on Paz's poems.

Flores, Angel. *Aproximaciones a Octavio Paz.* Mexico City: Joaquín Mortíz, 1974. An early collection of essays dedicated to Paz's work; gives a good idea of the critical reception Paz received at the height of his poetic career.

Gimferrer, Pere. *Lecturas de Octavio Paz.* Barcelona: Editorial Anagrama, 1980. A lucid study of Paz, written by one of the most important poets of the Hispanic world.

———, ed., *Octavio Paz.* Madrid: Taurus Ediciones, 1982. Good early collection of essays on his work.

Homage to Octavio Paz; Our 1982 Neustadt Laureate. In *World Literature Today: A Literary Quarterly of the University of Oklahoma* 56, no. 4 (1982). Collection in homage to Octavio Paz with important comments on his work.

Ivar, Ivask, ed. *The Perpetual Present: The Poetry and Prose of Octavio Paz.* Norman: University of Oklahoma Press, 1973. Good overall book on Paz's poems and poetics, written by sensitive readers of Paz's nuanced work. Of particular importance is the essay by Manuel Durán on *Blanco* and *Ladera este.*

Kushigian, Julia. *Orientalism in the Hispanic Literary Tradition: In Dialogue with Borges, Paz, and Sarduy.* Albuquerque: University of New Mexico Press, 1991. The best book to date on Paz's period in the Orient.

Magis, Carlos H. *La poesía hermética de Octavio Paz.* Mexico City: El Colegio de México, 1978. Takes as its point of departure the idea that Paz is a hermetic poet.

Phillips, Rachel. *The Poetic Modes of Octavio Paz.* Oxford: Oxford University Press, 1972. The first comprehensive book on Paz's poetry and one of the best.

Roggiano, Alfredo, ed. *Octavio Paz.* Madrid: Editorial Fundamentos, 1979. An important collection of essays on Paz's work, with a useful chronology.

Santí, Enrico Mario, ed. *Blanco/Archivo Blanco.* Mexico City: Ediciones El Equilibrista, 1995. A facsimile of *Blanco*'s first edition, the first volume contains a brilliant introduction to Paz's poem, along with samples of his correspondence, samples of his manuscript, and essays by translators. Indispensable not only for students of *Blanco,* but also for those interested in Paz's life in the Orient.

Sucre, Guillermo. *La máscara, la transparencia: Ensayos sobre poesía hispanoamericana.* Caracas: Monte Avila, 1975. One of the best books on Latin American poetry and poetics by one of its more lucid and sensitive readers.

Verani, Hugo. *Octavio Paz: Bibliografía crítica.* Mexico City: Universidad Nacional Autónoma de México, 1983. The best critical bibliography to date on Paz's works.

Wilson, Jason. *Octavio Paz.* Boston: Twayne, 1986. Very good introduction to the complete works of Paz.

————. *Octavio Paz: A Study of His Poetics.* Cambridge: Cambridge University Press, 1979. An excellent study of Paz as poet and essayist.

Xirau, Ramón. *Octavio Paz: El sentido de la palabra.* Mexico City: Joaquín Mortíz, 1970. Readings of Paz's work from a philosophical angle.

Yurkievich, Saúl. *Fundadores de la nueva poesía latinoamericana: Vallejo, Huidobro, Borges, Girondo, Neruda, Paz.* Barcelona: Barral Editores, 1971. (2d ed., rev., Ariel, 1984.) A classic book on Latin American poetry written by one of its most important critics. Yurkievich's book was the first comprehensive assessment of twentieth-century Latin American poetry.

Articles

Aparicio, Frances. "Epistemología y traducción en la obra de Octavio Paz." *Hispanic Journal* 8, no. 1 (1986): 157–67.

Bernard, Judith, "Myth and Structure in Octavio Paz's *Piedra de sol,*" *Symposium* 21, no. 1 (1967): 5–13.

Farajos, Mary. "Octavio Paz y Marcel Duchamp: Crítica moderna para un artista moderno." *Cuadernos Hispanoamericanos* 410 (August 1984): 79–96.

Goetzinger, Judith. "Thematic Divisions in *Libertad bajo palabra* (1986)." *Romance Notes* 1, no. 2 (1971): 226–33. Reads the evolution of *Libertad bajo palabra.* See also "Evolución de un poema: tres versiones de *Bajo tu clara sombra*" in Alfred Roggiano, ed., *Octavio Paz* (Madrid: Editorial Fundamentos, 1979).

Luciani, Frederick. "Octavio Paz on Sor Juana Inés de la Cruz: The Metaphor Incarnate." *Latin American Literary Review* 15 (July–December 1987): 6–25.

Malpartida, Juan. "El cuerpo y la historia: Dos aproximaciones a Octavio Paz." *Cuadernos hispanoamericanos* 468 (June 1989): 45–56.

Needleman, Ruth. "Hacia *Blanco.*" *Revista Iberoamericana* 74 (January–February 1971): 177–81.

Nugent, Robert. "Structure and Meaning in Octavio Paz's *Piedra de Sol.*" *Kentucky Romance Quarterly* 13, no. 3 (1966): 138–46.

Rodríguez Monegal, Emir. "Relectura de *El arco y la lira.*" *Revista Iberoamericana* 74 (January-February 1971): 35–46.

Santí, Enrico Mario. "The Politics of Poetics." *Diacritics,* no. 8 (Winter, 1978): 28–40. Important review-essay on Paz, his critics, and the relationship between poetry and prose in his work

Stanton, Anthony. "Octavio Paz, Alfonso Reyes y el análisis del fenómeno poético." *Hispanic Review* 61 (Summer 1993): 363–78.

Sucre, Guillermo. "La fijeza y el vértigo." *Revista Iberoamericana* 74 (January–February 1971): 47–71.

Weinberger, Eliot. "Octavio Paz." In *Works on Paper,* 107–10. New York: New Directions, 1986. Good, concise essay on Paz by the foremost translator of his poetry.

Index

193